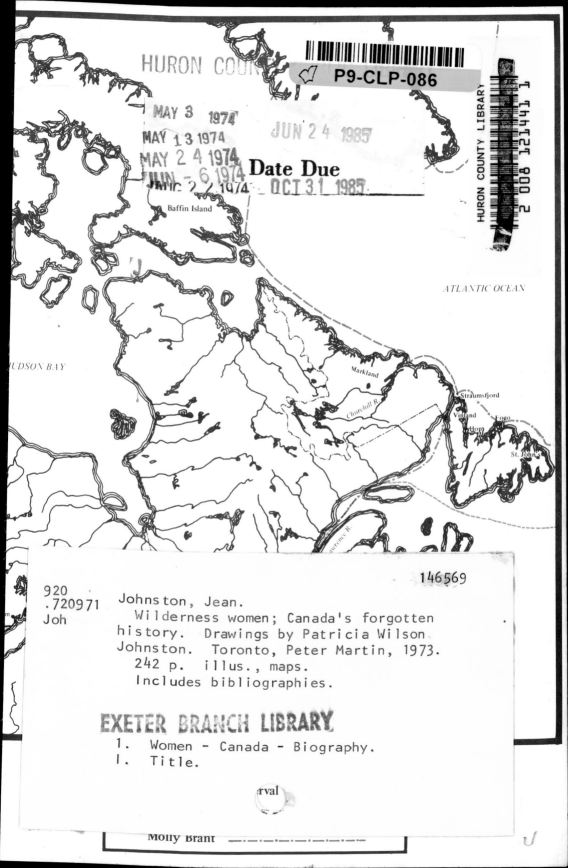

Baffin Island

ATLANTIC OCEAN

HUDSON BAY

Markland

Straumsfjord

Churchill R.

Vinland

Fogo

Hop

St. John's

St. Lawrence R.

Wilderness Women

Wilderness

Women

Canada's forgotten history

Jean Johnston

drawings by Patricia Wilson Johnston

Peter Martin Associates Limited

Design: Diana McElroy

©1973   Jean Johnston

ISBN: 0-88778-084-9

Printed in Canada by Web Offset

Peter Martin Associates Limited
35 Britain Street, Toronto, Ontario M5A 1R7

Contents

Introduction   vi

1. Gudrid   1

2. Marguerite de Roberval   23

3. Jeanne Mance   35

4. Molly Brant   73

5. Marie-Anne Lagimodière   121

6. Amelia Douglas   155

7. Charlotte Selina Bompas   179

8. Martha Black   209

9. The Quest Goes On   237

Acknowledgements   239

General Bibliography   242

General References   242

INTRODUCTION

Anyone who has been in a fur-trading post knows the sharp psychological line which separates it from the settlement. When women come, we clearly get into this next stage, for women are hostages to the new world. And when they are followed by children, we have crossed the line from mere settlement to colony.   A.R.M. Lower[1]

The first Europeans to come to America were entrepreneurs. They were men looking for profits from furs or fish, or simply responding to the appeal of the unknown. Women, not the men, were the colonizers. What kind of women were these first pioneers in the new world? Why did they come?

Gudrid, the Viking woman, was the torch-bearer. She was the first white woman to inhabit the new world — five centuries before Jacques Cartier saw the shores of the St. Lawrence. She conceived the first white child born in America.

Gudrid had all the determination, the hardness, the boldness and the colonizing zeal of the later women immigrants, and it was no fault of hers that the Viking expeditions to America failed.

The Viking expedition of 1007 A.D., of which Gudrid was a member, did not lack in daring and it was well-prepared. As a colonizing effort, its serious defect was its shortage of women. There were only five women, including Gudrid, to share the fortunes of the 160 men. How could a colony succeed when 155 men were hungering for the company of women, while five among them enjoyed the comfort of a wife? According to the Saga of *Eirik the Red,* "there was deep division between the men on account of the women, for the unmarried men fell foul of the married, which led to serious disturbances".[2]

Six hundred years passed before a successful colony was established in Canada by Europeans. Once such colonies had established a foothold on the Atlantic coast, they began to push inland following the beckoning St. Lawrence. Before the French reached the Great Lakes, they were joined by the British. With the native Americans as guides, the white men explored the intricate waterways that drained the rocky Laurentian Shield, that monstrous horseshoe of granite that covers half of Canada. The explorers left the Shield and crossed the vast plains, travelling by canoe along the broad winding rivers until they reached the Pacific Coast mountains. Over the mountains they went, still travelling by river, to the Pacific. Turning north, again by river, they found the Arctic Ocean.

For company on these long journeys and to console them in their tents and by their fires, the white men took as wives the sisters of their Indian guides. All the while, travelling close behind, almost within earshot, the white women followed, so that when the men reached the end of the land and thought to turn back to the settled communities they found white women with them. These women enjoyed much of the daring and boldness of the men and they assumed one other trait – stability. When they reached a stopping place, they made the land theirs.

These women were adventurers just as Champlain, La Verendrye and Alexander Mackenzie were adventurers. The difference was that as soon as the women came to a halt, they demanded something more permanent to live in than a tent – a result of their responsibility to provide for offspring. Therefore, the building of a permanent dwelling, no matter how simple, determines that the male must stop his roaming; comforts are assembled, land is cleared, churches and schools are built. The hunter and trapper vanish and there is a permanent community.

Although Gudrid was not able to make the land hers as the later colonists did, she was a bold forerunner of those women who colonized and settled Canada and the rest of North America. Gudrid and the seven other women included in this book are keys to the colonizing of Canada.

The expedition of 1541, of which Marguerite de Roberval was a member, failed dismally but she was able to show, though she was alone on a deserted island, that a European could live off the land. Champlain later used this concept of using the products of the new world when he established the first successful colony in North America.

Jeanne Mance helped to found a Christian mission at Montreal though the site was deep in hostile Iroquois country. Three times she saved the colony from foundering.

The settling of Ontario can be traced to the diplomacy of Molly Brant, the Mohawk wife of Sir William Johnson. During the American Revolution, her leadership kept the majority of the Six Nations loyal to the British cause, and so made Ontario a safe place for the loyalists to settle.

Marie-Anne Lagimodière was the first Canadian to follow her husband to the Northwest. After five years of wandering on the prairies, she persuaded Jean-Baptiste Lagimodière to settle on the Red River, near where Winnipeg is today. She, more than any other, succeeded in encouraging missionaries and school-teachers to come to the remote land of the nomads.

Lady Amelia Douglas, a Métis born in a remote fur-trading post, became the first First Lady of British Columbia. She kept open house for all who came and she spent her life tending the sick and the poor, before the days of hospitals and public welfare.

As the wife of the first Anglican Bishop in the far north, Charlotte Selina Bompas spent her mature years teaching Indians. She was the first white woman in the Arctic and, long before the gold rush, she brought a blend of feminine delicacy, charm and religion to the lonely miners who first prospected in the Yukon.

Martha Louise Black walked into the Klondike over the Trail of '98 and from that time, until her death in 1957, she was a part of all that happened there. She was called the Mother of the Yukon and as such is still remembered.

These women planted the roots of settlement in the New World.

Notes

1. A.R.M. Lower. *Canadians in the Making* (Toronto: 1958), p. xvi.
2. *Eirik the Red and other Icelandic Sagas,* selected and translated by Gwyn Jones (Toronto: 1961), p. 155.

Wilderness Women

1

Gudrid

Leif gave the country a name from its products, and called it
Vinland. Flatö Manuscript[1]

As soon as Gudrid heard of Leif Eiriksson's discovery of
Vinland, in 1000 A.D., she wanted to see these lands for herself.
Usually Viking women did not go to sea with their men, but
Gudrid contrived and persuaded until she achieved her goal.
Seven years after Leif, she too had reached the shores of North
America.

Although she was a principal character in the unfolding
drama of the Vikings' journeys to Vinland, we seldom hear
about Gudrid now. Yet her story is plainly told in the sagas of
Greenland and of Iceland.[2] There are discrepancies and differ-
ences in the various accounts, but the main facts agree and
confirm her historical role. Oral reporting and story-telling were
skilled arts among the Norse, and accuracy was the key to the
preservation of their folk-lore. The word "saga" means Norse
prose-writing or prose narrative. It does not mean fiction.

Gudrid was born about 980 A.D., a few years before Erik
the Red was banished from Iceland as the result of a blood
feud. Her father, Thorbjorn (pronounced Thorbiorn), a friend
of Eirik's, was a wealthy landowner with an estate on the west
coast of Iceland in the Snaefellsnes area.

Gudrid was a beautiful woman, according to her contemporaries, and "distinguished in everything she did".[3]

Her achievements and her extensive travels made her one of
the outstanding women of medieval Europe. Indeed, she had
scarcely an equal until 400 years later, when Jeanne d'Arc drove
the English out of France.

Iceland, in the Tenth Century, was in the main stream of
Norse events. Although the land has few trees, it has vivid
colouring in its rocks, mountains and glaciers and in the intense
blue of sea and sky. The climate is tempered by the Gulf
Stream.

Why should Gudrid want to leave this vital and interesting
land? What powerful urge incited her to leave comfort and
security, and to travel by open boat through unknown seas to
an unknown land?

Part of the answer can be seen in her own personality. She
was a curious, active woman. Another part of the answer is
found in the close friendship between her father and Eirik the
Red.

She spent her childhood and youth in the west of Iceland,
near Breidafjord, where Eirik had farmed and from which he
had been banished.[4] During her growing years, Eirik's quarrel
was one of the major concerns of the area. Since Gudrid's father
championed Eirik's cause, there is little doubt where her sym-
pathies lay. Eirik's sons were her playmates and she more than
likely climbed with them to the top of the mountains north of
Breidafjord. There, on a clear day, peaks of distant mountains
in the west could be seen shimmering across 190 miles of ocean.

When Eirik returned from his banishment, he came with
the exciting news that he had found good grazing land to
the west. He called this new land "Greenland". The Ice-
landers of the west coast were agog with the news, and
many were ready and willing to follow Eirik. Among these

were Gudrid's foster parents and her father, Thorbjorn.

.   .   .

By now, Gudrid was an attractive young woman, blonde and blue-eyed. She had already had one proposal of marriage which her father had scorned because the man, though wealthy, was low-born. About the time that Thorbjorn was deciding to go to Greenland, Gudrid had another offer of marriage from Thorer, a trader from Norway. He must have been a man of good family, for Gudrid's father did not object to this match.[5]

The number of names in the sagas derived from Thor is past counting. Gudrid's three husbands were Thors — Thorer, Thorstein and Thorfinn — and there are numerous other *Thor* compounds in the narrative. Most of them are distinct characters. However, less confusion might have arisen had the Norse not named so many of their children after the Viking god.

It was customary for Norse women to stay by the hearth when their men went trading or raiding. Not Gudrid. The effects of her childhood on the fjord, looking towards Greenland, and of her close relations with Eirik's family, created in her a great curiosity for the unknown, a hunger to see new things.

Gudrid's charm was enhanced by a bright mind and a tongue that could persuade and inspire. There was no reason for her new husband, Thorer, to go to Greenland. He was a trader, and there would be little trade in so new a colony. The sensible plan for him would be to take Gudrid and his trading profits back to Norway, leave Gudrid in his father's house, refit his ship, and continue to trade among the established settlements.

That would have been sensible. Instead, Gudrid persuaded Thorer to follow her father to Greenland — and to take her with him.

Unluckily, they ran into a storm during the voyage and their ship foundered on an island off the southern tip of Greenland. Their plight seemed hopeless. The ship was stranded on a tiny island in the northern ocean at the far edge of the known world.

Rescue of the fifteen marooned people would be a miracle. Yet the miracle happened. Rescue came in the person of Eirik's son, Leif, who according to one version of the Gudrid story was just returning from his momentous discovery of Vinland.

As a result of this discovery, and of his rescue of Gudrid and Thorer, Leif became known as Leif the Lucky.[6]

Leif took the castaways to his father's house at Brattahlid. Eirik the Red had already built himself a great house, probably as grand as those of any of the nobles in Iceland. To us, it would seem no more than a great barn. Because of the shortage of timber in Greenland, the walls were built partly of stone, and partly of sod, the sod acting as insulation. The only room divisions were draperies, and they were of the richest of materials — velvets, silks, tapestries. Cooking and heating arrangements were provided by large, primitive, open hearths. The floors were paved with flagstones. The only real convenience was a device for carrying running water through the hall.

This was the accommodation which Gudrid found waiting at Eirik the Red's. It was not too different from what she left in Iceland. However, if comforts were minimal, there was no lack of hospitality.

There were hard times in the new land that winter. Farm produce was scant, the hunt was bad, and fishing was poor; sickness was widespread and some men were lost at sea. The colonists decided to call in a prophetess to drive off the evil spirits.

Gudrid and her father were Christians,[7] and disapproved of witchcraft and augury. Thorbjorn absented himself entirely from the feast which had been prepared for the prophetess, and though Gudrid remained, she stood back as an onlooker.

When it became known that Gudrid was the only woman present who knew the chant "Varðlokur", necessary for the spells, the people begged her to lend her skill.

"You could be helpful to all these people," said the seer, "and still be no worse a woman."

Gudrid, though Christian, could not refuse. She was drawn into the circle of women surrounding the seer. When Gudrid recited the chant, she did it so well that those who were present praised her voice and her words.

The seer thanked her, and said that the spirits themselves had been drawn in to listen to her beautiful chant. The seer promised that the sickness which had stricken the settlement ". . . will go sooner than we had hoped. As for you Gudrid . . . . You will make a match here in Greenland, the most distinguished there is, but it will not last; for your ways lie out to Iceland where there will spring from you a great and goodly progeny. . . ."

Thorbjorn's skepticism of pagan practices was reinforced, for although the weather improved as had been prophesied, the sickness did not disappear before it claimed the life of Thorer, Gudrid's husband.

In the spring, Eirik gave his old friend, Thorbjorn, land at Stokkannes where there was some excellent farm land with good grazing. Here Thorbjorn is said to have built a stately house and lived the rest of his days. This area has been resettled in recent years by Greenlanders. It is still good farm land, with good grazing for sheep. In 1935, the same area supported a farming community of 125 people.

.   .   .

Following Leif's return from Vinland in the spring of 1001, there had been endless talk and conjecture about the new land, and the feeling grew that Leif's discoveries should be followed up. Leif's brother, Thorvald, was the first to decide to go. He outfitted a ship with thirty men in the spring of 1002, and had Leif's permission to use the buildings he had erected in Vinland.

Thorvald was entranced by the new land. Using Leif's Vinland for his base camp, Thorvald spent the next two years living off the land and exploring miles of coastline. He finally selected for himself a site where there was a beautiful bay with well-wooded shores. He planned to found a colony, but his plans never became more than dreams. It was in Thorvald's beautiful bay that the Norse had their first skirmish with the Eskimos, and Thorvald was fatally wounded by an arrow. Before dying, he asked to be buried at the spot he had chosen for his settlement, and to have a cross placed at his head. This cape, marked by the cross, became a landmark for future voyages.

Fate had dealt harshly with Thorvald, son of Eirik the Red, but it was not yet finished with the Eirikssons.

After Thorvald's death, his men wintered in Vinland, then returned in the spring to Eiriksfjord with their sad news. During their three years' absence, changes had taken place in Greenland.

"It had happened," says the sagaman, "that Thorstein of Eiriksfjord had married and taken to wife, Gudrid. . . ."

This seems to have been a love match. The sagaman says that the marriage "found favour with Gudrid and her father". Thorstein, another son of Eirik the Red, was well liked; he was astute, and he had property. Thorbjorn was delighted that his daughter should marry into the family of his old friend, Eirik. As for Gudrid, she had known Thorstein since those childhood days in Iceland.

Thorstein was deeply distressed by his brother's death. He immediately began to make plans to go to Vinland, to find Thorvald's body, and to bring it back to Greenland for a Christian burial.

That Gudrid encouraged him in his plans is certain, for it was her father's ship that was outfitted and made ready with a crew of twenty men.

Because this was neither a colonising scheme, nor a trading trip, but merely an exploratory trip with the main purpose of bringing back the body of Thorvald, the ship was outfitted with only the necessary weapons and provisions. It was no journey for a woman, yet Gudrid was determined to go. Using her feminine charm and her clever tongue, Gudrid talked Thorstein into taking her along.

As with Thorer before him, Thorstein was probably persuaded against his better judgement. It is surprising not only that Gudrid wanted to go, but that she was allowed to go. Nor could it be argued that she did not know what she was doing, for she had already had a stormy crossing from Iceland to Greenland, and had experienced a shipwreck.

Gudrid and Thorstein started out in high spirits, but were immediately caught up in a storm that drove them within sight of Iceland, and far enough east to encounter the birds of Ireland. Throughout the whole summer they were tossed about by storm or lost in fog, and in the autumn they returned deject-edly to Greenland.

Gudrid and Thorstein spent the winter comfortably on their own land, until a contagious disease swept the settlement. The attractive, capable Thorstein was struck down by the disease, and died. Gudrid was heart-broken and took her loss bitterly.

.   .   .

Leif took Gudrid into his home as if he were her father and "looked after her well". Henceforth, Gudrid made her home with Leif. Besides being twice widowed, she had also lost her father, for Thorbjorn too had died. She was now an heiress, for the whole of her father's estate passed into her hands, as well as that of Thorstein Eiriksson. Leif became her protector.

Eirik the Red was also dead now, and Leif was landlord at Brattahlid. In the autumn of that year, 1006, two ships put in at Eiriksfjord. The ships were traders from Iceland, and were operated under the partnership of four men. The most out-standing of the four was Thorfinn Karlsefni, a wealthy man of good family, with a good reputation as a merchant.

Karlsefni's ships carried goods from all over Europe; timber from Norway; wheat, honey and tin from England; glass, jewellery and weapons from central Europe; wine from France; silks and spices from the Mediterranean.

Leif invited Karlsefni, his partners, and the two ships' crews, altogether some eighty men, to winter with him at Brattahlid. Hospitality was open-handed between Leif and the partners, and all was good cheer.

In this pleasant atmosphere, Karlsefni soon discovered Gudrid. "She had a good outward appearance and was know-ing," says the sagaman, "and understood well how to behave with strangers." It is not surprising that Karlsefni fell in love with her, and courted her.

At Christmas, so sumptuous a feast was prepared that the visitors were amazed that it was possible in a land of such limited resources.

After the feast, Karlsefni went to Leif and asked for Gudrid's hand. Leif received the proposal favourably. Gudrid accepted, and the Christmas feast was prolonged into a wedding feast. Although Gudrid could not know it, her marriage to Karlsefni was the key to her great adventure in the New World.

Gudrid had not forsaken her ambition. During the winter, there was continuous talk about a voyage to Vinland. The saga-man says: "Gudrid and others persuaded Karlsefni strongly to the expedition."

When Karlsefni was finally convinced that an expedition to Vinland was a sane venture, he lost no time in organizing a full-scale operation, with the intention of starting a colony if conditions were favourable. The party consisted of 160 people, including five women. Gudrid and Karlsefni, and his partner, Snorri, fitted out a ship with a crew of sixty men, bound by an agreement for all to share in the profits. It was a large ship, for besides provisions and goods for trading with the Eskimos, it carried cattle. The other two Icelandic partners, Bjarni and Thorhall, joined the expedition with their ship, and with the crew that had served them. Then there was Thorvard, who was married to Eirik the Red's daughter, Freydis, and these two outfitted the ship that Gudrid's father had brought from Iceland. Freydis was a fierce woman, and she later played a violent role in the Vinland drama.

Karlsefni asked Leif for his houses in Vinland, but Leif preferred to retain ownership, and would lend them only.

.   .   .

Vinland lay in a sheltered cove in the northernmost tip of Newfoundland, on the coast where the Strait of Belle Isle enters the Atlantic Ocean. Looking away to the northeast from this cove, a visitor can see Belle Isle, the first landfall for ships making the northern approach from Europe to Canada. Northward can be seen the snow-covered mountains of Labrador, on the far side of the Strait.

Scholars have argued for centuries about the location of Vinland. It was not until 1961 and the following two years, when the Norwegian explorer, Dr. Helge Ingstad, dug up Norse remains dating back to the year 1000, that the site of Vinland on the south shore of the Strait of Belle Isle could be proven.[8]

The location is a perfect site for a colony. The climate is moderated by the sea, and protected from the Arctic Current by the Labrador projection. The scenery is magnificent, the meadows lush, the fishing good, and not only is there plenty of standing timber, but also driftwood, supplied by the main Arctic current.

Above all, there are quantities of *vinber* or wine-making berries; squashberries and blueberries grow in profusion.

One building, excavated by the Ingstad party, measured some fifty feet in length by forty-five in width. It consisted of a great hall and four rooms. There was evidence of stone fireplaces and ember pits, of a smith, nails and an anvil. The stones of the fire pits were just as the Vikings had left them and nothing had been disturbed. The nature of the buildings, their shape, contents and general layout resembled exactly the Viking sites in Greenland.

.   .   .

The Gudrid-Karlsefni expedition sailed up the western coast of Greenland, probably trading with settlements on the way. At the northern tip of settlement, about latitude 65°, the expedition sailed away from Greenland, travelling south or southwest.

The Viking ships were more seaworthy, but less comfortable, than the ships used five centuries later by Columbus, Cartier and Champlain. The ocean-going ships of the Norse were sailing ships, with a line of oars of moderately short sweep on either side for navigating in calms or shallow waters. There was no protection from the weather. The Vikings depended on an unclouded view of the sun or the stars to navigate by.

Luck was with Gudrid this time. After two days sailing across what we now call Davis Strait, the expedition sighted land. Boats were put ashore, and Gudrid would surely have been among the first to step onto the new land. This was probably at the southern tip of Baffin Land. The country was barren, covered everywhere by large flat stones, with arctic foxes the only life to be seen.

The expedition sailed on southward for two days, changed course to southeast, and found a well-forested land, inhabited by many wild animals. The Vikings called the land, "Markland". A traditional day's sailing in the time of the Vikings was 100 miles at four knots; in two days a ship might sail between 200 miles with a fair wind, and 340 miles with a very favourable wind and a good current. Four days of sailing from Greenland, with good winds, and carried by the Labrador Current, could have brought them well down the coast of Labrador, where tree growth begins.

The Gudrid-Karlsefni expedition followed the coast until they came to the area of Hamilton Inlet and Goose Bay where the land features are notable and prominent. Here, they found evidence of Thorvald's expedition — a broken keel placed as a landmark on a cape — showing that it was in this region of Labrador that Thorvald had been killed by Eskimos.

Gudrid and Karlsefni had brought with them two Scots, a man and a woman, who had been given to Leif as slaves and who were said to be "fleeter than deer". Their garments were alike, open at the sides and sleeveless, with a hood, and fastened between the legs by a button and loop. Karlsefni ordered the Scots put ashore to spy out the land. Three days later the messengers returned, one with a twig of *vinber,* the other with an ear of wild wheat.

Satisfied with this promising evidence, the expedition proceeded. They sailed into a strait at the entrance of which was an island surrounded by strong currents. Mistaking it for a fjord, they named it Straumsfjord — fjord of the strong currents. This was what we now call the Strait of Belle Isle. They had found Leif's Vinland, and Gudrid had reached her goal. She had come at last to the new world, where she was to stay for three years.

.   .   .

The Vikings unloaded their ships, and settled themselves in Leif's houses. This was to be their base camp. They had brought many kinds of livestock, including a bull, and as the pasture was excellent, the animals were allowed to roam. Eventually, they became wild and unmanageable.

Seduced at first by the goodness of the land and the ease of hunting and fishing, the expedition made no provision for the winter, and spent all of their time exploring. However, the weather fouled, and they found themselves short of food.

The period of scarcity did not last long, but it was serious enough to frighten them, and to make them more cautious. From then on they were never short of provisions, for they found good hunting on the mainland, fish in the sea, and an abundant supply of birds' eggs from breeding grounds on nearby islands.

During that autumn of 1007, Gudrid gave birth to her first child. "At this time," says the sagaman, "Gudrid, Karlsefni's wife, lay in of a male child and the child was called Snorri." In another account, the sagaman says, "Karlsefni's son, Snorri, was born there the first autumn. He was three winters old when they left."

This was the high moment of Gudrid's life. She was the first European woman to give birth to a child in America. She was also the mother of the first European colony in the new world, and the colony had been successfully launched.

During the first winter, wood and *vinber* were gathered and stored. In the spring, Karlsefni and one of his partners, Snorri, with about forty men, sailed off to the south on an exploratory trip. Straumsfjord belonged to Leif, and as he was not disposed to give it up, Gudrid and Karlsefni had to look elsewhere for a place to settle.

Now that Gudrid had a child, she was no longer carefree. She could not travel easily with a small infant, so she stayed at Straumsfjord to look after the settlement. With her, Karlsefni left one of his partners, Bjarni, and about 100 men. There is no hint in the sagas that Gudrid was content with these arrangements, but as someone had to stay behind in charge of the base settlements, it made sense that she, the wife of the commandant, should do so.

For the first time, Gudrid saw an expedition go off without her.

Sailing south, Karlsefni came to what he thought would be a favourable site for a colony. There was a bay which the men named "Hop" (pronounced *hope*), a word which meant a land-locked bay, salt with high tide, fresh with low tide; and such it was. It was a peaceful and fertile spot. The men found wild grasses where the land was low, and *vinber* where the land was hilly. There was a brook full of fish, and they dug pits in the sand to trap halibut as the tide went out. Many wild animals and game were found in the forest.

Hop was almost certainly in the vicinity of White Bay, on the east coast of Newfoundland, and was probably on the bold promontory at the top of the eastern shore of the Bay. To-day, the names in the area suggest a good land — Green Point, Paradise Point, Baie Verte.

For the first fortnight, all went well at Hop. Then, one morning when the Vikings looked out to sea, they saw a great number of skin boats approaching, propelled by poles which seemed to wave in a sun-wise motion. The poles were, of course, double-bladed paddles, unknown to the Norse. The cumulative effect of a large number of these paddles in rapid action is almost like looking into the spokes of a revolving wheel. Karlsefni and his men were amazed.

"What does this mean?" asked Karlsefni.

"Maybe it is a token of peace," his partner, Snorri, said. "Let's take a white shield and carry it toward them."

The Eskimos or *Skraelings* came ashore, curious no doubt to see the strange blond creatures and their unfamiliar equipment. The sagaman describes the Eskimos: ". . . dark ugly men with coarse hair on their heads; their eyes were conspicuous and they were broad across the cheeks. They stayed for a while marvelling, and then rowed away south beyond the cape."

Karlsefni and his party spent only a few months in the vicinity of Hop. This had been a scouting party. When they returned to Straumsfjord, where Gudrid and Bjarni had been in command, the settlement was in good order, with supplies well-stocked for winter. Gudrid's son, Snorri, was now about a year old, toddling about. The livestock was allowed to range, and they found their own grazing all that winter, for there was almost no snow.

Early one morning in the following spring, the Vikings saw a multitude of skin boats or kayaks, so many that the bay looked as if it had been sown with charcoal. They came around the headland from the south, and from each boat the poles were waving in the same sun-wise motion as before. Karlsefni took this as a good omen, and he and his men carried out their shields to show welcome.

They were unable to talk to the visitors, but they traded. The Eskimos traded their furs for pieces of red cloth which they tied around their heads. When the cloth began to run short, the Norse traders cut it into finger widths, but the Eskimos were still eager. They would have bought swords and spears too, but Karlsefni and Snorri forbade the men to dispose of their weapons. When most of the red cloth had been traded, Gudrid and the other women brought out dairy products to trade. Once the Eskimos had tasted the cheeses and butter and milk, they were no longer interested in the cloth.

In the midst of the trading, however, the bull belonging to Gudrid and Karlsefni, rushed out of the woods, bellowing. Completely terrified by this beast, the Eskimos gathered up their bundles of pelts, rushed to their kayaks, and paddled off to the south. "They carried their profits in their stomachs," says the sagaman.

Karlsefni now decided that a protective fence should be built around the habitation, to strengthen its defence. When the Eskimos returned a few weeks later, they were in greater numbers than before, and they brought more bundles of pelts. Gudrid and the women brought out their dairy products which the Eskimos liked so well. This time trading was done over the fence.

While the trading was going on, Gudrid sat watching from the door of her house, beside the cradle of her small son. A shadow passed over her, and a strange woman appeared, wearing a black kirtle or cloak with a snood over her hair. She was short, with golden hair, pale skin and eyes that were too large for a human head. She went to where Gudrid was sitting and asked, "What are you called?"

"I am called Gudrid. What are you called?"

"I am called Gudrid," the stranger said.

Gudrid, of our story, put our her hand towards the stranger to welcome her and to offer her a seat, but there was suddenly a loud noise and the strange woman vanished. At the same moment, one of the Eskimos, who had been about to steal a weapon, was killed by one of the Norsemen. The Eskimos quickly withdrew, leaving behind some of their goods and clothes.

No one but Gudrid had seen the strange woman. Did Gudrid truly think she had seen the apparition? Or, more likely, was this Gudrid's subtle way of warning the superstitious men that their security measures were lax? In any case, the story of the spirit woman was taken to be a warning.

"We must be cautious," said Karlsefni, "and take counsel, for I am sure they will come a third time. If they come again, it will be with hostility, and there will be many more of them. We will plan to send ten men out to the cape to show themselves there. The rest of our men will go into the woods and make a clearance for our cattle and wait until the enemy appears. We will put the bull in front of us."

When the Eskimos returned, as Karlsefni had predicted they poured into the bay in a multitude, with great shouting, their poles whirling madly.

The two parties clashed, the Eskimos using war-slings or throwing-sticks. Before the Norsemen could bring out their concealed cattle to frighten the Eskimos, the latter brought out a secret weapon of their own. They raised on a pole or harpoon, a great ball-shaped object, blue-black, which looked like an inflated sheep's paunch. This primitive balloon was hurled inland over the heads of the foremost Norse warriors and exploded with a terrific bang in their midst.

This time it was the Norsemen who flinched and ran. The noise stunned their senses, and they thought that the Eskimos were upon them from all sides. They ran up the river valley to the cliffs before they rallied.

It was a woman who saved the day. The fierce daughter of Eirik the Red, Freydis, came out of her house when she heard the explosion. Furious to see the Norsemen retreating, she shouted, "Why are you running from wretches like these? Fine fellows you are! I thought you would have knocked them on the head like cattle. Why, if I had a weapon, I think I could put up a better fight than any of you!"

The Greenlanders paid no attention to her.

Freydis tried to follow, but she was slow because she was pregnant. She kept on towards the forest, with the Eskimos close behind her. She found a dead Viking in her path, a sharp stone protruding from his head and his unsheathed sword beside him. This she took up to defend herself. When the Eskimos approached, she bared her breasts and she whetted the sword on them. The vision of such an amazon terrified the natives even more than the bull had, and they fled to their boats.

Karlsefni and the rest of the warriors reappeared, and praised Freydis loudly for her valour. Two of the Vikings had been killed and many of the natives. Altogether, the Vikings felt shamefaced about the whole affair.

A third winter of the Karlsefni-Gudrid expedition was spent at Straumsfjord. By now, there was discord among the Greenlanders. Jealousy over the women was at the root of it. There was discontent among the 155 men who did not have wives, and distrust among the five who did. A council was held and it was decided to return to Greenland. The reason given was that although the land was good, the attempt to form a colony was too dangerous due to the unknown temper and numbers of the Eskimos. Discord over the women was played down.

The sagaman does not tell how Gudrid felt about the failure of the expedition to settle a permanent colony. Apparently, she bowed silently to events, knowing that a successful colony could not be built upon discord. Perhaps, in some future time, another attempt might be made.

Young Snorri passed his third winter in America. Nothing is recorded of Freydis' child. It probably did not live.

.   .   .

In the spring, the whole expedition sailed away from Vinland with a south wind which took them to Markland. Here they found a party of five Eskimos, a man, two women and two children. Karlsefni's men managed to capture the two boys but the adults escaped. The two boys were brought to Greenland where they were taught to speak the Norse tongue, and where they were baptised. There is no further mention of these two Eskimo boys, but it would seem in character for Gudrid to continue to show an interest in their well-being after the expedition arrived back at Leif Eiriksson's. They were living mementos of her three years in Vinland.

There were two tragic sequels to the Karlsefni-Gudrid expedition. One was the loss of one of the three ships on the return journey to Greenland. The ship was blown eastward towards Ireland and sank; Bjarni, who had been co-commander at Straumsfjord with Gudrid, was drowned, as were half of his men.

The other sequel is more gruesome. Freydis, the ungentle daughter of Eirik the Red, and half-sister of Leif and Thorstein, arranged a partnership with two Icelandic traders for yet another voyage to Vinland; this voyage was purely for trade with the Eskimos, and to bring back timber. At the end of the winter, when the ships were well loaded, Freydis pretended to her husband that she had been abused by the Icelandic partners and goaded Thorvard into avenging her. The men of the Icelandic party were surprised while sleeping, and all were killed. However, none of Freydis' men would touch the Icelandic women, so Freydis cried, "Give me an axe," and according to the sagaman, she, herself, hacked the five women to pieces.

Although Freydis tried to bribe her people to keep silent, the story leaked out when they returned to Eiriksfjord. The account of the grim killing came at last to the ears of Leif.

"I cannot treat my sister as she deserves," he said. "But this I will foretell — that their posterity will never survive."

If this tragedy had occurred during the previous century, when paganism prevailed, Freydis' bloody act would have been the prelude to an almost endless feud. As it was, Freydis and her husband were treated with contempt and were ostracised by the rest of the colony.

This act not only soiled the bright name of the Eiriksson family, but dampened enthusiasm for future expeditions to Vinland. There are hints of other trips to the west for timber, and perhaps for pelts, but these were carried on as straight business ventures. The glamour of colonization in Vinland was gone.

When Freydis arrived back from her ill-fated expedition, she found Gudrid and Karlsefni still in Greenland, their ship almost ready to sail for Norway. Karlsefni, the astute merchant, had spent the winter trading among the settlements in Greenland, and it was a common saying that, "never a richer ship sailed from Greenland" Greenland exports, at that time, were walrus ivory, ropes of walrus leather, and furs; Karlsefni's ship was heavily loaded with these, as well as with fur pelts from America.

Gudrid was now a rich woman. Even so, she left Greenland with a heavy heart, as the story of Freydis' treachery began to be whispered from ear to ear. Gudrid's expedition had been a joyful success; but this final act, this anti-climax, had darkened the memory of Leif's Vinland.

.   .   .

Karlsefni and Gudrid sailed directly to Norway without incident. Karlsefni spent the winter trading and selling and, "He and his wife were held in high esteem by the best people in Norway." In the spring, the ship was fitted out for Iceland.

Karlsefni bought land at Glambae, in the north of Iceland, and here he lived until he died, a man of wealth, prominent in the affairs of Iceland. Besides Snorri, who had been born in Vinland, Karlsefni and Gudrid had a second son, Thorbjorn, named for Gudrid's father.

Gudrid's adventures were not yet over. Karlsefni died before his sons reached manhood, and Gudrid took over the management of the estate. After Snorri was married, Gudrid, not yet surfeited with travel, went off on a long journey to the south. It was said that she went as far as Rome.

Her arrival in Rome must have caused a stir. Although travel between Iceland and Rome was a common occurrence in Gudrid's day, Rome could have had few visitors who had lived in the new world beyond the Atlantic, and none with the daring, the wealth and the beauty of Gudrid. Certainly, after this time, the Vatican took a deep interest in Greenland's affairs.[9]

When Gudrid returned to her home at Glambae, she found that Snorri had built a small monastery. Eventually, she entered this monastery, and lived a life of seclusion until her death.[10]

It is easy to picture Gudrid in her old age; around her, the snow-capped mountains of Northern Iceland which reminded her of those further mountains across the northern sea in Greenland — those mountains that had called to her in her youth. During the long summer evenings, one of her grandchildren, perhaps Snorri's daughter Hallfrid, would come to talk to her in the quiet monastery, and Gudrid would tell the story of the voyages to Vinland.

It is not told who, among Gudrid's descendants, first put her stories of Vinland in writing. However, the writing of the *Book of Iceland* was begun when Hallfrid's son, Thorlak, was a comparatively young man. Thorlak, who was the Bishop of Skálholt, was an educated man. He was also the grandson of Snorri, the first white child born in America.

Notes

1. R.F. De Costa, *The Pre-Columbian Discovery of America* (Albany, N.Y.: 1890), p. 104.

2. The two principle sagas which share the title of *Eiriks Saga Rauða* are known, in English, more often by their sub-titles, *Saga of Thorfinn Karlsefni* and *Saga of the Greenlanders*. Why some details are accepted as historically genuine, and others discounted by scholars of Icelandic antiquities, seems to depend on the favoured theory of the critic. Gwyn Jones, in *The Norse Atlantic Saga,* treats the controversy with restraint

and common sense. The discovery of the Norse site at L'Anse aux Meadows at the northern tip of Newfoundland by Helge Ingstad, in 1961, settled many of the old arguments.

3. Gwyn Jones, *Eirik the Red and Other Icelandic Sagas* (Toronto: Oxford University Press, 1961), p. 130. Quotes and conversations from the sagas are from this text or from *Precolumbian Discovery of America.*

4. Eirik the Red was banished by the *Thing,* the assembly of law, because of his part in a lengthy, blood feud. Many of his supporters, including Gudrid's father, thought that he had been unfairly judged.

5. Many scholars are doubtful of this first marriage of Gudrid. It is told in the *Saga of the Greenlanders,* but not in the *Saga of Thorfinn Karlsefni.* However, Thorer is mentioned a number of times quite specifically. To include Thorer as one of Gudrid's husbands, and as an historical figure, does nothing to distort the chronology of main events.

6. Leif's rescue of Gudrid and Thorer is told in the *Saga of the Greenlanders* but not in the *Saga of Thorfinn Karlsefini.*

7. Christianity had only recently been introduced to Iceland. Leif introduced Christianity to Greenland in the year 1000. Eirik the Red was of the old religion, but his wife was a Christian and built the first church in Greenland.

8. The Norse site on the northern tip of Newfoundland was officially recognized by the Smithsonian Institute on November 5, 1963.

9. In 1121, Bishop Eirik was sent to Vinland to establish a mission. What became of him, or his mission, is not known.

10. Among Gudrid's descendants were at least three bishops, a governor, a noted scholar, and several prominent women.

Bibliography

Arbman, Holger. *The Vikings.* London: 1961.

Barrett, Elizabeth. "Did the Vikings reach here first?" *Evening Telegram,* St. John's, Nfld., Aug. 24, 1962.

Carson, Rachel. *The Sea Around Us,* Chapter 12. New York: 1960.

Danielson, Hjalmus. "Iceland's Golden Age Literature." *The Icelandic Canadian,* Vol. 14, No. 3 and 4. Winnipeg: 1956.

De Costa, B.F. *Precolumbian Discovery of America.* Albany: 1890.

Hermannsson, Halldor. "Problem of Vinland". *Islandica.* Ithica: 1936.

Jones, Gwyn. *Eirik the Red* (translation). Toronto: 1961.

Jones, Gwyn. *The Norse Atlantic Saga.* Toronto: 1964.

Mallet, Paul H. *Northern Antiquities.* London: 1755, trans. 1770.

Mortensen, Karl. *A Handbook of Norse Mythology.* (trans. by Crowell) New York: 1913.

Munn, W.A. *Vineland Voyages.* St. John's, Nfld: reprint 1946.

Oleson, T.J. *The Norsemen in America.* The Canadian Historical Association, Booklet 14: 1963.

Reeves, A.M. *The Founding of Wineland the Good.* London: 1890.

Stefansson, V. *Northwest to Fortune.* New York: 1956.

Stefansson, V. *Greenland.* New York: 1942.

Whitaker, Ian. "Vinland Discovered". Address to the Newfoundland Historical Society, published in *Daily News.* St. John's, Nfld: Oct. 26, 1962.

2

Marguerite de Roberval

So there they were, and they set up a menage, and built a lodging of leaves and made beds of the same until they had skins of the beasts in abundance, of which they ate the flesh: and they lived on fruit, for bread they could not have.

Andre Thevet[1]

Gudrid's expedition to Vinland was not forgotten.

A curious incident occurred while Gudrid and Karlsefni were trading in Norway. In addition to the goods from Greenland, Karlsefni had brought exotic wares from Vinland, fur pelts, *vinber* and *massür-wood*. Karlsefni had had a piece of this massür-wood, probably maple, carved into a house-bar — an ornamental gable-post — which had much the same import to a Norseman that a hearthstone had for an Englishman.

While waiting in harbour for a favourable wind, Karlsefni met a man from Bremen who became interested in the house-bar. This man wanted to buy it but Karlsefni refused. However, so tempting an offer was made that Karlsefni could not resist and

the stranger from Bremen took away the house-bar of massür-
wood.

The first written account of Vinland came from Adam of
Bremen, rector of a Cathedral school in Bremen and a noted
geographer-historian. Adam wrote two books in the 1070's,
sixty years after the episode of the sale of the house-bar in
Norway.

Adam says, "He [the King of Denmark] told me of yet another island, discovered by many in that ocean, which is called
Wineland because grapes grow wild there, producing the best of
wine. Moreover that self-sown grain abounds there we have
ascertained, not from fabulous conjecture, but from the reliable
report of the Danes [Norse]."[2]

This information came from King Swen of Denmark. However, Adam must have heard rumours of the lands beyond the
ocean long before his talk with King Swen. Anyone from
Bremen in 1070 would know about the exotic house-bar. He
would also have heard about Gudrid and Karlsefni and Vinland.
The man from Bremen who bought the house-bar would not
have kept this marvelous story a secret.

The story of Vinland was told and retold by the story-tellers
of Iceland and preserved for the archives of the Vatican by men
like Adam.

John Cabot and Christopher Columbus both went to the
Danish and Norse seamen for their sailing directions across the
Atlantic. Cabot followed the old Gudrid-Karlsefni sailing route,
making his landfall somewhere near the Strait of Belle Isle and
Leif's Vinland. Columbus sailed far to the south because he was
looking for China and not the uninhabited wilderness of Gudrid's new world.

After the Vikings, the second known attempt to colonize in
North America was not until the time of Jacques Cartier, in
1541. Again, there were a few women included, and again a
white child was born in the new world. The enterprise began
with a great flourish, and ended two years later in a fizzle.

During the whole ill-managed, ill-tempered expedition,
there was only one person whose behavior was heroic, and
that was a woman. She was Marguerite de La Roque de

Roberval, the niece of the commander, Sieur de Roberval.

. . .

Jacques Cartier discovered the Gulf of St. Lawrence in 1534. Seven years later, on January 15, 1541, Jean-François de La Rocque de Roberval[3] was commissioned by the King of France to found a colony in the newly discovered land. Roberval was made viceroy to the King, François I, and Cartier was appointed his lieutenant.

There was conflict between these two men from the start. Jacques Cartier had planned to found the colony himself, but he was superseded by Roberval, who had more influence at court. Roberval, a professional soldier, was a courtier and a personal friend of the King. Being a friend of François I seemed to be his chief qualification.

The King was excited about the new lands and put some of his own money into the enterprise. The expedition was to consist of ten ships, provisioned for two years, 400 sailors, 300 soldiers, materials for twenty small gunboats, a company of artisans—men and women recruited from the prisons of France—and some livestock. According to André Thevet, Geographer Royal, Roberval was hopeful that "even if this country did not bring him great profits, at least it would bring him immortal glory, and God willing, he would save a savage people from the depth of ignorance. . . ."[4]

The story of Marguerite de La Roque who went on this expedition, was first written in a journal of court gossip by Marguerite de Navarre,[5] the clever sister of François I. Some years later, André Thevet retold the Roberval story in his *Cosmographie Universelle*. The two accounts are almost the same except for some unimportant details. Thevet's story is livelier and more intimate. He claims to have been a personal friend of Sieur de Roberval and also of Jacques Cartier, and he says he got his story from Marguerite herself. Some time after her return to France "this poor woman came to the town of Nontron in Périgord when I was there and she told me what happened".[6]

Jacques Cartier, with five ships, sailed in the spring of 1541 but Roberval was delayed and his expedition did not sail until the following year. While waiting for his ships to be fitted, Roberval decided to invite his niece, Marguerite, to come along on this daring adventure. He was extremely fond of Marguerite and considered her almost a daughter. Jean-François and Marguerite were co-seigneurs of a property at Pontpoint near Senlis, northeast of Paris. The La Roques were an old, noble family from the south of France, but the Roberval properties were in Picardy in the northeast. La Rocque de Roberval was heavily in debt to most of his relatives, and possibly he was in debt to Marguerite. This is merely supposition, but might help to explain his later actions. There is no doubt that he was a harsh commander.

Marguerite, however, was tempting fate. Unknown to Roberval, there was a handsome young man in the expedition "who came more for the love of the damoiselle than for the service of the King or respect for the Captain".

The young man's name is not mentioned by Thevet or by Navarre.

Roberval's three ships, with their cargo of humans, provisions, livestock and ordnance, set sail April 16 from La Rochelle but suffered from contrary winds so that they had to put into harbour off the coast of Brittany. They were further delayed by bad weather and did not drop anchor at St. John's, Newfoundland, until June 8. In the harbour, Roberval found seventeen fishing ships and became involved in a quarrel between French and Portuguese fishermen. The time taken by this quarrel and to provide the ships with fresh water cost another three weeks. It was at this moment that Jacques Cartier arrived from the St. Lawrence, homeward bound.

Cartier reported to his chief that, "he could not with his small company withstand the savages which went about daily to annoy him". Roberval ordered Cartier to return to Canada and Cartier complied sulkily. They left St. John's at the end of June and sailed north for the Strait of Belle Isle.

·   ·   ·

During this eight week voyage, the two lovers had little to do but enjoy one another's company. The three weeks at St. John's, with no duties and with spring in the air, was an unexpected gift. They climbed the rocky hills, gathered blueberries, hunted caribou and fished for salmon, away from the confinement of the ship. In their indiscretion, they were abetted by Damienne, a trusted old servant of Marguerite. Damienne acted as a guard for the lovers.

Word of the affair got to Roberval and he was furious. He was far angrier with his niece than with the young man, for he thought she was disgracing the name of La Roque as well as insulting him personally. Was not this the girl he had treated as an intimate, almost as a daughter?

Roberval thought of separating them by putting them on different ships, but when a warning had no noticeable effect, he decided otherwise. He held his patience until the small fleet had left St. John's and approached Isle des Demons. There is evidence that Isle des Demons is now called the Island of Fogo, a large island off the north-east coast of Newfoundland.[7]

According to Thevet, this island called by the sailors Isle des Demons, "is the largest and nicest, but now inhabited by great apparitions and ghosts, which can be seen there by tricks of the devils, as experienced by the Christians themselves, and that is why it is called the Island of the Devils or Demons. It is a shame because it is so pretty and attracts more than any of the other islands. We go there to fish during the day and also to hunt but if one gets lost. . . "

This was the island that Roberval chose for Marguerite's exile. It is unlikely that he knew or gave any thought to the sailors' talk about demons. The island was one that he happened to be passing on his way north to the Strait of Belle Isle. In order to accomplish his purpose without interference, Roberval ordered Jacques Cartier to sail ahead. In this manoeuvre, Roberval was outsmarted, for Cartier, eager to return to France rather than spend another miserable winter in the new world, headed straight for St. Malo.

Roberval's plan was to punish Marguerite but not to harm the young man. Anchoring off the Isle des Demons, the Captain put

down a boat and ordered Marguerite into it with her old servant, Damienne. He told Marguerite that this was the place he
had chosen for her punishment. She had brought it upon herself
by her reckless behavior and now she must atone for the scandal
she had brought to the name of La Roque.

Sieur de Roberval provided her with four arquebuses and
some ammunition, so that she could defend herself against wild
animals. Then he ordered the boat off to the island.

It is unlikely that he meant the exile to be permanent.
French, Portuguese and English ships were fishing regularly in
these waters and the chance that Marguerite and her old servant
would be picked up by one of them was within reason. At least,
a man in Roberval's position might have rationalized that this
would happen.

In any case, he probably cared very little about what would
happen to her. These were feudal times, when common man,
and all women and animals, had little value. Life was cheap.
Only a few years before, Henry VIII of England had beheaded
his wife, Anne Boleyn. Besides, Roberval argued, Marguerite
had humiliated him. If she had no concern for him, why should
he have any for her?

Whatever plans he might have had for her later rescue were
immediately changed, however. The nameless young man
panicked. He was afraid that he would be put on another island
and separated from Marguerite. Hastily, he gathered up some
clothes, a few tools and his arquebus, and jumped into the boat
along with Marguerite and Damienne.

In Marguerite de Navarre's version of the story, it was the
young man who roused the ire of the Captain because of in-
subordination. When Roberval ordered the offender to be
removed to the deserted island, Marguerite begged to go with
him. Whichever version is correct, there is no doubt that the
two young people were in love and that they had courage. Poor
Damienne probably had no choice.

After depositing the party of three on the island, the most out-
lying island on the whole North American coast, Roberval sailed
away to Cap Rouge, on the north shore of the St. Lawrence
River, a few miles upstream from the site of Quebec city.

Thevet attempts to justify Roberval's action, arguing that he was:

Distressed by the harm his relative had done him, and pleased to have been able to punish them without staining his hands with their blood.

So there they were, and they set up a menage, and built a lodging of leaves and made beds of the same until they had skins of the beasts in abundance, of which they ate the flesh: and they lived on fruit, for bread they could not have.

.   .   .

The first summer passed comfortably. They built themselves a log cabin and slept on cedar boughs covered with furs. With plenty of wild game, fresh fruit and birds' eggs, their life was a kind of utopia.

It was only at nights that the spirits or demons terrified them ". . . as they tried to knock down their lodging, and took on shapes of all sorts of frightful animals". Christian faith gradually overcame the evil spirits, Marguerite said, and the hauntings ceased except for the loud cries at night which sounded like the noises and confusion of a busy market place. These noises may have been the night calls of American species of birds, many of which were quite unknown to Europeans. Most of these birds migrated south for the winter; as they departed, the unfamiliar frightening noises dwindled.

The first tragedy struck Marguerite's colony after she had become pregnant and was becoming big and awkward. They had been on the island for eight months by then, but had not seen a single ship, nothing whatever that could even have given them hope of rescue. The young man became depressed; as his morale drooped he became physically ill and he died. Marguerite's sorrow was intense but she was made of tough fibre. She had Damienne and the child to care for, so she learned to use the arquebus, a matchlock gun light enough for a woman to hold. She became so skilful, in fact, that on one day she killed three bears, so she told Thevet. One bear was white as an egg and was probably a polar bear. Polar bears are known to reach

Newfoundland, floating down from the north on ice pans.

After Marguerite's child was born, she baptised it herself. There was little ceremony.

A year went by, with Marguerite providing the food and defending her little party from the wild animals. A constant look-out was kept for passing ships, but no ships came.

.   .   .

Roberval's colony at Charlesbourg Royal on Cap Rouge was a disaster. Roberval himself was a bad-tempered, harsh commander, as well as a poor administrator. Scurvy nearly wiped out the colonists and the Indians were hostile. The Indian chief, Donnacona, whom Jacques Cartier had abducted and taken to France, had died in Paris and his people were not satisfied with the French explanations. La Rocque de Roberval, surrounded by suspicious natives, and by dying and surly Frenchmen, appealed to France for help and two ships were sent out to him. What was left of the colony and the high hopes of glory were taken back to France.

But no ships came to Isle des Demons. Marguerite continued to be optimistic, however, and managed to keep her small party in good spirits until the sixteenth or seventeenth month of their stay on the island. Then, in rapid succession, the old servant and the child died. This time, Marguerite had no one to help her mourn, nor to help her bury the bodies in the rocky soil. It was the autumn, and ahead of her lay the long winter which she had to face alone. For a time she nearly lost her courage, she told Thevet, for there was no one to talk to except the wild things and she kept seeing visions, "stranger than man could imagine". But she was a good Christian and she prayed to God; she believed that he renewed her courage and the strange visions vanished.

For a year, she lived on the island alone.

.   .   .

Then, one day – more than a year after the death of Damienne and the child, two years and five months after she had been left on the island — Marguerite saw ships: passing her island in full view were ships fishing for cod. She ran to the seashore and lit a smoke fire and signalled. Afraid that this was not enough, she ran up and down the shore, shouting and waving, but the fishermen thought she was one of the dreaded spirits and kept off shore.

Perhaps the fishermen, who were Bretons, saw something remarkably human in her desperation for, at length, one boat cautiously approached the island. They were amazed to find not an evil spirit but a woman, and a Frenchwoman at that. First, Marguerite had to show the fishermen her wood hut and the parts of the island where she had lived out her exile. Then, when the men were about to take her off to their ship, she was overcome with remorse and sorrow for her lover, her child and her servant. She said that she could never leave the place but wanted to die on Isle des Demons.

The Bretons persuaded her that she would be more sensible to return to France, and when they left she accompanied them willingly. However, when she talked to Thevet sometime later in the town of Nontron in Périgord, she told him that at times she wished she were back on the Isle des Demons with the three she had left buried there.

This is the end of the story as André Thevet tells it, but Marguerite de Navarre has a little to add: "They brought the poor woman with them straight to La Rochelle where they arrived after the voyage. There, when they made known to the inhabitants the fidelity and perseverance of this woman, she was received with great honour by all the women, who voluntarily brought her their daughters so she could teach them how to read and to write. In this honest way, she earned enough to keep her the rest of her life."

It is pleasant to think of Marguerite with her small pupils; occasionally she could have added some drama to her lessons by telling the little girls how a young woman could shoot three bears, "one white as an egg". No doubt she made a better teacher because of her venturesome youth.

One should question the phrase that she "earned enough to

keep her the rest of her life". Her ancestral properties were in Périgord and unless her uncle had bankrupted her, she need only teach for pleasure.

It is interesting to imagine her travelling to Nontron, a place 100 miles east of La Rochelle, to talk to the Friar, André Thevet, who knew Roberval and Jacques Cartier. Thevet had travelled to the Americas, and could understand when she talked of the sights and sounds of the new world. And, just possibly, he might have visited her island and seen the lonely graves.

·   ·   ·

Just as Gudrid's story was put into a book, so was Marguerite's. The stories were read and remembered. Marguerite's ability to take care of herself, alone, in the alien atmosphere of an unknown land proved that a person could live in the new land, depending on its resources, and survive.

It was not many years after the publication of Marguerite's story that Samuel de Champlain became Royal French Geographer. As a successor to André Thevet, Champlain had access to the latter's files which contained the story of Marguerite's exile on Isle des Demons. It is a remarkable tribute to Marguerite de la Roque that Champlain's success with his colony at Port Royal was founded on the theory that a colony could live off the land. Port Royal was the first colony in North America to succeed, and it was the first to use the products of the new land.

Marguerite's two years and five months on Isle des Demons had not been wasted.

Notes

1. André Thevet, *Cosmographie Universelle* (Paris: 1575), pp. 1019-20.
2. H.R. Holand, *Westward from Vinland* (New York: 1940), pp. 47-8.
3. The family name was La Roque. La Rocque de Roberval spelled his name *Rocque*.

4. Thevet was a Franciscan Friar who travelled extensively in the Americas in the 16th Century, and was the first French historian to describe America. Later he became Royal Geographer and chaplain to Queen Catherine de Medici. He was long considered a bogus scholar, but has recently been up-graded. Thevet himself never came to Canada but he talked to explorers who had — see the *Dictionary of Canadian Biography*, pp. 679-80. His story of Marguerite de Roberval is basically the same as that written by Marguerite de Navarre in *L'Heptameron*.

5. Marguerite de Navarre, *L'Heptameron* (Paris: 1559), pp. 392-5.

6. Quotes are from Thevet except where indicated.

7. According to Eric S. Jones, Member of the Newfoundland Legislature for Fogo in 1962, André Thevet's map of Isles des Demons is the present Island of Fogo *if* the top of the map is treated as south rather than north. Only recently has there been a convention among map-makers to put north at the top of the map. Folklore has usually placed Isle des Demons in the St. Lawrence, at the mouth of the Rivière Saint-Paul.

Bibliography

Biggar, H.P. *Early Trading Companies of New France,* pp. 231-42. Toronto: 1901.

Cartier, Jacques. *Jacques Cartier and his four voyages to Canada,* Translated by H.B. Stevens. Montreal: 1890.

De Costa, B.F. *Pre-Columbian Discovery of America.* Albany: 1893.

Denys, Nicolas. *Description and Natural History of the Coasts of North America (Acadia),* translated by W.F. Ganong. (Champlain Society) Toronto: 1908.

Hakluyt, R. *Voyages* (Divers Voyages Touching the Discovery of America). New York: 1965.

Holand, H.R. *Westward from Vinland.* New York: 1940.

Lescarbot, Marc. *Histoire de la Nouvelle France* (Paris: 1609), Champlain Society edition with English translation by W.L. Grant. 1907.

La Roque de Roquebrune R. "Marguerite de La Roque", *Dictionary of Canadian Biography,* pp. 425-6. Toronto: 1966.

Thevet, Andre. *Cosmographie Universelle.* Paris: 1575.

Trudel, M. *Dictionary of Canadian Biography,* Vol. I. Toronto: 1966.

Winsor, Justin. *Narrative and Critical History of America.* Boston: 1884-89.

3

Jeanne Mance

Scarcely a day without alarm.

Dollier de Casson.[1]

Why did Jeanne Mance, a sensible Frenchwoman, join so absurd a venture as the founding of a mission-colony at Montreal, deep in the Canadian wilderness? She knew some of the dangers. By 1641, every woman in France with a convent education knew the tragic story of Marguerite de Roberval.

It was true that Champlain had founded a small, durable colony at Quebec near the site of Jacques Cartier's failure, and that recently some Ursulines and some Augustinians had gone there as missionaries. But Montreal? Montreal was far from the sea, near the warpaths of the Iroquois. The *coureurs de bois* had penetrated up the St. Lawrence to the Great Lakes, and Jean Nicolet had reached the far shore of Lake Michigan, but this was the farthest west that Europeans had gone.

Jeanne Mance, a warm-hearted, friendly, young woman, was fired with the same enthusiasm for New France that affected so many others. She was born in Langres in Champagne, the province of Jeanne d'Arc, in 1606. Picturesque Langres, built high on a rocky promontory, was one of the oldest cities of France. It had been a religious centre for centuries; churches and convents crowded within its walls.

The Mance family was bourgeois of honourable stock. Jeanne's father, Charles Mance, was an attorney. Jeanne probably received her education in Langres at the Ursuline Convent which opened when she was seven years old. When she was nineteen, her mother died and Jeanne helped her father in the rearing of small brothers and sisters. Maître Mance was a religious man but he was affectionate and he put no restraints on his daughter's vocation. Jeanne was also religious but she was drawn away from the cloister to the world of healing. Her gift was nursing, and she learned her craft during a harsh period of war and plague.

During the 1630's, a plague swept Europe in the wake of the Thirty Years' War, striking the diocese of Langres more than once. After France entered the war in 1635, the great armies of Europe rolled over the countryside of Champagne, bringing desolation and plague as their passport. In the year 1637, over 5,500 people died in the neighbourhood of Langres. In that year the Bishop of Langres founded a hospital of charity and established an "association of pious ladies for the works of social charity". Although there are no registers surviving which prove that Jeanne Mance served with this association, it is believed that her voluntary nursing during these troubled times gave her the experience which lead to her vocation.

Jeanne, somewhat delicate in health, was an attractive woman of about average height, elastic of step, and quick in action. She had a warm personality with a persuasive tongue; on many occasions she was able to win others to her point of view. She never lacked friends and they came from all orders.

Jeanne had a cousin, Nicolas Dolebeau, who was chaplain at Sainte-Chapelle in Paris. While visiting his home town of Langres in April, 1640, he talked to Jeanne of the mission work being done by the Church in New France. The Dolebeau family were prejudiced in favour of the new colony, for one Dolebeau had gone to Quebec as one of the first Recollet missionaries, and another, an active Jesuit, was on his way to serve in the new mission. Nicolas Dolebeau, a learned ecclesiastic and a doctor of the Sorbonne, knew the world of Paris and beyond. From him Jeanne learned about the establishment of the Augustinian Hospitalières and the Ursulines in Quebec the previous year. He may have told her of *La Société de Notre-Dame de Montréal.*

Jeanne's first impulse to serve in Canada came as a result of her talk with Nicolas Dolebeau. She was thirty-three, and her father having died, she no longer had any responsibilities in Langres. She had a small annuity which gave her independence. But, she wondered, was her health up to it? We are not told what her indisposition was, but her indifferent health worried her; however, whenever she raised this matter as a possible obstacle to her fitness to serve in Canada, the thought was swept aside by her counsellors. Bad health was to be ignored as one would ignore a bothersome gnat. Her counsellors must have been right, for once she reached North America, the poor health vanished.

After her cousin returned to Paris, Jeanne, full of doubts and indecision, went to her spiritual advisor. He suggested that she go to Paris and talk to Père Lalemant who had the charge of the Jesuit mission in New France. Jeanne left for Paris on May 30, 1640. She told her friends and relatives that she was going to visit her cousin, Mme. de Bellevue, only sister of Nicolas Dolebeau, the Chaplain. Jeanne Mance never returned to Langres.

The Chaplain introduced her to those who could help her and she soon found herself among many interested people. Her interview with Père Lalemant was successful. She next called upon the Rector of the Jesuit Novitiate, Sainte-Jure. Nothing came as a result of this interview and three months slipped by before she saw him again. This period of waiting was a stiff trial and perhaps a necessary one. Although her courage was undiminished, her eager spirit was swamped with doubts and indecisions. Was her health fit? Was she, an "unknown", fit for such holy work? Did she have the necessary zeal? And where would she serve?

At last came a second interview with Père Saint-Jure, a long one; after this, he declared that she was a fit apostle; that he saw the will of God in her vocation; that she should declare openly her decision.

She declared her intentions to her family, and as she expected, they were horrified. But among the elite of Paris, she became a sensation. Everyone wanted to meet this young woman who was about to do such an extraordinary thing. It was noble, exciting, adventurous and pious. The ladies of Paris were inspired merely by talking to her. She met all the great ladies, the Princess de Condé, Charlotte de Montmorency, Madame the Chancellor, and even the Queen, Anne of Austria.

The militant zeal of the Jesuits had created a vogue in France; to work for New France was to work for the glory of God. Everyone from the King and Queen to the humblest unknowns in the provinces felt an urge to "do something" to help Christianize the Indians. To them, Indians were savages — Iroquois, Huron, Algonquin, Micmacs, all Indians were savages. Geography was irrelevant. The fact that the Island of Montreal was 1000 miles inland from the Atlantic and 150 miles up-river from Quebec, along a route almost impossible to defend, was not understood. Montreal was an exciting name, a mountain top above a mist. As for the Indians, God must have put them there to be converted.

Jeanne had made her declaration. She was committed to go to New France. Then, after the first flurry of excitement was over and the months passed by with no concrete opportunity offering itself, her self-doubts began to emerge again. Her declaration hung before her like an overripe berry. She was embarrassed. Perhaps she had been mistaken to attempt such a venture.

It was not until March, 1641, ten months after she had left Langres, that Jeanne Mance found her answer. In the preceding January, a distinguished Recollet, Père Rapine, had arrived in Paris. Jeanne was acquainted with him and so she went to him, telling him of her indecision. He approved of her ambitions and he assured her that it was only right that others should provide the means.

A few days later, Père Rapine sent word to Jeanne asking her to be ready to visit Angélique Faure, a distinguished Parisian and the widow of Claude de Bullion, Marquis de Gallardon, a former Minister of State. Madame de Bullion was immensely wealthy.

Jeanne was sent for in the afternoon and when she arrived at Hôtel de Bullion, she found Père Rapine already there. Madame de Bullion asked Jeanne about her ambitions and plans but the conversation was otherwise impersonal. On the second and third visits, much the same pattern was maintained, but on the fourth visit Madame de Bullion asked Jeanne if she would be willing to take charge of a hospital in New France, for she intended to endow one; she also asked Jeanne to make enquiries about the cost of the hospital already established at Quebec.

Jeanne was staggered by this offer. From the beginning, her thought had been to serve in a hospital as a lay nursing sister. She had no ambition to organize an operation. She temporized. She told Madame de Bullion that her health was unsatisfactory and she was afraid of taking on so much responsibility under such circumstances. Yet Jeanne was tempted. To have a whole establishment to herself, to run as she thought right! Perhaps, during her years as a volunteer at Langres, she had seen some gross mismanagement. Her fear of poor health melted before the challenge. She evaded the matter of health by telling Madame de Bullion that she placed herself entirely in the hands of God, and she went off to find out the cost of building in New France.

Although no words were said about Montreal, the two women were thoroughly aware of the *Société de Montréal*. Both knew that the hospital was meant for the projected mission-colony to be established at the site of the summer trading post begun by Champlain thirty years before. They both knew that it was a daring venture for, unlike other European colonies in America, Montreal was far from the seaboard. Besides, in all of New France there were only about 250 Europeans.

La Société de Notre-Dame de Montréal pour la Conversion de Sauvages de la Nouvelle-France had been founded as a mission-colony by Sieur Jerome Le Royer de la Dauversière, a man obsessed by good causes. In 1640, La Dauversière negotiated a transfer of property rights of the Island of Montreal to his *Société* which was then reformed into the *Compagnie de Montréal*. Paul Chomedy de Maisonneuve, a soldier noted for his coolness and his bravery, was appointed Commander and first Governor of the Island of Montreal. Like Jeanne Mance, Maisonneuve was without family ties and free to devote his life to the new colony.

Jeanne went again to Père Saint-Jure to consult him. She spent ten days in retreat and then, assured by him that her decision was sound, she returned to Madame de Bullion to accept. A contract was drawn up for the establishment of the *Hôtel-Dieu de Ville-Marie.* Arrangements were also made with the Company of Montreal for the inclusion of Jeanne Mance and her hospital in the proposed mission-colony.

As for the endowment, Madame de Bullion wished to be an unknown benefactor and asked Jeanne to communicate with her only through Père Rapine. This request for secrecy was to cause problems as time went on.

The last days in Paris slipped by, days full of preparation, business, farewells. Jeanne had an interview with Jean Jacques Olier, the founder of the Sulpicians and one of the first Associates of the *Société de Montréal.* L'abbé Olier was to have a profound effect on her life many years later. Jeanne also paid a final visit to Madame de Bullion who gave her a purse of 1,200 *livres.*

"Take this," she said, "as a token of our good will, until the business matters are completed."

She also gave to Jeanne, as personal gifts, a miniature framed in gold and inlaid with pearls, and a piece of valuable jewellery.

.   .   .

Jeanne left Paris in April, 1641. Her relatives wished to accompany her to Dieppe on the English channel where some of the ships of the Company were loading. But Jeanne would have none of this. She wanted at all costs to avoid a long drawn-out farewell and chose to go to La Rochelle which was more than twice the distance. She knew that Maisonneuve was at La Rochelle making his last preparations, and perhaps she hoped to see La Dauversière there as well. Although Jeanne Mance had thrown in her lot with this group of dreamers, she had not yet met any of the principals.

The trip from Paris to La Rochelle on the Bay of Biscay was long and tiring but her treatment at the inns along the route was embarrassingly kind. Dollier de Casson, the historian of Montreal and a contemporary of Jeanne Mance, says that she was so well received wherever she went that the innkeepers often hesitated to take her money.

Jeanne called at the Jesuit Residence at La Rochelle as soon as she arrived. The next morning, on her way to church, she encountered La Dauversière, the pious enthusiast. Although they had not met before, there was an instant recognition.

La Dauversière told her his plans and his ultimate aims but he confessed that the Company of Montreal had one great lack. They had Maisonneuve to lead the colony and to defend it, but they needed someone to supervise the stores, to organize the household, and to care for the sick and wounded until the hospital could be built. Would Mademoiselle Mance undertake that responsibility?

Jeanne hesitated as she had hesitated over Madame de Bullion's proposal not so many weeks before. This time the condition of her health did not trouble her but she wondered if the added responsibilities might not make her too bound by the disciplines of office. She might lose her freedom of action.

"If I do this," she said to La Dauversière, "I will become dependent on others and I will be depending less on Providence."

After this conversation at the church, La Dauversière called at her lodging, urging her to accept his proposal. He told her that the Company had already spent 75,000 *livres* on the project, and that they did not know where the next *sol* would come from. Truly, he pointed out, they were dependent on God, otherwise the project could not go on.

Jeanne Mance weakened. More than likely, she feared that her hospital would fail along with the whole grand design if there were not someone with practical ability in a position to administer the business. Was this to be her task? She told La Dauversière that she would write to Père Saint-Jure, and to her family, for advice.

"Lose no time," La Dauversière said. "Write by the next post to Père Saint-Jure." So Jeanne wrote.

Jeanne was next introduced to Maisonneuve and to Baron de Fancamp, one of the chief contributors. They both urged her to accept the Company's proposal. She learned that she was to sail on a small ship with Père de Laplace and twelve men. Maisonneuve and twenty-five other recruits would sail at the same time in another ship. She balked when she heard there would be no other women on the ships bound for the new colony but a timely letter arrived from Dieppe where the third ship was loading. On this ship, two of the men were taking their wives and a young girl had joined them. Montreal would have four women.

Word came from Père Saint-Jure, and from her relatives, advising her to accept the Company's offer. When she made her acceptance known to Maisonneuve, La Dauversière and Fancamp, they received her as an associate of the Company, "a gift from heaven". She was the eighth member of the *Société,* which was later augmented by many more. La Dauversière and Fancamp had contributed most of the original 75,000 *livres;* Mademoiselle Mance and Sieur de Maisonneuve contributed their services.

Before leaving La Rochelle, Jeanne persuaded La Dauversière to put the objects of the Company in writing and to have copies made. She herself wrote letters to enclose with the statement and sent them to the notable patrons she had met in Paris, begging for subscribers. La Dauversière carried out all of her suggestions and within a year forty-five new members had been enrolled, ensuring the financial support of the colony.

Thus, even before leaving France, Jeanne's talent to persuade, combined with her sound practical sense, shored up the Company on its shaky foundations. Jeanne's sensible mind would not be satisfied with La Dauversière's blithe attitude. Jeanne must know where the next *sol* would come from. After all, she was responsible for the founding of a hospital, not a castle in the air.

.   .   .

The two ships carrying the people and goods of the Company of Montreal sailed from La Rochelle, June 1, 1641. Two years before, Marie de l'Incarnation and Madeleine de La Peltrie had set out for Quebec to found the Ursuline Convent. With them had gone the Augustinian Hospitalières.

Mère Marie's work was as an educator among the young girls, French and Indian. She was a stern, self-disciplined individual, and like Jeanne Mance she was practical. Madame de La Peltrie, who financed the establishment of the Convent, was like La Dauversière, a pious enthusiast, full of good works but flighty. Together, Marie de l'Incarnation and Madame de La Peltrie founded an institution so sound that it has lasted to this day.

Like them, Jeanne was to establish a sound institution, but to accomplish this she had to return three times to France to help reorganize the affairs of the Colony and the hospital.

The ship in which Jeanne was passenger had clear sailing and reached Quebec on August 8, but that in which Maisonneuve travelled became separated from its partner and ran into fierce storms.

Jeanne's welcome at Quebec was not as ecstatic as that of the Ursulines and Hospitalières had been two years earlier. She was faced with unexpected problems as soon as she set foot ashore, and she was unusually vulnerable because she was still weak from prolonged seasickness. However, Père Le Jeune observes in the *Relations* of that year, that she "found at Quebec more [health] than she had when she left la Rochelle".

So Jeanne Mance unwittingly found her way into the *Relations,* the "Journal of the Jesuits", and became part of the mystique created by the Jesuits in the first half of the 17th Century. Jeanne did not consider herself a heroine, nor of any special fibre. She was simply following an impulse, a call, which seemed urgent to her; yet by arriving in New France at that romantic time, she helped build the legend of the saints and heroes.

In Quebec, Jeanne found an awkward situation. The Company ship from Dieppe had arrived before her and the men were already constructing a warehouse, but Maisonneuve had not arrived. Concerned for his safety and for the fortune of the whole venture, Jeanne also found that the people of Quebec were not at all sympathetic to the Montreal scheme. It was dubbed *la folle enterprise.* Governor de Montmagny had decided that Montreal would be too difficult to defend, and many feared that it would have an advantage in the fur trade. All these people tried to divert Jeanne from her purpose of establishing a hospital on the Island of Montreal. They tried to persuade her that the Island of Orleans would be more suitable. Downstream, but within sight of Quebec, Orleans was a large fertile island, and one large force could defend either community.

This suggestion was sensible, but Jeanne Mance was not to be swayed. Her contract called for her to go to the Island of Montreal and there she would go.

We are not told that she was housed with the Ursulines during those first weeks, but quite possibly she was, for Madame de La Peltrie, one of the founders of the convent, soon began to identify herself with the Montreal cause. The Governor's habitation, built on the sharp cliffs of Cap Diamond, gave a commanding view of the river, and Jeanne must have gone there regularly to watch for the coming of Maisonneuve.

It was not until August 20 that Maisonneuve reached Quebec, his ship battered but afloat. He had lost several men overboard during the storms. One of these was the surgeon, but Maisonneuve had been able to replace this necessary member of staff as a result of a chance encounter at Tadoussac. There, on a ship returning to France, Maisonneuve found a ship's surgeon willing to go back to Canada.

Jeanne Mance quickly told Maisonneuve about her problems at Quebec. Maisonneuve called first on the Governor to make his arrival official, and then on the Jesuits. From all sides he heard the same arguments which Jeanne had heard.

"You know that war has broken out again with the Iroquois," said the Governor of Quebec to the new Governor of

Montreal. "As they broke the peace in a way which shows that they are more active than ever, you will hardly consider establishing yourselves in so remote a spot. You must change your plans; if you like, you can have the Island of Orleans. In any case, the season is too far advanced for you to reach the Island of Montreal this year, even if you thought of doing so."

Maisonneuve replied,

> Sir, what you tell me would be excellent if I had been sent to look about and select a place. But as it had been decided by the Company who sent me that I should go to Montreal, my honour obliges me to go there and found a colony were every tree on the island changed into an Iroquois — And you will, I am sure, approve my decision. Since the season is so late, I will content myself to reconnoitring the place, before winter, with the most active of my men, so that I may see where I can plant my people next spring.

So it was decided. Governor de Montmagny, relieved to discover in Maisonneuve more prudence than he had expected, proposed that he should accompany the advance party to help choose a site. They went up river that autumn, and on October 15, took possession of the Island of Montreal in the name of the Company of Montreal, and chose the site which Champlain had used for his trading post, *Place Royale,* as the best spot for the first buildings.

While Maisonneuve was exploring the Island of Montreal, Jeanne remained at Quebec, attending to the needs of the Montreal colonists. Quebec, 1641, was no showplace. Champlain, its founder, had died six years before. Although more than thirty years old, the colony was still half trading post, half mission, a clutch of log buildings set on the edge of wilderness. Overlooking the colony, on top of the blue-green prominence of Cap Diamond, was the fort, built so to command the river, upstream and down.

Most of the buildings were in Lower Town, but by 1641, the year Jeanne Mance arrived, building had begun in Upper Town under the protecting shadow of the fort.

The Ursulines and the Hospitalières had brought a

conspicuous social change to the few inhabitants, for until their coming there had been only a handful of women; Marie Rollet, the widow of Louis Hébert, being the most prominent. Even with these *religieuses,* however, Quebec was nothing more than a raw, wild outpost, ugly and uncomfortable; homes were almost without furniture, and sometimes there was scarcely enough to eat.

Jeanne's immediate problem was to provide her people with winter quarters. An old man, Pierre de Puiseaux, who had become wealthy as a fur-trader, owned a farm just outside Quebec, close to Sillery. Impressed by the unselfish motives of the Company of Montreal, Puiseaux threw in his lot with the Montrealers giving them everything he owned—two houses, his farm, his cattle and his dock at Ste. Foy. Wealthy Madame de la Peltrie, who had founded the Ursulines at Quebec, became so enthused with the new scheme that she, too, joined the Montrealers. She left the Ursulines and went to live with Jeanne Mance at the Puiseaux house.

Mère Marie de l'Incarnation, the Superior of the Quebec Ursulines, writing to a friend in France in September 1642, had this to say:

> The persons who came last year to establish a colony in Montreal, who are a gentleman and a young lady from France, had no sooner arrived than our good foundress, who had with heroic generosity brought us to Canada, joined them. She afterward took her furniture and many other things, which were used for the church and which she had given us. To say she did wrong, I cannot before God; because, as she goes back into the world, it is right that she should have what suits her station; and finally, she has such piety and fear of the Lord, that I cannot doubt but that her intentions are good and holy.[2]

This letter shows masterly restraint under extreme provocation. Mère Marie knew that Madame de la Peltrie's motives were pure, even though her enthusiasms were unstable. She had brought the Ursulines to Quebec, and helped them build the convent. That was behind her. The needs of the Montrealers were now greater. Jeanne Mance did not need Madame de la

Peltrie's money, but she did need company — and what was a little furniture?

The Montrealers were thankful to have the Puiseaux home for winter quarters. Puiseaux also gave them permission to use trees from his stand of oaks to build their transports for the trip up the St. Lawrence. Jeanne spent the winter at "Puiseaux" with Madame de la Peltrie, Maisonneuve, and Puiseaux himself. Jeanne was in charge of supplies for the house, and of munitions. She spent a considerable amount of time with the Hospitalières who were then nearby at Sillery, and learned what she could about hospital treatment for Indians. She also made a start at studying one of the Indian languages.

By May 8, the Montrealers had loaded two vessels which had been built during the winter. The river was free of ice. The sun was warm. The buds were leafing. The time was propitious.

The Chevalier de Montmagny joined the Montrealers when all was ready and escorted them up the St. Lawrence, wide, silent and deep, between the banks of green foliage. For ten days, the forty colonists in the two vessels moved up against the strong current, camping on the banks at night, beside the still forest. They saw no unfriendly Iroquois, but for the first time these dreamers faced reality. In the depths of such wilderness, many a foe could be silently watching and, as silently, slip away without being seen. As the number of days of travel through the silent land reached ten, the Montrealers must, at last, have realized how truly bold they were, and how thin and vulnerable was their link with civilization.

During the last few days of the journey, distant blue peaks of the Appalachians could be seen to the south; the silent blue ranges of the shield stretched to the north. The travellers did not get their first glimpse of the blue dome of Mount Royal until they were but a few hours away. Prominent and bold, to match their spirit, it was like a fortress set in the wilderness and seemed to offer comfort and protection.

In the late afternoon of May 17,[3] they arrived on the island and tents were put up. The next morning being Sunday, Madame de la Peltrie and Mademoiselle Mance contrived an altar "setting it up in the neatest possible way" and the first mass was celebrated by Père Vimont, the Superior of the Jesuit Mission. As they thanked God for bringing them safely to their destination, this little band of forty men and women may well have wondered at their own courage. Had God really intended them to come? Once the mass was celebrated, however, they were committed. There was no turning back.

The party lived under canvas until the first rude buildings were built. For their protection, a palisade of pickets was put up and enclosed by a ditch. The site chosen had been used by Champlain as early as 1611 for a trading post and had around it a considerable amount of cleared land. On one side of the fortification, there was a little stream and a meadow filled with many birds and wild flowers. On the other side was marshy and inaccessible ground, easy to defend. The St. Lawrence flowed past the front of the fortification.

When the stockade was completed, Montmagny and Père Vimont returned to Quebec, with about half of the Montrealers, to bring up the rest of the stores and furniture. Madame de la Peltrie and her servant remained with Jeanne Mance as did Sieur de Puiseaux.

Twenty men remained at the fortifications, to guard the settlement and to erect buildings. Jeanne had a provisional hospital within the fort and she was also sacristan of the chapel. Some friendly Indians visited them on July 28, and the first baptism was registered, with Jeanne as godmother. The Iroquois, during those first months, seemed to have been totally unaware of the incursion and there were no surprise attacks or ambushes.

In August the ships from France arrived with good news as well as twelve new recruits. The good news was the report of the improved financial position of the Company with the increase of the Associates to forty-five members, highly gratifying to Jeanne. Future supplies were assured and the Company now basked under the protection of *Notre Dame de Montreal.*

A report by the Company to its Associates in 1643 stated that the Company had built a fort, a hospital and a lodging capable of holding seventy people. There were two Jesuit priests and a chapel called Notre-Dame. The projected townsite would be called Ville-Marie. Meanwhile, the people lived in one community, as if at an inn, the whole being a religious brotherhood. Jeanne thrived in this frontier atmosphere.

Quebec had begun its life as a business enterprise. The colony at Montreal was established primarily as a religious mission, and during its first years there was a religious community of goods. It differed from the religious communities set up by the Puritans in New England which were essentially escapist. The Montrealers were missionaries, seeking to convert the Indians to Christianity; the Puritans were running away from persecution, trying to establish a way of life removed from unwelcome interference. No colony, however, would turn up its nose at a little profitable trade, and in time, Montreal became one of the greatest fur trade marts on the continent.

.   .   .

In December of that first winter, the St. Lawrence overflowed its banks and inundated the entire settlement. Maisonneuve made a vow that if the waters would recede, he would lead a pilgrimage to the top of Mount Royal and plant a cross on the summit. The waters receded before Christmas and so, in fulfillment of his vow, Maisonneuve with Mlle. Mance led a procession of the whole colony up the forest paths to the mountain top. It was January 6, 1643, the Feast of the Epiphany. An altar was built and Père Vimond said Mass. To-day there is a splendid illuminated cross, one hundred feet high, standing on the same spot to commemorate the event, and to remind the modern Montrealers of their missionary beginnings.

On March 19, the Feast of St. Joseph, the main work had been completed on the fort, and cannon were mounted and fired to celebrate the *fête* day. It was a time of rejoicing, for with the completion of the fort, the workmen could begin on the houses and the colonists could soon hope for something better than the drafty, crowded quarters they had been living in.

With the coming of the ships in spring, there arrived a present from the King of a small ship with armaments. There was also a notice telling of the arrival in Quebec of Chevalier Louis d'Ailleboust with his wife and her sister. D'Ailleboust, an engineer, had been sent by the Company. He arrived in Montreal in August, and by autumn he had built solid bastions around the fort.

The arrival of Madame d'Ailleboust and her sister meant company for Jeanne, so that Madame de la Peltrie no longer felt herself needed and returned to the Ursulines in Quebec, but not before she tried to persuade the Jesuit priests to send her to one of the Huron missions. There is no hint about Jeanne's feelings towards Madame de la Peltrie. Jeanne must certainly have been grateful to have her company on the Island during that first winter. When Madame de la Peltrie left, however, Jeanne may have felt relieved. Madame de la Peltrie was good and generous but impulsive. Her whims, no matter how well-meant, must sometimes have been disturbing to Jeanne's sensible mind.

Jeanne had other problems more deflating than Madame de la Peltrie's departure. Sieur de Puiseaux, suffering from old age and illness, also wanted to leave. He wanted to return to France where he hoped to get better medical care, and asked the Company for the return of his property. This was a stunning request, for the Puiseaux property had been absorbed into the Company of Montreal. Mademoiselle Mance and Sieur de Maisonneuve promised Puiseaux, therefore, that they would keep careful account of all the Puiseaux property in New France and that the Company of Montreal would look after him in France as long as he lived. Dollier de Casson says that the Company did care for him until his death, though probably not in the style he could have demanded if his wealth had still been in his own name.

The first two years slid by without incident but in June, 1643, forty Mohawks killed three colonists and took three captives. In March of the following year, 200 Iroquois surrounded the settlement. There had been grumbling among the men about Maisonneuve's policy of defence, slurs cast on his personal courage; so he, in person, led thirty men out of the fort to attack. From this time on, the colony was almost continuously under siege. The colonists could never work their fields without carrying a gun or posting a guard. The bell of Hôtel-Dieu tolled in warning at each new attack, and the bell tolled frequently.

The French had made permanent enemies for themselves in 1610, when Champlain with a party of Huron and Montagnais had surprised the Iroquois, killing some of their chiefs. The French had taken sides in a tribal war and the Iroquois did not forget. From then on, beginning with the Jesuits, French authors increased the already unfriendly relations by writing Iroquois horror stories.

Jeanne Mance wrote about this time, "The Iroquois have now turned entirely against us, with more pride and insolence than they ever before showed. They encircled us so closely and their attacks were so sudden and frequent that there no longer was safety for any of us. They killed several of our people, and burned down the houses in the very vicinity of Ville-Marie. Our hospital was far from being in security, and we had to place a strong garrison in it to protect it."

Should they give up, these mad Montrealers? Certainly not. Besides, Jeanne now had her hospital. It had been completed in the spring of 1645. The four or five acres of land where it stood had been given by the Company, and was sufficient for a small farm. The building, sixty-five feet by twenty-five feet, was about ten minutes walk from the fort, and was itself strongly fortified by a picket-palisade and a ditch. It was sometimes called the house of Mademoiselle Mance, and she lived there until her death. The building contained a kitchen, a room for Mademoiselle Mance, a room for her servants, and two large wards for the sick. It was first built of rough logs which still had their bark, but it was later made snug with clapboard. There was also a small hospital chapel. In time, there was a small stable built to hold five cattle and twenty sheep.

Jeanne Mance was able to write to Madame de Bullion, her patron, "as soon as the house in which I now am, was finished, it was at once filled". The hospital was well equipped for its time and place, with mattresses, bed linen and other linen, copper and tin cooking pots, medicines and surgical instruments.

In a new contract made in 1648 when Madame de Bullion increased her donation, the latter stipulated that Mademoiselle Jeanne Mance was to remain as administrator until her death; after Jeanne Mance's death, a community of Hospitalières should replace her, to serve gratuitously and not at the expense of the Foundation. The Foundation was to provide for the hospital and its upkeep, but not for its staff.

In her contributions to the hospital, Madame de Bullion always had a singleness of purpose. She would not allow herself to be side-tracked by conflicting demands, no matter how worthy. La Dauversière, a worthy, charitable man was, unlike Madame de Bullion, impractical. He was a romantic do-gooder, and followed a will-of-the-wisp trail of activities, all pure in motive, but too diversified. If he had devoted his life to the founding of the mission on the Island of Montreal, he would have been a great man, but he became involved in many other charities in France. He established a hospital at La Flèche, but not content with this, he established three more hospitals in France. He next became involved in raising funds for the needy in Paris. He became ill. His own fortune was mostly gone and he was reported to be bankrupt. Since La Dauversière was financier and commissary for the Company of Montreal, this was a grim predicament, the more so because the Associates had been reduced from forty-five to nine. The Company was on the point of collapse.

Paul de Chomedy, Sieur de Maisonneuve, and Mademoiselle Jeanne Mance never knew when they were beaten. With the Iroquois at their gates, and their house in financial collapse, they could have given up with honour. Instead, Jeanne went off to France, hoping to inject a little life into the dying company. She was concerned both for the Company and for her hospital. La Dauversière was also manager of her endowment, and feared that his bankruptcy might cause the loss of her capital.

She sailed from Quebec, October 13, 1649, for France. In Paris she called first on Père Olier at St. Sulpice and spurred him to rally the remaining members of the Company. On March 31,

1650, there was a reorganization meeting of the Company. La Dauversière had recovered and was present, as was his faithful associate, Fancamp. Père Olier was elected Director and there was a new Secretary. The task now, Jeanne knew, was to renew the flagging interest of the wealthy patrons, "for after all, it had begun with common interests and much money had been spent, where would it all end?" if the Montreal project was abandoned for some other enthusiasm.

La Dauversière had avoided his creditors, Jeanne found, and the hospital endowment was safe. She visited Madame de Bullion and was assured that her patron would continue her support, even though the intermediary, Père Rapine, had died.

When Jeanne returned to Montreal with this satisfactory news, she was stunned by the shocking story of the massacre of the Hurons, and of the martyrdom of the Jesuits by the Iroquois who

> . . . had waited long
> For this event. Their hatred for the Hurons
> Fused with their hatred for the French and priests
> Was to be vented on this sacrifice.[4]

"From this time on," writes Dollier de Casson, "the Iroquois began to attack us in earnest, and with such obstinacy that there was scarcely a day without an alarm."

One day, forty Indians surrounded the hospital palisade and three colonists escaped capture only because the double gate had accidentally been left open. A few months later, 200 Iroquois entrenched themselves in the ditch surrounding the hospital, which they besieged. By August, the attacks came daily. "We saw nothing but enemies," says Dollier de Casson. "No one dared to open his door at night and in the daytime no one dared go more than four steps from his house, without his sword, gun or pistol."

Maisonneuve finally ordered all the colonists to take refuge in the fort and Jeanne Mance had to abandon her hospital and return to her old quarters within the fort.

How could Ville-Marie survive? Thirty of the seventy colonists had been killed, captured or disabled by the Iroquois.

Among those killed was Augustin Hébert, a Norman, who had arrived with Jeanne in 1642. He was an ancestor of Sir Wilfrid Laurier.

Jeanne Mance had been given an endowment of 44,000 *livres* by Madame de Bullion for the Hôtel-Dieu. Jeanne now questioned the use of the endowment if the hospital and the colony were lost. It would be better, she reasoned, to sacrifice a part to save the whole. She told Maisonneuve that she would buy from the Company of Montreal 100 arpents of land, for which she would pay 22,000 *livres*. With this money Maisonneuve was to recruit one or two hundred soldiers in France, and bring them back to save the colony.

Of this transaction, Jeanne said later, "I did not believe it was a sale because I saw very well that it was not worth the sum I was furnishing, but I had regard only to save the whole by this part." She was sure that Madame de Bullion would consent.

Maisonneuve accepted the offer, and a contract was signed in August, 1651, ratified at Montreal, and later by the Associates of the Company in Paris. There was one problem to be overcome. Since the death of Père Rapine, the intermediary between Jeanne Mance and Madame de Bullion, it was difficult for anyone other than Jeanne, herself, to approach Madame de Bullion, who still insisted on remaining the "unknown benefactor". Jeanne had to confide her secret to Maisonneuve. Later in Paris, Maisonneuve succeeded in seeing Madame de Bullion, and with the utmost tact, informed her of the dire needs of the colony. She made it known to him that she was in agreement with the transaction of the 22,000 *livres* and, moreover, increased her donation by a further 20,000 *livres*. Maisonneuve then proceeded to find soldiers.

He had told Jeanne, "I will try to bring back 200 men, which we badly need to defend this place; if, however, I cannot get at least 100, I will not return and the whole enterprise must be abandoned."

Maisonneuve had left a scanty garrison of seventeen Montrealers, augmented by a detachment of ten men from Quebec, to guard the fort at Montreal. During this period, the Montrealers defended themselves so vigorously, according to

Dollier de Casson, "that as soon as a musket-shot was heard anywhere, people immediately ran there at top speed. Here people ran to shots as to a good meal."

There were casualties however. One woman, called Primot, was captured. "As she had no weapons but hands and feet," continues Dollier de Casson," she caught hold of this monster so forcibly by a place which modesty forbids us to mention, that he could not free himself. He beat her with his hatchet over the head . . . until she fell unconscious to the earth, and so allowed the Iroquois to flee."

Primot survived.

Another survivor, Chiquot, was a Frenchman who had been scalped and left for dead. He was brought back to Jeanne in the fort and tenderly nursed. The nursing care he received from Jeanne and her small staff was so excellent that he survived and lived for another fourteen years.

Maisonneuve did not return in the summer of 1652, but he sent letters to say that he had been successful and was gathering up men. By the following spring, Jeanne, in a restless, anxious mood, left Montreal for Quebec to meet the supply ships from France. En route, she stopped overnight at Trois-Rivières, and then went on down the river. She missed by a day the appalling massacre of the French at Trois-Rivières by 600 Iroquois.

After the attack at Trois-Rivières, the whole of New France, even the stronghold at Quebec, became desperate for news of Maisonneuve and his soldiers. It was an agonizing wait, for he was delayed for forty days by adverse winds, and did not arrive at Quebec until September 22. He had with him 105 men, hired to serve the Company for five years.

He also brought with him Marguerite Bourgeoys who became the first schoolmistress in the colony of Montreal. She founded the Congrégation de Notre Dame, which is still flourishing to-day. Marguerite Bourgeoys, like Jeanne Mance, was a religious woman who served as a lay person. The two women became fast friends.

With the coming of the soldiers, Jeanne Mance was able to leave the fort and return to her home. A larger hospital was built, and she was then able to move into the original, modest Hôtel-Dieu.

With the peace following the arrival of Maisonneuve's soldiers — soldiers financed by Jeanne — the Colony at Montreal began to rally, even prosper. In 1654, there were thirteen marriages and, in 1655, Jeanne was godmother to six French children. (Before her death, she was godmother to forty-one French children as well as to many Indians.) Four orphan girls whose parents had been killed by Iroquois in 1655 were placed in her charge. One of these girls, Marie Moyen, remained with Jeanne for twelve years.

Maisonneuve, at the urging of Jeanne Mance, went to France once more in the interests of the Colony. His purpose was to encourage a number of Sulpicians to come to Montreal as permanent parish priests. In 1657 he returned with four Sulpicians. Jeanne offered them a part of her home until their own building was ready.

Another problem which attracted the attention of Maisonneuve and Jeanne Mance was arranging for the Hospitalières at La Flèche to come to Montreal to assist at the Hôtel-Dieu. Before this was solved, Jeanne was to cross swords with the powerful Bishop Laval.

.   .   .

During January of that same year, Jeanne had a fall. While hurrying to the hospital after Sunday morning chapel she slipped on the ice. The physician, Etienne Bouchard,[5] was called. When he reached her house, he found Jeanne unconscious on her bed. She had suffered a slight concussion, as well as a fractured forearm. He attended to the fracture, but unfortunately did not discover until months later that her wrist had been dislocated. By this time her whole arm had begun to shrivel and she suffered intense pain whenever the arm was touched.

Describing her injury, Jeanne wrote, "I remained deprived entirely of the use of my right hand, and moreover I suffered dreadfully. I had to carry my arm in a sling all the time, as I was not able to hold it otherwise. Since the moment of the fracture, I could not use my hand in any way, nor take the least freedom with it; so much so that I had to be dressed and served as if I were an infant." To be helpless was more disconcerting to Jeanne than to be in pain. To be served, and not to serve, was scarcely a part of her plan.

Moreover, Jeanne was worried about the coming of the Hospitalières, for nothing had been arranged for their endowment and her contract with Madame de Bullion limited the use of hospital funds to the operation and upkeep of the hospital alone.

Finally, Jeanne spoke to Monsieur l'abbé Gabriel de Queylus, the Sulpician Superior, who readily agreed that she should go to France to arrange for her Hospitalières, and to try to get medical treatment for her injured arm. As she was about to leave for France, two nuns from the Augustinian Hospitalières at Quebec arrived, evidently at the request of l'abbé Queylus. This created an extremely awkward situation, for Jeanne knew that, should she leave them in charge of her hospital, the Hospitalières from La Flèche would be ousted.

Jeanne herself felt that l'abbé Queylus was trying to outmanoeuvre her, hoping to establish the same order in both Montreal and Quebec. It might have been a wise plan, for the establishment at La Flèche did not have resources behind it, whereas the Augustinians did, but Jeanne was annoyed at the idea of Queylus taking advantage of her absence.

L'Abbé introduced the Augustinians by saying, "Here are two good hospital nuns, come because one of them needed a change of air."

Jeanne made the sisters comfortable, saying simply, *"Vous venez, mes mères, et moi je m'en vais."*

She went immediately to Maisonneuve to explain the situation. He had been astounded that Jeanne should have invited the nuns without first consulting him.

When all was made clear between them, these two old friends were able to laugh at the predicament. Before leaving for France, Jeanne delegated her position as administrator to Madame de la Badrillière, her assistant, with the advice that she was to give comfort and hospitality to the two visitors, but not to surrender her authority.

Marguerite Bourgeoys had begun the building of the Chapel of Notre Dame de Bons-Secours, but she postponed this work in order to accompany Jeanne Mance to France. Marguerite knew that Jeanne, because of her arm, would have immense difficulty travelling alone. They left Montreal on September 9, 1658, and after eight days in Quebec, they sailed for France on October 14. It was a rough crossing.

After landing at La Rochelle, they went on to La Flèche by sedan chair. Here they rested a week. They saw La Dauversière and reported to him their predicament, and the unhappy interference of l'abbé Queylus.

La Dauversière is reported to have said, "Monsieur de Queylus acts in vain."

Mance and Bourgeoys continued on to Paris where Marguerite Bourgeoys left Jeanne with her Dolebeau cousins. Marguerite then proceeded on to Troyes where she hoped to find recruits for her teaching staff.

Jeanne attended a general meeting of the Company of Montreal and received full support and approval for her various projects. The members were concerned about her arm and arranged for her to visit some of the most distinguished physicians that Paris could offer. All these doctors said the same thing.

"They assured me," said Jeanne, "that there was no means of restoring the use of my arm or hand; all that could be done was to prevent the natural heat of the arm from disappearing, so that my arm might not dry up entirely and become dead."

There seemed little left to do in France, other than arrange for the Hospitalières from La Flèche to embark for Montreal. Madame de Bullion had again solved the financial problem by giving the Hospitalières 20,000 *livres* as an endowment. Invested at five percent, this would keep the hospital nuns comfortably. Three nuns were chosen, Soeur Catherine Macé, Soeur Judith Moreau de Brésoles and Soeur Marie Maillet. Each of them later played a prominent role in the Hôtel-Dieu de Montréal. Marguerite Bourgeoys had meanwhile found four young women for her teaching staff, as well as twenty-eight other women who would go as colonists – the "King's Daughters".

Before leaving Paris, Jeanne asked the Superior of the Sulpicians if she might be allowed to visit the tomb of the deceased Monsieur Olier, the founder of the Sulpicians and the priest from whom Jeanne had had such constant support over the years. The Superior arranged for Jeanne to visit the chapel alone on the day of the feast of the Blessed Virgin. The Superior said Mass for her, and she received Holy Communion. After the Mass, he gave her the casket which held the heart of Père Olier. Then he left her.

Jeanne held the casket reverently in her left hand, then placed it on top of her bandaged right arm. As she did this, a great emotion swept over her. "My heart was so full that I cannot now express myself." Then, amazingly, she began to feel a wonderful warmth spread through the withered arm, down to her finger tips.

She walked out of the chapel and back to the house of the Dolebeaus, and hardly able to speak, she showed her restored arm to her sister and to her cousin.

An hour later, Jeanne and her sister returned to the Seminary to report her cure to the Superior. A public thanksgiving was held among the seminarians and Jeanne later wrote, in the presence of the Superior and the other Sulpicians, the following with her right hand:

JESUS, MARIE, JOSEPH
The 2nd of February, 1659, in the chapel of the Seminary I write these words after Holy Mass, with my right hand of which for two years I had not had any use.
Jeanne Mance

Two weeks later Jeanne wrote a long declaration:

In the name of the Most Holy Trinity. Amen.
I, Jeanne Mance, recognize and confess in the presence of My God having received the grace of the use of my right hand by the merits of the late Monsieur Olier . . .

There are several pages of details telling of her fall, of the various treatments and of the diagnoses of the Paris doctors. In conclusion she declares,

Having taken hold of this precious depository with my left hand I placed it on my right arm all covered as it was, and in my arm sling. I thought of the grace which God had placed in this holy heart [Monsier Olier's] and I was wholly astonished that from the moment I placed the holy depository on my hand I felt it free and that it upheld without my assistance the weight of the leaden box in which the heart was enclosed. This surprised and astonished me marvellously. . . . I felt at the same time an extraordinary warmth spread itself through my arm to the tip of my fingers.

The use of my hand from this moment was restored to me, although my hand is always dislocated, which is still most wonderful and I serve myself without any suffering. I declare that all I have written on these two small sheets is true and sincere. In faith of which I have written and signed it with the same hand of which I have received the use, at Paris, this February 13, 1659.

Almost the only writings of Jeanne Mance which survive, are official and they tend to give a chilling impression of their author. Jeanne was a warm-hearted, active person, and it is a pity that these documents throw such a cold shadow over her.

As for the miracle, Jeanne was a woman of her time, deeply and simply religious. She believed in the miracle with all her heart and with all her heart she was thankful to God.

Jeanne's cure was lasting, and of course such a marvel caused great excitement. Soeur Morin, who served under Jeanne Mance and was the first historian of the Hôtel-Dieu, writes, "She was worn out with speaking of it. . . . There was great zeal among the ladies as to which should have her in their homes. They said that she was a saint. Some cut her clothing in adulation."

Jeanne herself said, "They made me suffer a kind of martyrdom, as if I had contributed to this marvel other than by my misery and infirmity. . . . I felt that I should leave Paris and go where I was unknown." To the sensible Mademoiselle Mance, this adulation was an absurdity.

There were still business matters to attend to in Paris and she was plagued by many annoying obstructions. Bishop Laval, who had been newly appointed Vicar Apostolic of Canada and was soon to leave for his new diocese, urged delay in sending the three Hospitalières from La Flèche to Montreal. In reply, La Dauversière said, "If they don't go this year, they will never go." The bishop of the diocese of La Flèche refused permission for the three nuns to leave France.

In the midst of this controversy, La Dauversière became ill and, since he was the director for the Hospital of La Flèche, the Hospitalières could do nothing but wait. A rumour got about that La Dauversière was forcibly taking the women to Montreal against the will of their parents, and there was a near riot. Fortunately, La Dauversière, who suffered from gallstones, recovered his health in time to smooth the tempers and to escort the nuns from La Flèche to La Rochelle, where Marguerite Bourgeoys was waiting with her party of thirty-two young women.

Jeanne left Paris on horseback, travelling the same route she had travelled when she first left for Canada eighteen years before. Within a day of La Rochelle, her horse was frightened by a pack of dogs and threw her into a ditch. In falling, her newly healed right arm took the impact but was unharmed. Jeanne was almost as amazed at this as she had been at the recent cure. It seemed to accent the miracle. Word got back to Paris and a witty writer could not resist the taunt, *"Le miracle est demiraclé."*

.   .   .

Jeanne found her whole party waiting for her at La Rochelle. They were to sail on the *Saint-André,* a light sailing ship previously used as a troop ship. There were 110 passengers, most of them recruits for Montreal, including two Sulpicians, Marguerite Bourgeoys' young women, and a young carpenter named Etienne Truteau. He was a boy of 17, from north of Bordeau.

Eight years after arriving in Montreal, Etienne Truteau married Adrienne Barbier, a 14 year old girl who had been educated for four years by the Hospitalières. Etienne and Adrienne had 13 sons and one daughter. They settled at Longueuil on the south shore of the St. Lawrence, opposite Montreal, but not until the Iroquois threat had diminished. All the Trudeaus in North America are descended from Etienne

Truteau and Adrienne Barbier, including Canada's Prime Minister, Pierre Elliott Trudeau.

La Dauversière's illness, coming on top of Bishop Laval's interference with Jeanne's plans during the spring, had delayed their sailing for nearly three months and had depleted the Company's funds. The party did not have enough money to pay the passage in advance, and the ship's captain refused to take them.

Jeanne Mance again came to the rescue of the Montrealers by raising a loan from a merchant at La Rochelle, and the *Saint-André* sailed on June 29. They were scarcely out of sight of the coast of France when typhus broke out among the passangers. The ship, which had been used for two years as a hospital troop ship, had not been disinfected. At first, the Master of the ship would not allow the nursing sisters to attend to the sick. After ten people had died however, he was forced to consent. From this time on, the Hospitalières with Marguerite Bourgeoys took charge of the sick and, although many were smitten by the disease, no more passengers died. Jeanne Mance *fut à l'extrémités* and probably suffered from her usual seasickness. Later she herself took the fever and was still ill when the ship docked at Quebec, on September 7, 1659. Complicated by miracles, near riots, and deadly fevers, it could not be said that Jeanne's visit to France had been dull.

Marguerite Bourgeoys departed immediately for Montreal with her party. The three Hospitalières were received by Bishop Laval and, after a short delay, they received his permission to go to Montreal. Jeanne, quarantined in Lower Town, urged them to go on without her. En route to Montreal, the La Flèche Hospitalières passed the two Augustinian Hospitalières who had at last been recalled to the Hôtel-Dieu at Quebec. The La Flèche sisters arrived at Ville-Marie, October 20. They were welcomed whole-heartedly by the colony and given temporary quarters in the house of Jeanne Mance. They took possession of Hôtel-Dieu of Montreal on November 20.

Jeanne returned to her home a few weeks later, and had scarcely taken over her position of administrator when she received the disquieting news of La Dauversière's death, and of his bankruptcy. The news of his death was serious enough, for he was director and supplier for the colony and the hospital, but his bankruptcy threatened the financial structure of the whole undertaking. Even worse, Jeanne was to discover that the 20,000 *livres* which Madame de Bullion had given as an endowment for the Hospitalières from La Flèche had been gobbled up by the creditors.

Although the three Hospitalières had no possible means of income, they chose to stay in the Montreal colony. Jeanne Mance, Maisonneuve, the Sulpicians and the citizens, now about 400 persons, rallied round and gave what small assistance they could. Jeanne was able to beg a little here and there; the citizens brought food; the Governor presented the sisters with 100 acres of wooded land which would supply them with fuel — if they could afford to have it cut. The most dramatic gift was in the person of Mathurin Jouaneaux, who deeded himself and all his property and livestock to the Hospitalières. He became their foreman and a member of the Community. Soeur Macé's brother sent them 400 or 500 *livres* a year, and was eventually able to secure a donation of 30,000 *livres,* but not until they had lived for some years in great want. Their years of poverty endeared them to the citizens who had no more, no less, than they did. What disturbed Jeanne Mance most of all was the refusal, for many years, of Bishop Laval to recognize their community officially.

The Indians were again on the attack. Rumours came that there were 600 Iroquois about to descend on Montreal, Trois-Rivières, and Quebec. It was at this time, 1660, that Dollard des Ormeaux and his band of seventeen sacrificed themselves at the Long Sault on the Ottawa River, and temporarily diverted the Iroquois from Montreal. Iroquois attacks were to continue for five more years.

During these years, Marie Morin from Quebec joined the Hospitalières of Saint Joseph at Montreal as a postulant. She was only thirteen years old, and was the first postulant to take her vows. Soeur Morin later became the historian. Writing of those years, she says:

I believe that death would have been far sweeter for me
than a life filled and over-filled with such alarms for ourselves, and such compassion for our unfortunate brethren
whom we saw so cruelly treated. . .

Each time that any one of our people was attacked, the
tocsin was rung to call the inhabitants to the rescue and to
warn those who were at work in exposed places to take
refuge from danger . . . which they always did at the first
sound of the bell. Sister Brésoles and I went up to the
belfry in order not to employ a man, whose help might be
needed against the enemy. From our point of elevation we
could see the fights going on, close at hand, which pro-
duced a sense of terror in us; and we often came down
trembling and believing our last hour on earth had come.[6]

Although constantly in terror, these Hospitalières, and the
other women of the community continued to busy themselves
with their daily chores, without thought of giving up.

Sometimes the patients were wounded Iroquois. Although
some of these warriors were grateful to the sisters for their
nursing care, this was not always so. One Iroquois drove Soeur
de Brésoles into a closet and tried to choke her to death but the
sick and injured in the ward heard her screams and came to her
rescue, beating the man with crutches and chairs.

In 1663 came the great earthquake. It was one of the most
severe earthquakes of modern times and was felt violently over
a large area of the continent. The people were terrified. Père
Jérôme Lalemant writes in the *Relations,*

We saw near us great openings made and a prodigious
amount of land swallowed up; we saw ourselves surrounded by upheavals and ruins, without losing even a
child, nor the hair of a head hurt. While the surrounding
mountains were laid low, we had only a few chimneys
upset.

Many, of course, wrote of the earthquake, but Soeur Morin's
remarks have a pleasant naivety:

At Quebec the churches were filled all day and all night
and the priests were kept busy with confessions. The de-
votion was not so great in Montreal, because each remained at home, and the door of our church was kept
closed; and maybe we had not so much need of con-

fessions, for at that time life was very good and innocent in all Montreal.

Jeanne Mance was absent at the time of the earthquake, as she had been absent at the time of the other great catastrophe — the massacre of the Hurons and the Jesuits. She had a more complex catastrophe of her own to solve. The financial affairs of the Company of Montreal were again in a shambles.

Sometime before the earthquake, Mademoiselle Mance went again to Paris. Sieur de Maisonneuve had started out with her, but the Governor at Quebec persuaded him to remain at Montreal. Jeanne sailed for France in the autumn of 1662, and was gone for two years. During that time, acting on behalf of the Company of Montreal and of Maisonneuve, she signed a "cession" of the Charter of the Company of Montreal over to the Seminary of St. Sulpice in Paris, on March 9, 1663. Apart from the Seminary, there remained only five members of the Company of Montreal. It seemed right that the Sulpicians who had supported the venture from its inception should now become the lawful seigneurs.

.   .   .

Times were changing. The Company of One Hundred Associates, *La Grande Compagnie,* had been required to resign its charter. The colonies of New France were to be governed directly by the crown. The new Seigneurs of the Island of Montreal had their commission ratified by the colonial government in 1664.

One of the first results of the change of government was the recall to France of Paul Chomedy de Maisonneuve, who had been Governor of the Montreal colony for twenty-three years. Now there was to be a central government at Quebec, and no place at Montreal for a man of Maisonneuve's rank. At the time of his departure, it must have seemed to Jeanne Mance that all she had fought for was lost. But this was not so.

The Colony of Montreal and Ville-Marie slowly grew. The Indian threat lessened. The Hôtel-Dieu was established and the Sulpicians made good landlords. Perhaps Jeanne Mance missed the earlier battles.

Although fully occupied as administrator of Hôtel-Dieu, Jeanne Mance always kept an active interest in people. Besides caring for some of the children orphaned by the Iroquois, she assisted a number of families who emigrated to Montreal, by providing passage money. Records in Montreal archives give some of the names of the families assisted and the deeds of obligation by which these colonists agreed to repay Mademoiselle Mance. Some of the names are well-known names in Quebec to-day — Charbonneau, Cardinault, Coyet, Roy, Thibaudeau, Ricaud, Pelletreau, Guiberge, Beojan, and Gougnon.

The coming of the Marquis de Tracy's soldiers brought new life to Montreal, as well as to Quebec; they also brought money. The forts along the Richelieu had to be supplied from Montreal. François Dollier de Casson, the soldier-priest and historian, arrived with three other Sulpicians in September of 1666. He was sent as chaplain with Tracy on an expedition against the Mohawk and later he spent a winter at Fort Ste. Anne on Lake Champlain. Here he found the soldiers dying of scurvy and lack of supplies. Word was sent to Montreal where the Sulpician priest, Monsieur Souart, and Jeanne Mance rapidly assembled several sleigh loads of supplies to send to the Fort. The men who had been sent to Montreal for help "came back well supplied, since Monsieur Souart and Mademoiselle Mance sent several sleighs loaded with all kinds of food such as purslane, salt-pork, onions, poultry, and a quantity of Touraine prunes".

These timely supplies saved the garrison. Dollier de Casson later says, "I must further add that the Hospital of Montreal distinguished itself by the crowd of invalids it took in from there [Ste. Anne] to whom it devoted so much care."

Jeanne's hospital organization had been proven not only willing but flexible. The Hôtel-Dieu cared for the enemy-Iroquois along with the battle-worn French, and its machinery was versatile. Her organization was able to cope with the urgent problem of sending fresh foods to an inland post in winter, although the military supply lines had broken down. This is another instance of Jeanne Mance as a great administrator and persuader.

The life in the colony begun by Sieur de Maisonneuve and Mademoiselle Mance was changing. When Jeanne died in 1673, Montreal was on the way to becoming a great fur mart. There were nearly 1,500 inhabitants. In a good year, some 800 canoes would arrive for the annual fair from the whole area of the Great Lakes, the Ottawa and the Richelieu systems. The stream of Indian and French traders would be met by local traders, clerks, seamen and officials from Quebec and abroad. The Governor would make his annual appearance.

A tent town of birch bark dwellings and booths would spring up on the common. The fair was a time of abandon and festivities for those from the wilderness, keynoted by excessive drinking by both white men and natives. The fur traders had introduced brandy to the fur trade and this was a subject of great concern to the clergy and many government officials. Montreal's days of innocence were past.

Jeanne was undoubtedly concerned about the changing atmosphere of her beloved Ville-Marie. Another shadow fell across her last years. Bishop Laval had finally recognised officially the Hospitalières de Saint Joseph at the Hôtel-Dieu, but he persisted in his belief that Jeanne had done wrong to use her endowment of 22,000 *livres* to buy "100 arpents of land" from the Company of Montreal. Laval had not been in Canada at the time that the little colony was diminished to seventeen defenders and he looked at the transaction from a legal point of view. As he was administrator of diocesan funds, he felt an inquiry was called for.

The matter was brought before the Privy Council of the King and Maisonneuve represented Jeanne Mance at the hearings. Madame de Bullion had died, and although there was considerable evidence to show that Jeanne's decision had had the approval of the Company and of Madame de Bullion, there was no piece of paper for proof. The Council judged that "Mademoiselle Mance had not sufficient authority to commit the Hôtel-Dieu" but "the Seminary was not bound to any restitution to the Hôtel-Dieu".

Bishop Laval persisted in his attitude that Jeanne had been imprudent, up until 1680 when he retired. His successor,

Monseigneur de Saint-Ballier, then let the matter drop.

But Jeanne had died seven years before, her last years saddened by her Bishop's disapproval. If she could only have foreseen that the 100 arpents (approximately 100 acres) were one day to become a wealthy source of income for her beloved Hôtel-Dieu, she would have died more happily.

The 100 acres, called the fief of Nazareth in the district of Ste. Anne, lie in downtown Montreal, and to-day include the Montreal City Hall, the Court House, Champ de Mars, the Bonsecours Market and the Chateau de Ramezay. All these lands have long ago been sold to help provide for the new hospital built on the side of Mount Royal.

The last official act of her career, shortly before her death, was to take part in the laying of foundation stones of the Parish Church of Notre-Dame de Montréal. Five stones were laid — one by the Governor General, one by the Superior of the Seminary, one by the Intendant, one by the Governor of Montreal, and one by Jeanne Mance.

Even if Jeanne's judgement was questioned on one matter of her thirty-year administration, she knew she had founded her colony well. Biographies have been written by many writers who sense the drama and the drive of this astonishing woman, but the writings are usually cluttered with pious verbiage so that one cannot see the woman behind the words. The writings of her contemporaries, particularly Dollier de Casson and Soeur Morin, cast her in a role of intense seriousness. She was a religious woman with one dominant purpose, yet she was warm-hearted and people loved her. She was called the "Angel of the Colony".

She was generous with others and undemanding. She gave many people, humble and not so humble, shelter in her house; she gave freely of her time and of her sympathy, and she asked nothing for herself in return. However, she was not afraid to beg for the people of the colony, "her people", and when she did beg, she was successful.

Almost nothing of what Jeanne Mance wrote, herself, has survived. Anything in the way of memoirs or letters, was burned in one of the fires which have three times destroyed the Hôtel-

Dieu. It is a pity that we do not have more of her own thoughts, rather than the remote, stylized writings of her contemporaries.

Of the human side of Jeanne Mance, little is known. We know that she was quick-moving, but was she ever angry? We know that she was generous and persuasive, but had she a sense of humour?

It is unreasonable to think of her as humourless. She had many warm, long-lasting friendships, beginning with La Dauversière, Madame de Bullion, and Maisonneuve. She captured Madame de la Peltrie from the Ursulines. There were Monsieur Olier of the Sulpicians, Marguerite Bourgeoys and the Hospitalières, to say nothing of the influential patrons in Paris, or Monsieur de Priseaux who gave her his whole fortune. All of these people did anything she asked of them.

If she had been an essentially humourless person, it is unlikely she would have had such influence with the Associates of the Company of Montreal. The only person Jeanne Mance had any jarring disagreement with, during her long career as administrator of the affairs of the Hôtel-Dieu and of the Colony of Montreal, was Bishop Laval, and Laval was not famous for his sense of humour.

It could be said that Jeanne Mance's achievements stand for all to see in the great pile which is the Hôtel-Dieu de Montréal. One of Montreal's great hospitals, it stands today a little below the crown of Mount Royal overlooking the harbour of Montreal, Isle Ste.-Hélène, and the first site of the Hôtel-Dieu by the waterfront, north-east of the old Notre Dame Church. Between the Church and the Hôtel-Dieu, for a good part of the way, runs a street called Jeanne Mance.

Jeanne Mance would prefer to see her achievements in the life of the institution — not only the hospital but the associated congregation of Saint-Joseph, the nursing school, and all the fifty-six Houses in Canada, the United States and France which call *le Monastère de Saint-Joseph de l'Hôtel-Dieu de Montréal* their Mother House. These form Jeanne Mance's monument. They also prove her to be one of the greatest of the women colonizers who followed Gudrid. Her roots went deep in the new land. Her efforts at Montreal prepared the way for one of

the descendants of the Iroquois, Molly Brant, who helped to
establish a British colony on the shores of Lake Ontario.

Notes

1. Dollier de Casson, *History of Montreal,* translated by Ralph Flenley
   (Toronto: 1928). All quotes are from this title unless otherwise indicated.
2. Translation from Letters of Marie de l'Incarnation by Madeleine Reeds.
   See also the passage in *Word from New France,* edited by Joyce Marshall
   (Toronto: 1967), p. 115.
3. The official celebration of the Founding of Montreal has always been
   held on May 18, the date given in the accounts by Dollier de Casson
   and Soeur Morin. Père Vimont in the *Relation* for 1642 gives the date
   as May 17. There is a continuing scholarly argument as to which is right.
4. E.J. Pratt, *Brebeuf and His Brethren* (Toronto: 1940).
5. J.J. Heagerty, *The Romance of Medicine in Canada* (Toronto: 1940).
   Etienne Bouchart, one of the first physicians in Canada, remained in
   Montreal for 25 years. He contracted with the principal inhabitants of
   Montreal to serve each person for one dollar a year.
6. Soeur Marie Morin, *Annales de l'Hotel-Dieu de Montreal.*

Bibliography

Allard, Mère r.h.s.j. *Marraine Mance.* Montreal: 1962.

Atherton, W.H. *Jeanne Mance.* Montreal: 1945.

Daveluy, Marie Claire. *Jeanne Mance.* Montreal: 1934.

Dollier de Casson, François. *A History of Montreal,* edited and translated
    by Ralph Flenley. Toronto: 1928.

Faillon, Etienne Michel. *Histoire de la Colonie Francaise en Canada.* Ville-
    marie: 1836.

Foran, J.K. *Jeanne Mance.* Montreal: 1931.

Heagerty, J.J. *Romance of Medicine in Canada.* Toronto: 1940.

Marie de l'Incarnation. *Word from New France,* selected letters translated and edited by Joyce Marshall. Toronto: 1967.

Montreuil, Anna B. *There Came Three Gifts.* Toronto: 1955.

Morin, Soeur Marie. *Annales de l'Hôtel-Dieu de Montreal.*

Jesuit Relations.

Repplier, Agnes. *Mère Marie of the Ursulines.* Garden City: 1931.

4

Molly Brant

One word from her is more taken notice of by the Five Nations than a thousand from any white man.
Daniel Claus to Governor Haldimand, 1779[1]

The mantle of Gudrid does not fit as neatly over Molly Brant as it did over Jeanne Mance, for Molly was a native American. She was a Mohawk, one of the Confederacy of the Six Nations.

When Molly joined her brother, Joseph, at Fort Niagara in 1777 at the time of the American Revolutionary War, she was following Iroquois tradition as had her mother about thirty years earlier. The accepted custom among the Iroquois was for widows and orphans and the ill to seek shelter with their relatives, preferably a brother.

Today there is a pall that hangs over the name of Brant. It seems that the more Molly and Joseph Brant are honoured by the white people, the less they are esteemed by their own people of the Six Nations.

The loyalty of the Brants and the Six Nations at the time of the Revolutionary War provided the secure base upon which the loyal British were to found the new province of Upper Canada. The great influence of the Brants among their own people was the stone upon which the founding of English Canada rested. The government realized this and rewarded both Joseph and Molly with pensions and lands.

For one of their people to receive rewards from a foreign power was judged as an act of betrayal by the Six Nations. Once Joseph and Molly accepted gifts from the British, the Brant influence began to wane. They were suspect. The older generations of Iroquois remained loyal to the Brants during their lifetime, but the younger people began to ask questions. Had the Brants sold out to the whites?

The argument still goes on. The Brant brother and sister were great, without doubt, but they tried to live in two worlds and fell between. Who is to judge that they were wrong? A new nation was to be created and Molly and Joseph were the instruments.

.   .   .

Molly spent her youth in the valley of the Mohawk, that beautiful river which flows in an almost east-west course, separating the northern part of New York State from the more populous south. The main routes of the Montreal-Albany-Niagara triangle are the same now as they were 300 years ago. The Mohawk, flowing deeply and quietly between its wooded hills and fertile flats, is the southern side of the triangle now, as it was for the Indians before white men came; the Mohawk links Lake Ontario, by an interior system of lakes and rivers, to Lake Champlain, the Richelieu River and the St. Lawrence.

This great triangle of lakes and rivers and portages was the main highway for the Iroquois war canoes when the Iroquois were masters of the northeastern quarter of North America. In the nineteenth century, the Mohawk was the chief artery of the Erie Canal. Today the New York Thruway from Niagara to New York City travels the length of the Mohawk, and so majestic is the valley, that the motor route scarcely disturbs its serenity.

Nowhere else in the interior of North America are there white settlements with a longer history than those situated on the Mohawk. Henry Hudson was exploring the Hudson River in 1609; in the same year, Champlain was discovering Lake Champlain in company with his Montagnais allies. By the year 1614, the Dutch had a fort at Albany and traders were established on the Mohawk at Schenectady. Soon after 1710, several thousand Palatinate Germans who had been persecuted for their faith were settled on the rich flats in the upper part of the Valley, under the patronage of Queen Anne of England. These were followed by Scottish and Irish settlers.

The Iroquois, therefore, were among the first of the North American natives to feel the impact of the white man. They were acute enough to realize the value of their services to the white people. Their strategic position on the Mohawk River, between Canada and the Anglo-American colonies, placed the Iroquois in the balance-of-power position, and it was not until the English had defeated the French, and the Americans had defeated the English, that the Iroquois lost their position of power.

The Iroquois,[2] or the Confederacy of the Six Nations of the Longhouse, were a sophisticated people — intelligent, honest, brave and proud, with a superior form of government, so ingenious in its unity that the founding fathers of the United States borrowed some of the Confederacy's principles.

The Confederacy was matrilineal. The children belonged to the mother's clan which would have a totemic device, such as a wolf, bear, or tortoise. The old women had much power, sitting in the councils as advisers. Some of the chief women had authority to choose the political chiefs or sachems from among their own offspring, although the war chiefs were usually chosen by the warriors, sachems, and "men of sense". No man married into his own clan but he might and often did marry into a distant tribe or league.

Sir William Johnson, writing in 1771 to Arthur Lee, observed:

> The Indians taken collectively, did certainly a few centuries ago live under some more order and government

than they do at present . . . for their intercourse in general being with the lower class of our traders, they learn little from us but our vices.

The fierce Iroquois warriors were dreaded by both the French and American colonists, yet the Iroquois were hospitable and trusting until they felt themselves betrayed or insulted. Their revenge could be horrible but not as horrible as some white historians would have us believe. English, French and American commanding officers who used the Indians as allies knew well enough what their Indian allies were doing and made use of the fierce reputation of the Iroquois warriors to smudge over white men's atrocities.

During Pontiac's War, for example, General Jeffery Amherst urged the distribution among Indians of blankets from a smallpox hospital. Whether or not he actually did it, the Indians believed he had. A decade later, a group of Cayugas (Six Nations) from a village on the Susquehanna were invited to a feast by some whites and treacherously slain — both men and women. As a result, their chief who had until then been a friend of the whites, became their bitter enemy. In 1782 at Gnadenhutten in the Ohio Valley, sixty-two adults, one-third women, and thirty-four children, were massacred. These were peaceful Moravian Delawares whose only crime was that they would not fight. This kind of genocide continued in the United States for over two centuries. The extermination of Indians was often United States government policy.

Scalping was not a common practice among the Indian people until bounties were paid by the *white* French and English commands. "In 1675 for the scalps of two men, two women and six children which the "Heroine", Hannah Dustin brought in a single-handed, the colony (Connecticut) gave her f50." In Canada, in about 1688, ten beaver skins were paid for each scalp "red or white, Christian or Pagan". Scalps were easier to carry than heads when it came time to collect the bounty.

Although they tried to remain neutral, the Iroquois were dragged by the force of their geography and their own interests into the white wars of the seventeenth and eighteenth centuries. Because they chose to ally with the English against the French, and later with the English against the American Revolutionaries, the Iroquois were hated by those they opposed. Most of the stories we read about them come from biased French and American historians.

For the most part, patient with their ruthless, violent and inconsistent white brothers, the Iroquois, besides being a semi-settled and agricultural people, were also the great middlemen in the fur trade between the Europeans and the more distant Indians. When they made common cause with the English, the Iroquois turned the balance of our early history. This is the more remarkable because they probably never assembled an army of more than 2,000 warriors at any one period.

.   .   .

We are curious about Molly Brant, the Mohawk matron whose actions affected so many people, white and red. Was she merely the spokesman of a remarkable people? Was she a diplomatic genius? Surely both.

Molly was an aristocrat among the Mohawk who were the aristocrats of the Six Nations. Her grandfather and her brother, each in his time, was received at the Court of St. James. Molly herself was for fifteen years the hostess and consort of one of the wealthiest and most powerful men in North America, Sir William Johnson. Military necessity rather than choice forced her to become a colonist in the frontier area of what was later to become Ontario.

The use of the name of Brant among the Mohawk goes back to the seventeenth century when a Briton named Brant[3] reached Albany, perhaps as early as 1665. His offspring apparently inter-married with both Dutch and Mohawk; some of the Mohawk adopted the name for legal purposes. For example, one sachem of the Mohawk used "Brant" with his totemic signature of the wolf on a property deed.

In 1710 Colonel Peter Schuyler, a member of one of the early Dutch families at Albany and much beloved by the Indians, took four sachems to England to the Court of Queen Anne. Three of these were Mohawk, one called "Brant" from

Canajoharie Castle.[4] The four sachems created a sensation in London and were much feted and were mentioned in the *Tatler* and the *Spectator*. Records tell us that during Brant's visit to England, he saw a large group of Palatine Germans, Protestants who had been persecuted for their faith and had sought protection with Queen Anne. The Mohawk, Brant, was appalled by their wretched condition and invited them to share his lands along the Mohawk River. It was this invitation to the Germans which brought them to the Mohawk, to the area later called German Flats. After the visit to England by the four sachems, a large council was held in Albany, and Brant and the other sachems persuaded their Iroquois brethren to throw in their lot with the English.

"King Brant" or SagayeanQuaTraTon was a dominant personality. Because of his skill as a warrior chief, his tribe had survived the Frontenac incursions into the Five Nations territory. Brant, a Mohawk by adoption, had married the daughter of a Mohawk chief. Because the Mohawk were a matrilineal society, Brant's wife inherited through her mother, not her father, the privilege of choosing the *Tekarahogea*. This was a political title and meant something like president of the council. The Matron who inherited the privilege of bestowing this powerful position could name anyone of her choice, a son, a nephew, whom she believed would make a suitable chief of the tribe. Brant's wife chose her own son who became the great Hendrick, famous during the French and Indian wars of 1754-1763.

Two generations later in the family of Hendrick, sachem of Canajoharie, was born a girl called Degonwadonti, which means "many opposed to one". Degonwadonti became known by the English name of Mary or Molly Brant and her brother, Thayendanega, as Joseph Brant. Molly and Joseph were born on the Ohio River where their parents had gone for several seasons' hunting – Molly in 1736, Joseph in 1742. One winter when Molly was ten or eleven years old, her father died of fever. Isolated at the time of his death from others of their tribe, the small family spent a winter of desperate hardship before they were released by the spring break-up. The mother then returned with her children to the home of her youth, Canajoharie Castle, on the Mohawk River, and to the protection of her brother, Nickus Brant, sometimes called "Old Brant", and a son of Hendrick.

The name Canajoharie means "boiling pot" or the "pot that washes itself clean", a descriptive reference to the swirling cauldron near the mouth of Canajoharie creek. The creek itself tumbles down from the great sweeping hills which reach southward towards the Catskills. The Indian village, Upper Castle, was a few miles to the west on the edge of a prominence overlooking the valley.

Molly was accustomed to white people. European traders and settlers had been established on the lower Mohawk for over 100 years. Many of the Mohawk had intermarried with whites and were farming independently. Farming was a natural occupation although social life was usually communal and the men would go hunting in the winter. Long before European influence, the Iroquois had developed indigenous crops, particularly "the three sisters", corn, beans and squash. During the French invasion of the 1680's, large acreages of corn were destroyed as well as a "vast quantity of hogs".

Growing up in the household of her uncle, Nickus Brant, a prominent sachem who became Tekarahogea after the death of his father Hendrick, Molly's life had many advantages. She had the comfort of a European-style wooden house as well furnished as those of any of the pioneer settlers. The Brant family was considered by white contemporaries to be one of distinction. Its members moved easily in two worlds and acted as interpreters for both cultures. With such a background, it is not surprising that Molly Brant was dominant among her contemporaries.

.   .   .

When Molly was 15 she began her schooling at Stockbridge Mission School in Massachusetts, probably at the insistence of William Johnson. This assumption is based on considerable evidence. Johnson was a young Irish trader on the Mohawk acting as agent for his uncle, Admiral Sir Peter Warren, RN. Sir Peter had contributed £700 towards a mission school at Stockbridge, run by the great American theologian, Jonathan Edwards, and William Johnson was asked to persuade his neighbours to send their children there.

In 1751 some 92 Mohawk made the long journey from the Mohawk River to Stockbridge. These included Hendrick, his brother Abraham, and his son, Nickus Brant. Nickus was among the first to arrive and was curious enough to remain for some months in the vicinity himself.

As the school was designed for both boys and girls, it seems probable that Molly and Joseph both attended it and studied for a time under Jonathan Edwards. Such a primary education at Stockbridge helps to explain how Joseph became a reasonably well-educated man, after two short years at Moor's Charity School (later Dartmouth College) under Dr. E. Wheelock. It explains also how Molly could later run the complicated household of Sir William Johnson and be described by an English visitor as "wellbred"; or if Dr. Wheelock can be credited, that she could write in her native language.[5]

Only a few years before William Johnson's interest in the Stockbridge school, Nickus was a war prisoner of the French at Quebec; he had been ransomed by the British in 1749, about the time that Molly, Joseph and their mother had returned from the Ohio to Canajoharie. While Nickus had been absent, his family had come under direct protection of William Johnson who was Colonel of the forces recruited from the Six Nations. It was he who had arranged for the ransom of Nickus and other Six Nations prisoners. There was therefore a close relationship between the Nickus Brant family and William Johnson from the time that Molly was a young girl. Nickus could scarcely have resisted Johnson's arguments persuading him to send his niece and nephew to the Stockbridge school.

Why do we know so little about Molly Brant? Much has been written about Joseph but very little about his sister who was six years his senior. Molly came to hold great power within the matrilineal Six Nations as a diplomat. Her influence can be attributed to her own abilities and to her relation with Sir William Johnson.

Although her guardian was a sachem, Molly did her share of cultivating the crops and of gathering the wild fruits, including wild cranberries abundant in that area. A young female had to prove herself in order to obtain the superior status of wise woman or "clan mother" in middle age.

She was full of fun. According to the traditions of the Valley, Molly was sixteen when she attended a regimental muster at Canajoharie as one of the spectators. The story goes that she begged a ride from a young officer who passed by on a spirited horse. The officer, not guessing that she could or would take him at his word, invited her to mount. Agile as a cat, Molly sprang onto the horse's back behind the rider. The startled animal took off at high speed around the parade ground with Molly hanging onto the officer, her eyes flashing, long hair flying, blanket flapping. The spectators thoroughly enjoyed the unplanned event, none less than the Superintendent of Indian Affairs, young Colonel Johnson.

Even at this early age, Molly's fame was spreading. There is a scrap of a note in New York Documents (VI p 589) which says "Johnson took Molly from her father in 1750. He enticed her and her mother to come down river in her bark canoe. Her father, Hendrick and Abraham were hostile. Molly prevailed upon them [to allow] her to become Col. Johnson's wife."[6]

This was straight gossip. Daniel Claus, writing in 1754, paints a different picture. Claus, a German immigrant who later became one of Sir William's agents and married one of his daughters, was living with Hendrick in order to learn the Mohawk language. Claus recounts a formal visit made by Hendrick and eleven companions to the Governor of Pennsylvania at Philadelphia. Among the eleven was Molly.

On the return journey, the party stopped at Albany "where Capt Stairs fell in love with Ms (sic) Mary Brant who was then pretty, likely not havg (sic) had the small pox." So at eighteen, Molly was attractive, and clever too; otherwise her grandfather, Hendrick, would not have considered her suitable for participation in a diplomatic mission.[7]

In September 1755, William Johnson, as Major General, led the white militia and the Iroquois warriors against the French at

Lake George. The battle was conclusive and ended the menace from the north. There were many casualties, however. Hendrick was killed and William Johnson was severely wounded. Joseph, a boy of thirteen, fought in his first battle. As a reward for his brilliant victory, Johnson was knighted and rewarded with a gift of £5,000 by the Crown.

In 1759, the year of the fall of Quebec to the British, Molly Brant became mistress at Sir William's stone fortress-house. She was 23 years old. Her new life in the large, complicated household was not easy, but she was determined to succeed. One of her major problems was to win the approval of Sir William's children who were nearly as old as she was. In addition to at least two children by unknown women, Sir William had three children by Catherine Weissenberg. Catherine is a shadowy character. Probably she was a German bondservant who never learned to speak English well enough to act as Sir William's hostess. Her children, Nancy, Mary and John, were christened at Fort Hunter under her name, but in Johnson's will he names her as his wife. There may have been a deathbed marriage to protect the legitimacy of his heir.[8]

William Johnson was an uninhibited robust male and, typical of his period, had had plenty of women; his relation with Molly, however, was conjugal. They were married by Indian ceremony and although there is no document to show that they were legally married according to British law, the union was no light-hearted affair. Not only was there strong attraction between them, but they also needed one another's tact and support in their dealings with the Six Nations. In his will, Sir William calls Molly "my housekeeper". This was his way of protecting her rank as a Mohawk Matron. If Molly had taken his name, she would have lost prestige among her people and been refused a voice in the council. To the end of her life, she went under her own name, Molly Brant, although her children were all registered in the Loyalist Returns as Johnsons.

Molly's name begins to appear in the Johnson Papers in the summer of 1759. In Sir William's journal, written at Oswego, the September 17 entry includes "... By a Mohawk this day, wrote a letter to Nancy, another to Molly. ..." Molly fitted into the Johnson household without a lurch. Nancy, the eldest of the Johnson children, was about twenty, and had been in charge of her father's household. She would not have surrendered her position easily to the newcomer, not more than a few years older than she. However there is slight hint of dissension in the house, and the two Johnson daughters remained under their father's roof for several more years, even for a time following their marriages.

The first year that Molly lived at Fort Johnson, there was a small family upset when it was discovered that Nancy was in love with her father's agent, Daniel Claus, at that time posted in Montreal. Sir William wrote to him sharply disapproving of his "carrying on an Intrigue of the kind privately in my Family".

Did Molly help to smooth out the romance? She must have helped, for Nancy married Daniel in April of that year, and Claus was a true friend to Molly as long as he lived.

There was a considerable correspondence between Sir William and Daniel Claus at this time, mostly about the Indian trade, but occasionally a family item would be inserted. In the fall of 1760, Sir William wrote to Claus ". . . I would have you buy me some little curiosities there [Montreal] of no great value and send them by the first opportunity."

Sir William was hoping for something slightly exotic from the newly-conquered French town of Montreal to give to Molly. Sir William was by nature exuberant; he enjoyed the common folk, the Indians, the aristocrats, alike; he enjoyed reading and had an amazing library, including the most modern books of science and mathematics; he was partial to athletic meets and feats of prowess, and sponsored many matches with both whites and Indians participating. He was religious and built a number of churches. Most of all, perhaps, he was sociable and loved to be hospitable.

In Molly, Sir William found a hostess who had charm, spirit and tact, a matchless hostess for his wilderness barony with its blend of the urbane and the wild. To Molly, the girl who sprang to the back of a speeding horse, Fort Johnson was a challenge. She would show that she was not, like Catherine Weissenberg, a woman of shadows.

Before the end of 1759, Molly had borne a son for Sir William; the boy was christened Peter, for Sir Peter Warren, William's uncle. In all, Molly bore at least nine children, two sons and six daughters surviving infancy.

Sir William was often absent from Fort Johnson for long periods and these absences he laments in his letters and journals. In the summer of 1761, for example, it was necessary for him to meet the Ottawa Confederacy and other Indians of the Western Nations at Detroit. He was gone for months. Nearing home late in October he met Captain Etherington who, ". . . told me Molly was delivered of a girl; that all was well at my house, where they stayed two days."

While Sir William was away, Molly had to act on his behalf for the Mohawk in the Valley; she had to run a large, complicated household of servants, slaves, dependants, and employees; she entertained two gentlemen visitors who "stayed two days"; and she bore Sir William a daughter. And she loved it all. The fertile genes she had inherited from her ancestors were beginning to flower.

Now that he had Molly to come back to, Sir William had begun to think of home as something more desirable than Bachelor's Hall. Sportive amours belonged to the past; home had become a place of the heart, a place of elegance to be adorned. Fort Johnson had not been a family home, but Sir William was now a family man.

The Fort was a man's establishment. Downstairs on either side of the wide hall were large rooms, one a dining room and the other a parlor; behind each was a narrow room, one a pantry to serve the dining room, the other an office. The kitchen was in the rear in a separate building. Upstairs was the same arrangement, two large bedrooms, two very narrow bedrooms. These narrow rooms may have been used for storing munitions under lock and key, for this was, after all, a frontier community.

Surrounding the big stone mansion, part home, part office, part fort, there was a small village of separate dwellings, because by the 1750's, William Johnson was becoming affluent and important in his own right with many dependants. He still acted as his uncle's agent but he had his own lands, his own settlers and his own trading post; he was Superintendent of Indian Affairs for the Province of New York and a colonel of militia for the northern frontier; he held a seat on the provincial council. He had two or three secretaries or agents to help him handle Indian Affairs. His daughters had a governess. There were numerous servants and slaves. Officials and military people from Albany came and went, as well as Indians. The trading post, scarcely a mile away, was always busy with its staff of warehousemen and clerks. He retained a full-time lawyer and a family physician, a blacksmith, a tailor, a gardener, farm manager, and a few musicians. William and Molly entertained governors and common folk, British lords and Indian chiefs.

.   .   .

Sir William decided in 1762 to build another mansion more suitable to his family's needs, this one nine miles inland from the river, on the highlands to the northwest of Fort Johnson. Molly would rather have lived on the river where there was constant intercourse with the world, both white and Indian. By building inland, she knew Sir William was proclaiming his comfortable rapport with the Six Nations; that this would build up his image as trusted friend of the Indian and enhance his power. The move inland was daring, but good medicine, and the realist in her approved.

During the summer and fall of 1762, labourers began preparing timber for building, and actual building commenced in the spring of 1763. Both the stone mansion, Fort Johnson, facing the Mohawk River, and the frame mansion on the hills are still standing and well-preserved, magnificent examples of eighteenth century Colonial architecture.

Johnson Hall was built on the same plan as the Fort, though much more spacious and comfortable. It was built of timbers and framed, rather than of cold stone. Johnson planned a fifteen-foot-wide centre hall, running from back to front door, with the same size hall above, and a handsome staircase with mahogany balustrade connecting the two floors. On either side of the hall, both upstairs and down, were two rooms, each with an immense fireplace. The fireplaces were built back-to-back, so that only two large chimneys were needed, centrally positioned for the four upper and lower rooms to left and right of the hall. Johnson Hall had its kitchen in the basement. On the ground floor was a large parlor, a large dining room, a room for the children, and a room for Sir William which was both office and bedroom. Upstairs were four bedrooms, one of them for Molly and her children, as was clearly indicated in Sir William's will. In his very long will, Sir William shows without any doubt his affection for, and his responsibility towards, all his children as well as for Molly.

The new house was finished sometime in 1763 but the family had scarcely moved in before the Pontiac War erupted. To protect the household, two stone blockhouses were built. The house was further protected by a stockade. One of the block-houses was defended by a small cannon which Sir William's uncle, Admiral Sir Peter Warren, had captured at Louisburg and sent to his nephew as a present and trophy. Molly's firstborn was named for this uncle.

How did this new life of Molly's compare with her life at Canajoharie Castle? She was certainly not a girl who had grown up in a wigwam, as some writers have suggested. Both her uncle, Nickus, and her grandfather, Hendrick, lived in comfortable frame houses with implements and furniture such as any European settler might have. Nickus owned a good farm with livestock, close to Canajoharie, and farmed it as well as any of his neighbours. After Molly took over at Johnson Hall, she was said by the wealthy General Philip Schuyler, a frequent visitor, "to be a most accomplished mistress of such an establishment".

Johnson Hall could be said to be communal in somewhat the same way as was Canajoharie Castle, the main difference being that the Hall had one boss, whereas the Indian Castle was ruled by consensus. Eating facilities at the Hall were more refined but the food was similar. The slaves and white servants living in the cluster of small houses surrounding the main building, ate in much the same way as did the Indians. When Indians came to visit, Dr. Wheelock reported,

I have seen at Mount Johnson sixty or eighty Indians at one time lodging under tents on the lawn and taking their meals from tables made of pine boards spread under the trees. . . . These visits must have been very expensive to Sir William and he told me that never more than half their cost was defrayed out of the public exchequer.

Although Nickus was said to dress in European style, Molly always dressed in Iroquoian fashion, but she used European materials. Her children, however, she dressed in European style to protect them from inquisitive eyes. Her children were sent to the manor school at Johnstown, the village which grew up near Johnson Hall.

The greatest difference between her two lives was in the degree of responsibility. Under Nickus's roof the older women did the planning. At Johnson Hall, Molly did most of the ordering for the whole establishment. She was in charge of the welfare of all Indians, slaves and servants; she patched up quarrels, tamed rebellious help; she attended the sick and injured — sometimes using her medicinal herbs, sometimes calling in the family physician. Added to all this, Sir William often needed her counsel in dealing with the Six Nations.

Sir William met the representatives of almost all the Western Nations at a large Peace Council held at Niagara in July, 1764. There were 2,060 warriors and sachems present from the whole of the St. Lawrence and Great Lakes system and even a few from Hudson Bay. It has been said that from Niagara, Sir William ruled half of North America. Discussion of boundary lines at Niagara led to further negotiations at Johnson Hall.

In December 1764, Sir William wrote: "I have at present every room in my house full of Indians and the prospect before me of continual business all the winter." In the spring of 1765, the Johnson Hall establishment was taxed to the utmost to provide quarters and provision for 900 Indians who had come to meet in full formal council. It was at this council that the Ohio River Boundary Line became for the Indians the line of "no surrender" to further encroachments by the whites. The Indian Nations tried for the next three decades to hold this boundary line and in their arguments they always quoted the

Treaty made by them in 1765 with Sir William Johnson.

Molly, too, was deeply involved during these negotiations. She was always at hand as self-appointed interpreter. Though she was nearly overwhelmed by the tremendous demands on the hospitality of Johnson Hall, she always knew what her husband's intention was as to the rights of her people. Sir William's role as counsellor was undoubtedly strengthened by Molly's prestige among the Six Nations.

During these tumultuous years, there was other entertaining to be done besides providing for Indian ambassadors. In a stormy period in March 1763, Mary, second daughter of Sir William, married her cousin, Lieutenant Guy Johnson, thus making Guy son-in-law as well as secretary to her father. Apparently both Nancy and Mary (also known as Molly), whose husbands were constantly coming and going in the interests of the Indian Department, still called Johnson Hall home; and young Johnny, now a gay bachelor, still hung up his hat at his father's mansion. The household must have been harmonious, otherwise the two married daughters would not have stayed with Molly. A born diplomat, she knew how to get along with people.

Molly was also good company. In June of 1765, shortly after the Indian delegates had left Johnson Hall, Sir William and Molly entertained Lady Susan, eldest daughter of Stephen Fox, first Earl of Ilchester. Lady Susan had eloped with an actor, William O'Brien, and sailed for America. The young lovers spent some time with the Johnsons and later Lady Susan wrote ". . . Molly Brant was a well-bred and pleasant lady . . . who in many a ramble proved a delightful companion."

Another guest arrived before the departure of the O'Briens. Lord Adam Gordon, afterwards commander-in-chief of the army in Scotland, was on a pleasure tour of America and spent some days at Johnson Hall. When Lord Gordon returned to England in October, he took John Johnson with him, in order, according to Sir William, ". . . to try to wear off the rusticity of a country education."

There are other pictures of Molly which come out of this period. Anne Grant, who spent her youth in Albany, reflects the gossip of the town in her *Memoirs of an American Lady:* "Here this singular man [Sir William] lived like a little sovereign. . . . He had connected himself with an Indian maiden, daughter of a sachem, who possessed an uncommonly agreeable person, and good understanding."

There is yet another picture of Molly written by an anonymous English person. "Her features are fine and beautiful; her complexion clear and olive-tinted. . . . She was quiet in demeanor, on occasion, and possessed of a calm dignity that bespoke a native pride and consciousness of power. She seldom imposed herself into the picture, but no one was in her presence without being aware of her."

This was Molly at the age of thirty.

.   .   .

Indian affairs for a while after 1765 settled into a calm which left Sir William time to devote to his own domestic affairs. In 1766 he built stone dwellings, one for each of his two eldest daughters. Even in the great Johnson mansion, living space was growing congested as Molly's young ones began to grow. It was a relief to all to be able to live under separate roofs. When Sir John[9] returned from England in 1767, he also moved out of Johnson Hall to live bachelor-style at Fort Johnson.

Molly was grateful to have Johnson Hall to herself. Besides her concern for her four children, Peter, Elizabeth, Magdalene and Margaret, she worried over Sir William's constant zest for activity, knowing his exertions only aggravated his failing health. Sir William was subject to frequent attacks of dysentery as well as severe pain in his thighs from an old wound. In spite of poor health, he travelled to Oswego in July of 1767 to smoke a peace pipe with Pontiac, and then hurried back to Johnson Hall to play host to the Governor of New York Province, Sir Henry Moore, with his wife and daughter.

Trouble was brewing between the colonies and the Crown, but life at Johnson Hall was scarcely ruffled. In the summer of 1769, Sir William was kept in bed by illness for the whole season. His illness was somewhat alleviated by word received in royal letters patent of a large grant of 66,000 acres on the north side of the Mohawk River, "as a mark of appreciation for his services". Sir William and Molly had been waiting for nine years for the patent with the "mark of appreciation".

The royal patent was not a gift but merely approval of a gift from his neighbours. In the autumn of 1760, the Mohawk of Canajoharie in full council had made Sir William a present, in token of esteem and affection, of a large grant of land totalling 66,000 acres. This grant was so large that the Council of the Province of New York could not rightfully bestow the patent and had referred the matter to the British Crown. (Sir William purchased most of the rest of his land-holdings from white settlers, his total estate being more than 173,000 acres.)[10]

Did Molly have a fractious patient to care for during the long summer? We are not told, but certainly Sir William was not lacking in entertainment with his books on science and history, his popular literature, his music, his microscope and prism, and his visitors. Molly's charm and tact kept the tedium to a minimum. She was forceful enough to stop trifling problems from reaching him; she could scrap with the best when her family's interests were at stake. There is a hint that she had a sharp temper.

Life at Johnson Hall was like that of a small village. There was the "bouw-master" or farm manager who managed the ten or fifteen negro slave labourers. These lived not far from the Hall in small dwellings with their families. Besides the slaves, there were personal servants, secretaries and agents, a lawyer, a doctor and all had to be provided for. Two negro servants, Juba and Jenny, were specifically mentioned in the will as belonging to "Miss Molly" and they followed her to Canada. Molly herself was generally "Miss Molly" to those who loved and respected her.

Relations between the mother country and the colonies were worsening. Writing from his bed in September 1769, Sir William worried:

> I must confess that the aspect of affairs at home is very unpleasing and ought to give concern to every well-wisher of his country because whatever reason or justice there

may be in the late steps, there is probability of their being carried farther than a good man can wish for.

These were Johnson's thoughts, five years before the American Revolution. Molly's feelings were of the same cast as her husband's. Sir William and Molly said and kept on saying, "Let's be reasonable. Let's hear both sides of the quarrel."

Sir William had recovered his health by 1770 well enough to resume his strenuous duties as King's Councillor and Superintendent for Indian Affairs. Within a mile of the Hall a small hamlet had grown which was named Johnstown. Here Sir William erected a stone Anglican church and a school for the eighty families, and hired a teacher, Edward Wall. Miss Molly's three eldest learned their ABC's from Wall who was said to be severe with most of the pupils but rather indulgent with Sir William's children.

Sometime during 1772, Molly had her ninth child and also lost a child. One of the Seneca chiefs openly wept when he heard of Sir William's and Miss Molly's loss.

Molly's brother, Joseph, had settled down by this time as farmer-trader in the Valley. Earlier, Joseph had been sent by Sir William and Molly to Moor's Charity School for Indians[11] and he had done well. However the tribes were suspicious of the "westernization" of one of their potential leaders and persuaded Molly to have him recalled after less than two years. Joseph made full use of his education, slight as it was, for during his life he translated many passages from the gospels and from the Anglican liturgy into Mohawk. His use of English noticeably improved in later years and by the end of his life he was a master of English prose. On a more practical plane, Sir William employed Joseph frequently as interpreter.

The account books for this period show an enormous variety of items. There were fine wines, gun powder, blankets, a "piece of diaper napkin", books, nursery stock, shoes, and yards of materials for the seamstress to make into clothes for the household. The accounts include not only articles for the house, supplies for the servants – such as "shoes for the wench Diana" – but trading goods for the Indians. Although there appears to be little for Molly in most of these accounts, her name often is shown on lists "per Molly" because she did much of the ordering. Sir William was now the wealthiest and most influential man in the province and Molly, as his chatelaine, was an asset.

There was one more happy family event in the Johnson menage before the shadows fell. In June 1773, Sir William's son, Sir John, married Mary Watts in New York City. Mary Watts, usually called Polly, came from one of the best families of the City and Sir William was gratified, although poor health did not permit him to attend the wedding.

In the spring of 1774 a series of bloody encounters and reprisals, begun initially by some vicious white traders, took place along the Ohio. The Six Nations felt themselves involved and determined to go to the assistance of their Indian allies. By June 7 nearly 600 Indians had assembled at the Hall. Sir William, suffering from his old complaint, dysentery, and exhausted from weeks of continuous effort to appease the Indians, was in no condition to hold a council. Molly, too, was under great strain, torn between conflicting anxieties, the needs of her people and Sir William's health.

On the second day of the council, Sir William spoke for two hours with all the fire and vivacity of an Indian orator. It was a hot summer day and he stood for the whole two hours in the sun. When he retired he was so exhausted that he had to be helped to his library, and shortly after was seized by convulsions. His son, Sir John, nine miles away at Fort Johnson, was sent for. When Sir John arrived his father was past speaking and a few minutes later Sir William died. He was in his sixtieth year.

.   .   .

The story of the Valley is that Molly's death wail was taken up by her people. Their *Great Brother,* "Warraghiyagey", was dead. The Indians were stupified for not only was Sir William greatly beloved by them but he was their protector: the Six Nations Confederacy considered him a part of themselves.

In the first moment of blank dismay, the 600 Indians who were attending the Council at Johnson Hall were on the point of dispersing when Colonel Guy Johnson came to them and calmed them by promising, as the deputy to Sir William, that he would take charge of their affairs. For Molly, however, there was no deputy for Sir William. Her world had fallen apart.

Sir William was undoubtedly the outstanding figure in Anglo-America in the generation preceeding the Revolution. "Sir William never deceived us," said the Indians. His integrity stood out like a mountain of granite in the turbulent frontier world of shady quick-money speculators and it was this strict integrity, allied with a genius for organization, which was the basis of his success with the Indian and his influence in the Colonies.

The Revolution apparently wiped out in a few disastrous years the life-work of this unusual man, but on deeper examination it becomes evident that the community that Sir William welded together along the Mohawk — the Germans, Dutch, Scots, Irish, and the Mohawk — was the nucleus and foundation for the Province of Ontario. In a world of tricky balances, Sir William's Mohawk Valley people tipped the scales and kept Canada British.

The vacuum created by Sir William's death was filled by Molly, her brother Joseph, and Sir John Johnson, all in their thirties. These three provided the leadership needed by the Valley people, and transported them to Canada. Molly was the binding force which tied them all together.

Sir William provided liberally for all his children. Sir John succeeded to his father's title and principal estates. Sir William had for some years been concerned about this succession and in his will he makes particular reference to "my beloved wife, Catherine Johnson". To Molly he refers throughout the document as "my prudent and faithful House Keeper Mary Brant" and to Molly's children as "my natural children" or the "eight children of mine by Mary Brant". The distinction between Catherine and Molly suggests that Sir William was at once supporting Catherine's uncertain status as wife, and Molly's rank as Mohawk Matron. Besides providing for his eleven children by Catherine and Molly, he left property to William and to Brant, sons by unknown Indian women.

Molly and her children (the eldest, Peter, was only thirteen when his father died) were well cared for, not only in lands and money but by the appointment of seven guardians or trustees to look after their interests. Sir John and his wife Polly moved to Johnson Hall, and Miss Molly and her family moved back to Fort Johnson where she had first come to Sir William.

The swell of incidents which was soon to burst into armed rebellion against the Crown was rapidly reaching floodtide. Emotions were so charged that it became more and more difficult to remain neutral. It has been argued by American historians that if Sir William had lived he would have sided with the rebels or "patriots", but though he understood and sympathized with the grievances of the colonials, he was no hot-head and he believed in the British system of order. Sir William would have tried to remain neutral as his son, Sir John, tried to do, but would have been forced by the extremists to state his position. It is inconceivable that a man like Sir William would take up arms against his sovereign; as there were no neutrals, he would have been declared a Tory and thus an enemy. Molly and the Iroquois were also caught in a dilemma. They, too, expected to be neutral but were soon forced to choose sides.

The Johnson clan at this time included Molly and her eight children; Sir John, heir to the Johnson estate; Colonel Guy Johnson, Sir John's brother-in-law and Superintendent of Indian Affairs; Colonel Daniel Claus, another brother-in-law; Joseph Brant, Molly's brother, who was Guy Johnson's secretary; William and Brant, half-brothers of Sir John. For the most part, the people of the Valley were loyal adherents of the Johnsons and the Tory cause, excepting a hard core of Dutch who leaned towards the rebel side. Among the most loyal of the Johnson adherents were the Mohawk.

By June 1775, Colonel Guy Johnson was forced to leave the Valley. Joseph Brant and other Mohawk went with him to Canada. By January 1776, Sir John and some of the remaining Tory partisans were forced to flee; Sir John's wife was held by the revolutionaries as a prisoner. The Claus family had gone to Montreal.

Molly retreated to the Indian village of Canajoharie with her children. She was nearly destitute. Lieutenant Tench Tilghman, secretary and aide to General George Washington, visited the Valley in August, 1776, on a tour of inspection. Tilghman found Molly carrying on a small trade with the Indians. On August 15, he writes in his Memoirs:

> This morning we were honored with a visit from the favorite of the late Sir William Johnson . . . She saluted us with an air of ease and politeness, she was dressed after the Indian manner, but her linen and other Cloathes the finest of their kind . . . The Indians pay her great respect and I am afraid her influence will give us some trouble, for we are informed that she is . . . entirely in the interests of Guy Johnson who is now in Canada.[12]

Of course she was in the interests of Guy Johnson and all Johnsons. They were her interests. It did not occur to her that the Tories could be wrong or could lose. It was all miserably inconvenient and racking but it could not last forever and then all would be as it had been. Meanwhile she did her best to support herself and children. By doing a little trading with the Mohawk she retained some independence. It was far from easy. Some Oneidas in pay of the rebels constantly harassed her and often robbed her.

Prime sources give us other testimony of Molly's influence with the Six Nations. In 1778, Colonel Daniel Claus wrote to Sir John Johnson that ". . . a Joseph and Mary Brant will outdo fifty Butlers in managing and keeping them [the Indians] firm". In 1779, Claus wrote to Governor Haldimand, ". . . one word from her is more taken notice of by the Five Nations than a thousand from any white man without exception". Captain Alexander Fraser wrote in 1780 to Governor Haldimand that ". . . Miss Molly Brant's influence over them is far Superior to that of all the Chiefs put together".

Much pressure was brought upon the Six Nations Confederacy to ally itself openly with the British cause. Joseph Brant went to England in the winter of 1775-76 and was impressed by British resources and power. On his return to America, he conferred with Molly, and after this the Brants cast their lot and that of the Confederacy with the British.

Where were Sir John Johnson and Colonel Guy when the Iroquois made this decision? They were living in Canada as was Daniel Claus. Molly, and Molly alone of the Johnson clan, was living among the Iroquois and in a position to persuade. And she believed firmly in Sir William's King.

The British mounted a large-scale attack on the Mohawk Valley but were stopped at Oriskany. After the withdrawal of the British, Molly found her life in the Valley too oppressive, and she moved west with her children to live with the Seneca. She now openly favoured the British, and was known to have sent a runner to warm them of an ambush. When she found some of the Five Nations[13] "wavering and unstable", Molly held a public debate in council with one of the dissident chiefs.

She reminded the Seneca chief that it was the Americans who had driven her and many of the Mohawk from the Valley; that she had been insulted and robbed although she had been living peacefully, as in the past. She argued that the Americans wanted the Valley for themselves because it was the foodbasket of the rebellious colonies and that they would drive the Seneca and Cayuga from their lands when the time came. She also reminded the Seneca that Sir William had been their good friend and that he trusted the Great King. And now the Great King had promised that all the Six Nations' lands would be restored as soon as the present trouble was over — at the King's expense. Then she threatened that if the Seneca broke their covenant with the King, Warraghiyagey would cause the immoveable mountains to move, the silver chain to come loose, so that it fell into the hands of their mortal enemies.

Molly spoke with such eloquence that the chief and others present promised to abide by their engagements made previously with Sir William.

Molly settled with relatives at Cayuga[14], and would probably have remained there, but a number of Indian families, as displaced as she was, had begun to congregate around Fort Niagara at the mouth of the Niagara River. The command at Niagara which was then under Lieutenant-Colonel Mason Bolton ". . . sent her repeated and very pressing and encouraging messages to come and reside at Niagara."¹⁵

The British knew that Molly could conciliate the distraught Indians as no white man could, and probably no other Indian.

.   .   .

In 1777, except for an insignificant fur post at Fort Toronto and the military post at Cataraqui, the province we now call Ontario was not yet inhabited by Europeans. Almost all the big fur posts and fortifications – Oswego, Niagara, Detroit, Michilimackinac, Sault Ste. Marie – were situated south of the Great Lakes, south of the present international boundary between Canada and the United States. Cataraqui, at the entrance to the St. Lawrence, was a notable exception. When Upper Canada was first organized in 1791, that part of the province south of the French and Ottawa Rivers was aptly called the Iroquois Hunting Grounds; as a result of Iroquois tribal wars there were almost no Iroquois living north of the Lakes. The Mississauga, finding that no other nation had preempted old Huron and Neutral territory, began a southern movement during the middle of the Eighteenth Century so that by 1777 they were making claim for that portion of territory between Lakes Huron, Erie and Ontario earlier occupied by the Iroquois. Some Ojibway had migrated to the shores of Lakes Huron and Simcoe. The total Indian population in Southern Ontario at that time was thought to be about 1,000. It was into this almost vacant land – perhaps the only vacant land on the continent – that Indians and whites, displaced by the American Revolution, began to trickle.

Fort Niagara sat on the east bank of the Niagara River near its outlet into Lake Ontario. This old fort, now restored, is a museum at Youngstown, N.Y. It was begun by the French in 1725, and captured by Sir William Johnson for the British shortly before Molly went to live at Fort Johnson. In 1777, the fortification was of considerable size enclosing an area of six or eight acres. Facing the river was the "Castle", the original fortress built to look like a French manor house to deceive the Seneca about its military purpose. The Superintendent of Indian Affairs, Colonel Guy Johnson, had a handsome house within the enclosure. After the coming of the Indians and the Loyalists, houses for them were built by the government around the Fort. After the peace treaty, six years later, the whole British-Loyalist establishment was moved across the river to the west to what was to become Niagara-on-the-Lake.

When Molly arrived, it was an impressive refuge. She left Cayuga for Oswego late in the year 1777, and from there travelled by ship on Lake Ontario to Fort Niagara. She joined her brother Joseph at Niagara and spent the winter in Joseph's household. Joseph gave her £30 for immediate necessities and General Haldimand sent her £25. By summer she had her own establishment and was living in a house ordered for her by Haldimand.

In a letter written June 23, 1778, from Niagara to Daniel Claus, Molly said:

> Dear Sir; I have been favor'd with yours and the Trunk of Presents. . . . We have a report of Joseph having had a brush with the Rebels but do not know at what place. . . . I am obliged to you for the care and attention in sending me those very necessary articles, and should be very glad if you have any accounts from New York that you would let me know them, as well as of George and Peggy, whom I hope are agreeably settled in Montreal. My children are all in good health and desire their loves to you, Mrs. Claus, Lady and Sir John Johnson. I hope the Time is very near, when we shall all return to our habitations on the Mohawk River.

George and Peggy, mentioned in the letter, had been sent to Montreal to join their older sisters who were attending school there at government expense. The request for "any accounts from New York" came from Molly's anxiety about her older son Peter, who was a very young lieutenant serving with the British forces on Long Island and from whom she had not heard. Her unease had grounds. Peter had, in fact, died in 1777 at the age of seventeen. Although the circumstances of his death are uncertain, he was known for his courage for he had, alone and unaided, captured the notorious Ethan Allan.

Despite her troubles, Molly's sense of humour was sometimes impish. She told Colonel Bolton that she had had a dream: that she had dreamed she had been kicking the head of one of the Revolutionary Colonials around the ground. This dream motif was an Indian device for asking for something — in this instance, the head of Colonel Stacia, now a British prisoner, who had been insulting to her. Bolton knew and Molly knew that the request for Stacia's head was outlandish; they settled for some rum for the Indians.

Molly went back to the Indian towns among the Seneca in the fall of 1778 but returned to Niagara in November, agitated because she had heard nothing about her sons. She sent for the agent, Mr. Taylor of Taylor and Duffin, ". . . and told him she is under a great concern at the loss of her two Sons, being dear to her — were they still alive, she thinks one of them might be with her sometimes. She wishes to send you a true State of Disposition of the Six Nations."

Molly was now a servant of government. She was no longer a free spirit, free to roam the wilds or punish her servants as she willed. She had become a small cog in a big machine and she obeyed orders. A sharpness begins to show in her dealings with people. Although she and her children were provided for, life was thorny. She could be a stoic but she was far from content; and she desperately longed for Sir William's support.

Butler and his Rangers, and Brant and his Iroquois surprised the Cherry Valley that winter and completely destroyed the prosperous community which was deep in rebel country. Fearful retaliation came in the summer of 1779 when George Washington ordered General John Sullivan to destroy the Seneca and the Cayuga countries. Sullivan broke the Iroquois as a nation, although he secured no prisoners; ". . . the nest, but not the birds," said one Indian. The Seneca did what the Mohawk had done when Frontenac had invaded their country — they melted into the forests.

Molly was not at Niagara when the refugees began to arrive. At the invitation of Governor Haldimand she had gone to Montreal to see him and to visit her children who were in school. The governor himself had arranged for Molly's children to go to Montreal boarding schools.

By September 6, Molly had received the news of Sullivan's

campaign, of the disaster to the Seneca and the threat to Niagara. Claus writes to Haldimand on that date;

> Miss Molly since hearing of the movement of the Indians is very anxious to return among the Six Nations and says that her staying away at this critical time, may prove injurious to her character hereafter, being at the head of a Society of Six Nations Matrons who have a great deal to say among the young men, in particular in time of war.

Haldimand replies on the 9th, "As for Miss Molly, if she thinks her presence necessary . . . she must be suffered to depart. Colonel Johnson will of course provide for her Journey." Molly knew she was needed by her people at Niagara and by September 13 she was on her way back. At Haldimand's suggestion, she left her two youngest girls with Claus who made arrangements for them to join their older sisters at school.

On the same day that Molly left Montreal, Haldimand at Quebec was writing a note to Lord Germaine, Secretary of State for the colonies:

> His [Joseph's] sister who lived many years with Sir William by whom he had many children and to whose influence he was much indebted in his successful management of the Six Nations, was driven from her home with her family, took refuge at Niagara two years ago. Her situation there not being as comfortable as could be wished, she brought her family down to Montreal, by my desire, where I settled her to her satisfaction, but upon hearing of the Rebels advancing into the Indian country, thinking she might be of use in encouraging the Indians to preserve their Fidelity, she returned to Niagara.

Although her ancestor Brant and her brother Joseph had visited England, this mention in the files of the Colonial office was the closest Molly came to official recognition. She knew her importance as a negotiator, however, and played her role with poise.

.   .   .

On October 5, Molly herself wrote to Daniel Claus from

Carleton Island, an island in the St. Lawrence close to the present city of Kingston. Carleton Island had been selected by the
British the previous year as a military base. Molly was literally
stranded there. All transport was commandeered by the army.
"We arrived here the 29th last month," she said,

> after a tedious and disagreeable voyage, where we remain
> and by all appearance may for the winter. . . . The Indians
> are a good dale [sic] dissatisfied on Acct. of the Col's hasty
> temper which I hope he will soon drop. Otherwise it may
> be disadvantageous. I need not tele [sic] you whatever is
> promised or told them it ought to be performed . . .

The tactful allusions to Colonel Johnson and his "hasty
temper" show that Molly had her ear to the ground. It was not
long afterward that Colonel Guy Johnson was removed from his
position as Superintendent of Indian Affairs as being unsuitable
for the post. It was said he drank too much and made a poor
example for the Indians. He was succeeded by the capable Sir
John Johnson.

As she had guessed, Molly remained on Carleton Island. She
was made as comfortable as possible for the winter in the military barracks. It is uncertain how many of her family were with
her, though we know that the two youngest, Susan and Nancy,
were at school in Montreal, and probably Mary, Margaret and
George were there too. Besides her children, she had with her a
boy named William Lamb, who may have been an Indian
orphan or a negro; also with her were her three negro slaves,
Abraham and the two young sisters, Juba and Jenny. Molly was
forty-three years old, and her eldest daughters, Elizabeth, sixteen, and Magdalene, fourteen, were almost grown; these two,
according to Claus ". . . she would willingly see appear decent".
For a mother of growing daughters in a war-torn land, she held
an uneasy responsibility and her concern was natural.

On the official Loyalist Returns, Molly was listed as Mrs.
Molly Brant and the children as Johnsons. Her decision for this
distinction of names grew from her position as link between
two cultures which were in military alliance. By keeping her
matronymic of Brant, she held her status in the matriarchial
order of the Iroquois. By allowing her children to use the

patronymic of Johnson, she gave them their place in the patriarchial order of the British.

When large numbers of Indian refugees began to arrive at Carleton Island from Niagara, the commanding officer at the base found Molly's services so valuable that she was asked to remain permanently. In the spring, Captain Alexander Fraser wrote to Haldimand, full of praise for Miss Molly, saying that the Indians' good behaviour ". . . is in great measure to be ascribed to Miss Molly Brant's influence, which is far superior to that of all their chiefs put together". Also Captain Tice wrote in flattering terms of the "assistance she gave me in keeping the Indians orderly".

Although Molly was tucked away on Carleton Island, Haldimand had not forgotten her, for he wrote to Daniel Claus suggesting ". . . Miss Molly's influence may be useful." During the summer of 1780, Molly Brant again visited Montreal, leaving Carleton on June 30 in the company of Colonel John Butler. Captain Fraser was so afraid of losing her services that he wrote to General Haldimand in a quite transparent attempt to persuade the General that Molly should remain at Carleton. Phrases have been quoted from this letter out of context and are the only source anywhere that suggest Molly had a violent temper.

Captain Fraser wrote:

> She will probably wish to change her place of Residence and may want to go on to Niagara where she will be a very unwelcome Guest to Col. Bolton, and most of the other principal people in that quarter, and if she be not humoured in all her demands for herself, and for her dependants (which are numerous) she may by the violence of her temper be led to create mischief."

And then he adds:

> In case your Excellency would wish her to remain here, it were good that some little box of a house were built for her as it would be more comfortable to her family than living in a Barrack Room — I have at my own expense made a tollerable [sic] good garden for her and I have made her Situation as Comfortable as possible. Indeed she seems very pleased with her treatment and I have every reason to be satisfied with her conduct through the winter.

Obviously Fraser found Molly very helpful and was pleased with his methods of gratifying her. The garden was a spot where she could feel free of some of her restraints. If her temper sometimes did become hot, it was her only means of burning government red tape. The patient Indians at Carleton were evidence of her effectiveness.

Captain Fraser need not have worried about Molly leaving him, for Haldimand informed him through a secretary that Miss Molly's "inclination fortunately leads her to settle at Carleton Island rather than return to Niagara," and he was directed to build ". . . a house as will lodge Her and Family comfortably, chusing [sic] a favourable Situation, within a few hundred yards of the Fort."

When Fraser was relieved of his command at Carleton Island by Major Ross, Fraser reported to Haldimand, "I gave particulars regarding Miss Molly. She got into her new house and seemed better satisfied with her situation than I have ever known her before."

Besides using her influence with the Indians, Molly also collected information which she passed on to General Haldimand. During the winter of 1780-81, for example, she obtained information about rebel activities from Mary Aaron, an Indian beauty who had been General Schuyler's mistress but had deserted to join the Loyalists. Schuyler was one of those who had admired Molly a decade earlier when she had been mistress at Johnson Hall.

During the summer of 1781, Molly again went to Montreal and, according to Daniel Claus, took away her son George, and also Susan and Mary. They had all done well at school, particularly George who had shown a flair for mathematics. Molly sent her thanks to General Haldimand to which he replied through a secretary to Claus ". . . His Excellency is pleased to find his Intention in the education of Miss Molly's children has so well succeeded and that she appears sensible of the Benefit they have received, it being His Excellency's wish, as well on account of the Regard he bore the late Sir William Johnson, as to reward the Services of her Family, to show her every friendly attention in his Powers."

Was Molly happy at Carleton? She was content enough. Although Carleton Island was not the hub of the universe, none-theless it was a busy stopping place for everyone passing east or west from Niagara, Detroit and Michilimackinac to the seaports of Montreal and Quebec. Not only were Molly's own people continuously passing up and down the river, but the soldiers and fur traders also called on their way through. A two-day journey by ship would take her to Niagara and a week's journey by bateau or canoe to Montreal. Life at Carleton Island was perhaps as active and stirring as living at Fort Johnson on the Mohawk.

True, there was no Sir William whose loss Molly still felt deeply, nor was she a personage as she had been at Johnson Hall; but for a refugee, life was tolerable and interesting. A visit to Montreal enabled Molly to see her children and her husband's relatives. Although Guy Johnson's wife was dead and he had retired to England, Molly continued to have good relations with Daniel Claus and Sir John Johnson and she frequently visited them, as letters show. For example, Sir John, writing to Joseph Brant in June 1787, mentioned, "Your sister is here and Mrs. Kerr both with us and the children." Mrs. Kerr was Molly's daughter Elizabeth and the children were grandchildren.

Besides being a haven for her family, Montreal had another pull for her. Here she found herself in the midst of exciting talk of high adventure by the fur traders, many of whom she knew personally or at least by name. After the outbreak of the revolution, fur traders based at Albany or New York had moved to Montreal. There were the Ellice brothers with whom Sir William had done business at Schenectady; Simon McTavish had spent part of his youth on Johnson lands; Alexander Mackenzie's father fought in Sir John Johnson's "Royal Greens" and Alexander himself attended school in Montreal, perhaps with Molly's son George who was about the same age. There were the Frobisher brothers and Alexander Henry, James McGill, Peter Pond – all of these men were becoming prominent names in the fur trade. There was talk of a merger, the first joint-stock company in North America, a merger which became known as the North West Company. These men were the great explorers of the Northwest, the founders of the famous Beaver Club. Molly knew most of them.

The war years slipped by. Although the Loyalists sent no more large expeditions into New York, repeated scorched-earth raids were made by Sir John's "Royal Greens", Butler's Rangers, and Joseph Brant's Iroquois. These raids were so successful that the beautiful Mohawk Valley, the breadbasket of the Congress forces, was desolated and largely abandoned by the settlers. At least one quarter of the original rebel Valley militia had switched sides and joined the Loyalist forces based in Canada. Yet, despite these substantial successes by the Loyalists from Canada, the war was lost by the British in the south when Lord Cornwallis was forced to surrender 7,073 men at Yorktown, Virginia, in October, 1781.

The war dragged on in a desultory manner for another year before a peace treaty was signed in November, 1782.

.   .   .

In the treaty with the United States, Great Britain had made no stipulation on behalf of her Indian allies. This was the first rude shock that caused Molly Brant and her brother Joseph to suspect that the so-much-trusted British did not always keep faith. Were the Six Nations expendable now that they were no longer needed to fight the French or the Americans? In the great wars between the white people, the Iroquois had lost all their lands. Was the Great King dumping his faithful allies?

Although there was no provision made in the treaty, Sir Guy Carleton had pledged on behalf of the British Government that as soon as the war was over, the Six Nations should be restored to the condition that they had held at the commencement of hostilities; Haldimand, his successor, had renewed this pledge under seal. Because the Mohawk had lost their fertile lands along the Mohawk River and because they did not wish to reside within the boundaries of the United States, they now began to look towards the vacant land between the Great Lakes which had once been Iroquois territory.

The Mohawk first considered lands at the foot of Lake

Ontario around the Bay of Quinte. This region was the traditional home of Dekanawidah, the culture hero of the Iroquois.
However the Senecas, apprehensive about relations with the
United States, begged the Mohawk to choose land closer to
Niagara. Joseph Brant conferred with Sir John Johnson, the
able Superintendent of Indian Affairs, and the country around
the Grand River which flowed into Lake Erie, was chosen. An
area ". . . six miles on either side of the river, from the mouth
to its source . . ." was bought by the crown from the
Mississauga. In 1784, General Haldimand made a formal grant
of 786,000 acres, to be reserved for the Mohawk and others of
the Six Nations, who "with their posterity, were to enjoy
forever."[16]

The British, in the treaty with the United States, ceded away
all lands south of the Lakes and the St. Lawrence. This meant
that all the forts from Oswego to Michilimackinac, including
those on the Ohio, Niagara and Detroit, were lost. Not only the
Indians but the fur traders too were alarmed to be left without
British support.

This meant another move for Molly. The Fort on Carleton
Island was one of the first to be abandoned. The site of the old
French Fort Frontenac on the north shore mainland of the St.
Lawrence was chosen as a substitute, to be called Fort Cata-
raqui — now Kingston, Ontario.

Government was concerned to keep Molly happy. A large,
comfortable house was built for her near the mouth of the
Cataraqui River in the shelter of the bay, and at Haldimand's
suggestion, a house was also built for Joseph: ". . . I would have
a comfortable House Built for him and near as possible (but
distant from) to Molly's. It will give them both Satisfaction and
they can be gratified without any great Expense, as there are so
many workmen employed [available]."

The site of these large, substantial houses was on land near
the mouth of the Cataraqui River in the shelter of the bay. The
Cataraqui country, beautiful, clean, wild and rugged, was however not the Mohawk country with its fertile flats. The
Cataraqui drained from the Laurentian Shield and the soil was
thin over the pre-Cambrian rock with outcroppings of alluvial

limestone. Only here and there in pockets was the soil deep and rich. Yet the harbour was good and Cataraqui, which was to become Kingston, situated at the upper end of the St. Lawrence, soon became a busy port-of-call for all traffic between the Great Lakes and the ocean ports.

Commissioners were appointed by the Crown to inquire into the losses and services of the Loyalists, and sittings held at Saint John, Halifax and Montreal were begun in 1784 and were extended until 1790. Sir John Johnson was appointed to supervise the settlement of the disbanded soldiers and their families, the refugees from the Mohawk Valley and Upper New York Province — Sir William Johnson's people. Sir John was also responsible for the settlement of the Six Nations Confederacy, some of whom settled near Kingston, some on the Grand River Lands.

The Johnson clan fared reasonably well in the hands of the Commissioners. In March of 1788, Sir John testified on behalf of his half-brothers and half-sisters. Most of his testimony was a sworn declaration as to the value of the lands left to Molly's children by their father, Sir William Johnson. Molly had already received compensation for her own losses in several ways: her children had received educations at government expense; she had a comfortable house at Kingston and a pension of £100 per annum; she also had lands at Kingston, at Fredericksburgh and at Niagara.

Sir John Johnson got compensation of £47,000 and land grants for services and for losses amounting to £100,000. Joseph Brant was given 3,400 acres of land, £1,000 and military rank and pay. Sir John settled in Montreal, Molly remained at Kingston and Joseph eventually built himself a handsome house at Burlington, Ontario, modelled after Johnson Hall, where he lived in elegance "in the style of a gentleman". Brant House has been reconstructed and beside it has been built a splendid new hospital called Joseph Brant Hospital.

The three principals in the migration story of the Mohawk Valley people thus settled in the three key centres — Sir John in a headquarters position at Montreal and within easy reach of the Loyalists on the north shore of the St. Lawrence above Montreal; Molly near her people who had settled at Kingston;

Joseph near the Grand River Lands.

As soon as the Six Nations established themselves on the Grand River Lands, Joseph Brant erected a church and a school. The church was called Her Majesty's Chapel of the Mohawks, and was the first Protestant church in Ontario, if not the first church. The communion silver in the chapel is the silverware given by Queen Anne to the earlier Brant in 1712 for the first church on the Mohawk River. [17]

Overtures were made to both Joseph and Molly by the new republic. Joseph was offered sizeable land grants and Molly was promised that ". . . if she and Her Family would return to that Country . . . a sum of Money equal to the sum their lands were sold for by the Commission of Confiscation — that these offers altho' very great, were rejected with the utmost contempt."[18]

In these words of Molly's son-in-law, John Ferguson, one can almost see the snarl of her lips. Although she went back once to visit her beloved valley, she had no intention of living among those uncouth rebels, people who had driven her and her people from their land. She had nothing but scorn for them. Besides she had a new life to make, a new land to colonize.

.   .   .

Molly's days of alarms and excitements were finished now. Her great influence among her people and with her brother was no longer needed by the British government. Gone was the urgency to keep the Six Nations neutral *in favor of* the British, or to keep the Mohawk warriors primed and keen to fight against the Americans. After a lifetime of turmoil, prestige and power, Molly, at fifty, found herself unneeded politically. She was considered by her contemporaries as an "extraordinary person". She was a doer. How could she rest at being a cipher? She took her place in the frontier community in the way she knew best — looking after people. She was known throughout the whole of Kingston for her medicinal knowledge and her herbs. Proud of her heritage, she always wore Iroquois dress, though usually made from European materials. When very young, she and Joseph had been baptised as Anglicans. Nonetheless Molly understood and appreciated the Longhouse culture and religion. She lived in two worlds and made little distinction between red and white men, humble or proud.

In her last years, Molly lived with her daughter Magdalene who had married John Ferguson, member of the Legislature of Upper Canada for Kingston. All of Molly's daughters were part of the upper stratum of the society of the province. They were considered "lady-like, handsome women" and a grand-daughter, Kate Kerr Osborne, was "a queenly girl, beautiful, accomplished, proud of her Mohawk blood".

Molly's eldest daughter, Elizabeth, married Dr. Robert Kerr of Niagara, a prominent physician and magistrate. Ann married a naval officer, Captain Hugh Earl, for whom Earl Street in Kingston is named. Margaret married Captain George Farley of the 24th Regiment and Susannah married Lieutenant Henry Lemoine of the 60th Royal American Foot. Mary "a handsome spinster" remained single after being involved in a romantic tragedy. Son George married and settled on the Grand River Reserve near Brantford as a farmer-teacher. A big man, known as "Big George", he was said to drink too much, but was well-liked.[19]

Molly did not drink. It was a mistake, she thought. Following Iroquois tradition, she knew how to be firm with her daughters even if indulgent with a son. Once when the girls were dressed in full Indian costume for a ball, they met some British officers who mistook them for pretty squaws and offered to see them home. Molly replied tartly that she had taught her daughters to take care of themselves.

During these years a few friends disappeared. Colonel Guy Johnson of the "hasty temper", but always a friend to Molly, died in England in 1788. Colonel Daniel Claus, garrulous but helpful, had died a year earlier during a visit to Wales. His son William, who was a grandson of Sir William Johnson, succeeded as Deputy Superintendent of Indian Affairs, but was not as diplomatic as his father and grandfather. William Claus lived at Niagara with his mother who had been Nancy Johnson, the same Nancy whose romances had been Molly's first introduction into Johnson family affairs. Sir John Johnson continued for many years as Superintendent-General of Indian Affairs in British North America. He was also appointed to the Legislative Council of Quebec. He built a house outside Montreal which he called "Mount Johnson" and there his wife Polly was kept occupied producing eleven children.

In June of 1793, the American Commissioners who were proceeding to Sandusky to treat with the Western Nations Indians and the Six Nations concerning the Ohio Boundary were held up for some time at Niagara. One of the Commissioners, General Benjamin Lincoln, describes in his private journal the entertainment provided by his Excellency, Lieutenant Governor Simcoe, for the celebration of the King's Birthday, June 4. In the morning there was a levee, in the afternoon a muster, and in the evening a ball.

"What excited the best feeling of my heart," wrote the General,

> was the ease and affection with which the ladies met each other, although there were a number present whose mothers sprang from the aborigines of the country. They appeared as well dressed as the company in general, and intermixed with them in a measure which evinced at once the dignity of their own minds, and the good sense of the others. These ladies possessed great ingenuity and industry, and have merit: for the education they have acquired is owing principally to their own industry, as their father, Sir William Johnson, was dead and the mother retained the manners and dress of her tribe.

The general evidently did not know Molly Brant nor her determination that her daughters should "appear decent". Should Molly ever have read those words she would have been annoyed, and rightly so.

Elizabeth who lived in Niagara was likely one of the charmers who had caught the American General's eye. Molly and her other daughters were visiting in Niagara, for the preceeding day had been the wedding of Susannah to Lieutenant Henry Lemoine. As a Mohawk Matron, Molly would also have been present to have her say in the Council being held at Fort Erie and Niagara, in which Captain Joseph Brant was playing a leading part. The Indians were growing suspicious of the American intentions concerning the Ohio boundary.

In the following year, when the Western Indians were defeated by General Wayne on the Miami River, the Ohio boundary was the forfeit. The white men poured across the river and there was nothing for the Indians to do but to retreat slowly westward or be slowly surrounded, as the Six Nations were.

Molly was again in Niagara in the late summer of 1794, sick at heart and body over the collapse of the Indian Nations. Joseph and Molly had believed that they could introduce their people to the best of the white man's ways, the best of Christianity, the best of agriculture, good housing, good schooling, without loss of Iroquois identity. Now it seemed an impossible idea. Even Joseph Brant, proud Mohawk though he was, began to feel that his people could not be lifted to an easier way of living, or indeed survive, without integration.

Molly's own disillusionment was great. Mrs. John Graves Simcoe, wife of the Lieutenant-Governor, who was leaving Niagara for Kingston on the *Missassaga*, wrote on September 13: "Orders were given for my accomodation that no person would have a passage to Kingston in the *Missassaga* but I relented in favor of Brant's sister, who was ill and very desirous to go. She speaks English well, and is a civil and very sensible old woman."[20]

Molly was fifty-eight, but to Mrs. Simcoe, who was about thirty, Molly appeared old and perhaps she felt old. Her life had been momentous. She had lived in the midst of three wars, the French and Indian War, the Pontiac War and the Revolution; she had entertained the great of the land and she had been destitute; she had been adviser and chief diplomat among the Six Nations and had advised them to side with the British, only to see them lose their lands; she had been present at the Council which devised the Ohio Boundary, and now this too was a lost cause.

Perhaps on the boat trip to Kingston, Molly missed Sir William more than she had at any time since his death. It seemed that almost everything he had stood for had shattered; and yet, even in her depression, she could take comfort in her children, Sir William's children, whom she herself had raised and raised well, to live successfully in the white man's world; integrated, as the white man would say; dispossessed, according to the Indians.

.   .   .

Kingston had grown from a garrison to a small town of some fifty wooden buildings. Here, with her daughter Magdalene Ferguson, Molly lived the last few years of her life. Her only unmarried daughter, Mary, was with her.

It was to Fergusons' that Lieutenant Henry Lemoine came to ask for Mary's hand. Mary was not disinclined. Her sister Susan had died a year after her marriage to Henry and their child had died in infancy. The young man, bereft and lonely, had turned to Mary, but both Molly and Magdalene were opposed on religious and personal grounds to Mary marrying Henry. When Lemoine begged to see Mary, sister Magdalene was quite unyielding. In despair, he blew out his brains with a pistol, the bullet penetrating the wall of the parlour. Mary, the dark-eyed beauty, never married.[21]

Molly would have been living at Magdalene's during the spring of 1795 when Governor Simcoe was confined to his room for more than a month while on a visit to Kingston. He was so ill that Mrs. Simcoe could not leave him. He suffered from severe headache and "such a cough that some nights he could not lie down". Mrs. Simcoe turned for help to Molly Brant, who "prescribed a root – which really relieved his cough in a very short time". Molly could not bring back her daughter's dead suitor but she could help the living.

Our last glimpse of Molly is given by an English clergyman who visited Upper Canada in the 1790's.

> In the church at Kingston we saw an Indian woman, who sat in an honourable place among the English. She appeared very devout during the Divine Service and very attentive to the Sermon. She was the relict of the late Sir William Johnson, Superintendent of Indian Affairs in the Province of New York, and Mother of several children by him, who married to Englishmen and provided for by the Crown. When Indian embassies arrived, she was sent for,

dined at Governor Simcoe's and was treated with respect by himself and his lady. During the life of Sir William, she was attended with splendour and respect and since the war, received a pension and compensation for losses for herself and her children.[22]

Molly died on April 16, 1796, at the home of her daughter Magdalene. She was sixty years old. Molly's impress on the Canadian fulfillment is almost too subtle for analysis. We can analyse her character and ask: "What manner of woman was this Mohawk Matron who commanded the attention and respect of savages, soldiers, ordinary citizens, aristocrats, generals, governors and even the British Secretary of State?[23]

Why did she command this attention? What was the secret of her magnetism?

She was born to power but also inherited charm and tact and the knowledge of how to use power. After the death of Sir William, she was the only person of status among the Iroquois who could persuade the British; combined with this, she was the only person of status among the British who could persuade the Iroquois. Sir John, Colonel Guy or Daniel Claus did not have the influence among the Iroquois that Sir William had had. Neither did Molly, but she was a fit substitute.

An example of this double-persuasion is seen in her warning concerning Colonel Guy's "hasty temper". He was causing discontent among the Six Nations. She was able to persuade her people to be patient and at the same time she prompted the British to act. Only Molly had enough power among the Six Nations and knowledge of the British needs to convince the dissident Seneca chief to remain loyal to his British commitments, made to Sir William.

Even though events did not turn out as Molly had hoped, she did not regret her decision. Molly believed in the British order of things, as had Sir William, and in this order she saw the only hope for her people. The British desperately needed the Six Nations to help secure their northern frontier. Molly was the bond between the two peoples and the British knew it. Molly lived long enough to see a new society – Upper Canada – emerge upon the new frontier. A new nation was to be created and Molly and Joseph were the instruments.

There is only a trace of Molly's descendants to be found today. George had no children. The myth that he was the grandfather of Pauline Johnson, the poet, is untrue. The graveyard at St. Paul's, Kingston, is full of little Fergusons — Magdalene had no issue to survive. Ann Earl had three daughters, none of whom had issue. The Kerr family were prominent in the Hamilton-Niagara area for over three generations. Their descendants migrated to Winnipeg and are now scattered from Edmonton to Toronto. Margaret who married Captain George Farley had four children but this family also scattered, Daniel being the only one to remain in Kingston. The others went abroad. Before Margaret Farley went to join her children in England in 1831, she visited the Mohawk country to see once again Johnson Hall, the home of her childhood. She had been ten years old when forced to flee.[24]

Today there are no descendants of Sir William in North America carrying the name of Johnson and only a few abroad. (Sir John's heirs are in England.) Nevertheless there are some survivors with the Johnson blood if not the Johnson name who carry the heady genes of Sir William and Molly in their veins.

Molly left behind few of her thoughts in writing, so perhaps, to understand her more fully, we should turn to Joseph Brant whom she described as "an only brother whom I dearly love". Joseph and Molly always worked as a team and usually saw eye to eye.

In a letter to Thomas Eddy, philosopher and philanthropist, Joseph Brant says:

> I was, Sir, born of Indian parents, and lived while a child among those whom you are pleased to call savages; I was afterwards sent to live among the white people, and educated at one of your schools; since which period I have been honored much beyond my deserts . . . and after much exertion to divest myself of my prejudice, I am obliged to give my opinion in favor of my own people . . . In the government you call civilized, the happiness of the people is constantly sacrificed to the splendor of empire . . .[25]

In these words we hear the voice of Molly Brant.

The great influence Molly exerted on her own people and her untiring efforts on behalf of the new colony in Upper Canada were the stones upon which the founding of English Canada rested. It took another woman to bridge the wilderness of water and rock to help found a new Canadian colony on the Red River.

Notes

1. Haldimand Papers, B114 p. 63: Claus to Haldimand, Aug. 30, 1779. Dominion Archives.

2. Pre-European sites of Iroquoian people have been found on the St. Lawrence from Brockville to Trois Rivières. (W.J. Wintemberg: Bulletin 83, National Museum of Canada.) The tribes which gravitated towards New York State became known as the Five Nations of the Iroquois and were made up of a confederacy of the Mohawk, Oneida, Onondaga, Cayuga and Seneca. The Tuscarora were adopted into the Confederacy in 1722, making the sixth nation. The term "Longhouse" was symbolic of their religion as well as a description of their dwellings. The Onondaga were geographically at centre and were the "Firekeepers"; the Mohawk guarded the eastern door, the Seneca the west. The correct name for the Mohawk is *Canienga* or People of the Flint. Mohawk was a derogatory term given them by their enemies, the Mohicans.

3. British or Dutch—the name is spelled both "Brant" and "Brandt".

4. "Castle" was the term applied by white men to the Indian fortified village. Canajoharie Castle was 15 miles west of the present Amsterdam, N.Y.

5. Tench Tilghman, *Memoirs* (pub. by Munsel, 1876), p. 82; Rev. E. Wheelock, *Draper* F. 18 p. 77; *Johnson Papers* Vol. I p. 233; *Ontario History* "Molly Brant, Mohawk Matron" by Jean Johnston, June 1964; "Ancestry and Descendants", June, 1971.

6. For page references see: *Ontario History,* "Ancestry and Descendants of Molly Brant", June 1971, p. 87; "Molly Brant, Mohawk Matron", June 1964, p. 105.

7. *Narrative of his Relations with Sir William Johnson,* 1904 by Daniel Claus, p. 6.

8. *New York History,* 1937, "Sir William Johnson's Wives" by Milton Hamilton; *Draper Papers* F 15 p. 61.

9. Sir John Johnson was created a knight while in England in 1765-66, in recognition of his services in the French and Indian Wars. Sir William was pleased, for the knighthood of his son meant to some degree approval of the father and eased the nagging worry concerning the legitimacy of the Johnson children.

10. Paper, "Colonial Mansions of Sir William Johnson and his son, Sir John Johnson," Fort Johnson, New York. See "Sir William Johnson's Will", p. 10.

11. Moor's School became Dartmouth College. Brant's teacher, Rev. Doctor Eleazor Wheelock, became its first president. Joseph Brant always remained on good terms with Wheelock, and later sent his own sons to him for schooling.

12. For page references see: "Molly Brant: Mohawk Matron", *Ontario History*, (Toronto: June, 1964).

13. The original Confederacy was only Five Nations. The Tuscarora were adopted in 1722.

14. On Lake Cayuga, one of the Finger Lakes in northwest New York State.

15. Daniel Claus to Governor Haldimand. Claus and Haldimand Papers are to be found in the Dominion Archives. Ottawa.

16. Although much of their land has been sold or rented, often for very little, the Six Nations are still able to live in a cohesive group, some farming, some working in nearby cities but living on the Reserve. The Grand River Reserve near Brantford, is today, with its 43,000 acres and 7,000 people, the largest Iroquois Reserve.

17. Her Majesty s Chapel of the Mohawks, at Brantford, is Ontario's oldest church. Although nearly 200 years old, it is in excellent repair.

18. Upper Canada Land Petitions, F. 3, No. 41, 1797.

19. "Molly Brant", *Ontario History* (Toronto: June, 1964), p. 105.

20. *Draper Papers,* F. 13, p. 101-103.

21. *Draper Papers,* F. 13, p. 92.

22. *Draper Papers,* F. 11, p. 5; J.C. Ogden, "A Tour Through Upper Canada" (Litchfield: 1799), p. 61-62.

23. H.P. Gundy, "Molly Brant, Loyalist", *Ontario Historical Society,* XLV (Toronto, Sept. 3, 1953).

24. Jean Johnston, "Ancestors and Descendants of Molly Brant", *Ontario History* (Toronto: June, 1971).

25. "Molly Brant" *Ontario History,* (Toronto: June, 1964), p. 105.

Bibliography

Angus, Margaret. "Old Kingston Homes and Families", *Kingston Historical Society,* 1954/55.

Beattie, Jessie L. *The Split in the Sky.* Toronto: 1960.

Bond, Richard P. *Queen Anne's American Kings.* Oxford: 1952.

Bradley, A.G. "Lord Dorchester", *Makers of Canada.* Toronto: 1928.

Brebner, J. Bartlet. *Canada.* Toronto: 1960.

Campbell, Marjorie Freeman. *Niagara, Hinge of the Golden Arc.* Toronto: 1958.

Claus Papers. National Archives, Ottawa.

Chalmers, Harvey (in collaboration with Ethel Brant Monture). *Joseph Brant, Mohawk.* Toronto: 1955.

Draper MSS on Brant. Microfilm. Original at Wisconsin University.

Flexnor, J.P. *Mohawk Baronet.* New York: 1959.

Friederici, Georg. Skalpieren und Ähnliche Kriegsgebräuche in Amerika. Braunschweig: 1906.

Grant, Mrs. Anne. *Memoirs of an American Lady* (reprint). New York: 1845.

Griffis, W.E. *Sir William Johnson and the Six Nations.* New York: 1906.

Guillet, E.C. *Early Life in Upper Canada.* Toronto: 1933.

Gundy, H. Pearson. "Molly Brant, Loyalist", *Ontario Historical Society,* Vol. XLV, No. 3, Sept. 1953.

Haldimand Papers. National Archives, Ottawa.

Hale, Horatio. *The Iroquois Book of Rites.* Reprinted Toronto: 1963.

Hamilton, Dr. Milton W. "Sir William Johnson's Wives" *New York History.* New York: 1937.

Holden, Mrs. John Rose. "The Brant Family", Wentworth Historical Society, 1937.

Horsey, Edwin E. "Cataraqui, Fort Frontenac, Kingston", manuscript, Kingston Public Library. 1945.

Johnston, Charles M. *Brant County: a History.* Toronto: 1967.

Johnston, Charles M. "Joseph Brant Grand River Lands", *Ontario History,* Vol. LV, No. 4. December, 1963.

Johnston, Jean. "Molly Brant, Mohawk Matron", *Ontario History.* June, 1964. "Ancestry and Descendants of Molly Brant", *Ontario History.* June, 1971.

Johnson, Sir John. *The North American Johnsons.* London: 1963.

Kirkby, William. *Annals of Niagara.* Toronto: 1896.

La Rochefaucauld-Lioncourt. *Travels in Canada.* Republished Toronto: 1917.

McIlwraith, Jean N. "Sir Frederick Haldimand", *Makers of Canada.* Toronto: 1928

Military Files of 24th Regiment, and 60th Regiment.

Ontario Archives Report, 1904 (Report of Loyalist Commissioners).

Pound, Arthur. *Johnson of the Mohawks.* New York: 1930.

Parish Records, Old St. Paul's Church, Kingston

Reed, D.B. *Life and Times of Governor Simcoe.* Toronto: 1890.

Riddell, Hon. Wm. Renwick. "Was Molly Brant Married?" *Ontario Historical Society,* Vol. XIX. 1922.

Robertson, J. Ross. *The Diary of Mrs. Simcoe* (revised). Toronto: 1890.

Seaver, James E. *Life of Mary Jemison.* Reedited, Rochester: 1856.

Simms, Jeptha. *Trappers of New York.* St. Johnsville: 1835.

Simms, Jeptha. *History of Schoharie County.* Albany: 1845.

Scott, Duncan Campbell. "John Graves Simcoe", *Makers of Canada.* Toronto: 1928.

Stanley, George F. *Canada's Soldiers.* Toronto: 1960.

Stanley, George F. "Six Nations in War of 1812", *Ontario History,* Vol. LV, No. 4.

Stone, W.L. *Life of Joseph Brant.* Cooperstown: 1845.

Stone, W.L. *Life and Times of Sir William Johnson.* Albany: 1865.

Vrooman, J.J. *Clarissa of Tribes Hill.* Schenectady: 1950.

Wilson, Edmund. *Apologies to the Iroquois.* New York: 1959.

5

Marie-Anne Lagimodière

Our Canoe, a most beautiful craft, airy and elegant beyond description, was 35 feet in length . . . we started, the voyageurs singing and the Canoe almost flying thro' the water . . . the motion is perfectly easy & in fine weather it is the most delightful mode of travelling that can be imagined.

Frances Simpson[1]

Although Marie-Anne Lagimodière did not write the words quoted, she understood their meaning perfectly. In 1806, she travelled 2,000 miles from Montreal to the Red River along the old Voyageurs' Highway. She was the first white woman to come from Canada into the Northwest, called by the French-speaking *les pays d'en haut,* the land of plains, hills, grass, forest, buffalo.

Marie-Anne, sister in spirit to Gudrid, helped tame this nomads' land of Indians, Métis and fur traders. The white fur traders' world was a man's milieu of French *voyageurs,*[2] Scottish and English *bourgeois* and company clerks. Although often

121

lonely, sometimes terrified by warlike Indians, Marie-Anne adapted herself to the customs of *les pays d'en haut* and created a family. Jean-Baptiste, her husband, was not employed by one of the big fur companies but he was always a good provider. He was an independent, defined by the fur traders as a "freeman". In the winter he trapped, and in the summer he hunted buffalo. He was so skilful that he became known as the "Great Hunter".

Marie-Anne Gaboury grew up in Maskinongé in the diocese of Trois-Rivières. At the age of sixteen, she left her family to enter the service of Monsieur l'abbé Vinet-Souligny. For almost ten years she served in the solitude of the presbytère as assistant housekeeper. Marie-Anne, handsome and vibrant, felt that her life was dull. There were few parties and fewer young men. At twenty-five, she felt stifled and bored.

In the autumn of 1805, Jean-Baptiste Lagimodière[3] who had been five years in *les pays d'en haut* returned to Canada to visit his family at Maskinongé. The town was enlivened by this blond, blue-eyed man with his tall stories and his audacious spirits.

Marie-Anne was ripe to be charmed by the handsome, popular voyageur-hunter. What is more, Jean-Baptiste was charmed by Marie-Anne, by her blonde good looks and by her eager response to his stories of the Northwest. When Jean-Baptiste asked her to marry him, she accepted him at once. He was of good family and neither her family nor the priest had any objections. They were married April 21, 1806.

Everyone in the village had taken it for granted that Jean-Baptiste had come home to settle, to take up farming along with his relatives and neighbours in peaceful Maskinongé. Among those who had assumed that he would settle was Marie-Anne. Perhaps that had been Jean-Baptiste's intent when he first returned, but when spring came and ice flowed out from the rivers, when the fur brigades were assembling at Lachine and all was hustle and bustle, the call of the west, the great sky, the empty plains, the freedom, all proved too much for the spirit of a Jean-Baptiste. He felt as confined in the old community of Maskinongé as had Marie-Anne in the presbytère.

She begged him to remain, and she prayed. When she became

convinced that nothing would stop him, she felt that she had only one alternative. If her husband went off to the Northwest, she might never see him again. She decided to go with him.

This was an astonishing idea, and it must certainly have astounded Jean-Baptiste, for never before had a woman left the security of the St. Lawrence community to go into the nomads' land of *les pays d'en haut.* Marie-Anne knew there were great hardships to be faced, for her brother, Pierre Gaboury, had spent two years in the west. Her parents objected strongly, fearing that they would never see their daughter again, but the curé advised her that if she had the courage to follow her husband she should do so. He warned her, though, that there were no missionaries, no churches and no schools in the land to which she was going.

So what could Jean-Baptiste do? He had married Marie-Anne because of her high spirits and sense of adventure. Now that she was determined to go and had the blessing of the priest, Jean-Baptiste could scarcely refuse — but he must have had many misgivings.

.   .   .

During the first week of June, less than two months after her marriage, Marie-Anne Gaboury said good-bye to her family and the beautiful parish of Maskinongé. If she had been able to look into the future to see the trials and dangers ahead of her, to realize that she would never come home again, she might have lost her courage.

However, she was young, in love, and seeking adventure.

The two travellers left by carriage for Lachine where the fur brigades set out for the Red River. From Lachine,[4] which was on the Island of Montreal but above the Lachine Rapids, trade goods were sent by canoe and portage 3,000 miles to Lake Athabasca and beyond, into the Mackenzie and Peace River systems. Lachine was also the trans-shipment point for furs destined for the markets of Europe.

It was at Lachine that Molly Brant embarked after visiting her children in the 1780's. And it was at Lachine that one could get a glimpse of the great Montreal canoe, the *canot de maître,* specifically designed to carry heavy trade goods from above the Lachine Rapids up the Ottawa River, up the Mattawa River to the French River, along the under-belly of the Laurentian Shield by way of Georgian Bay and Lake Superior, to the depot at Fort William.[5]

The canot de maître was nothing more than a frail basket covered with birch bark, glued together by pine gum and lashed with *wattape* or spruce root. If the canoe was not painted, there was usually some design on the high prow and stern. The ability of this frail craft to carry a five ton burden over one thousand miles, through turbulent water, seems not much short of the miraculous.

Although canoes were commonplace to Marie-Anne, she was impressed by the size of the Montreal canoe, and thrilled to see her countrymen deftly loading the ninety-pound *pièces* on the floorboards. Joking, singing, laughing as they handled the great bundles, these were romantic adventurers, the men of the Northwest.

For over a hundred years, the voyageurs and their birch canoes had been travelling the interior waterways of the Canadian transport system. They and their birch canoes *were* the transport system. The traders or *bourgeois* were the business men. To them, the country meant fur and fur meant profit. Mostly of Scottish origin, these traders were a hardheaded, efficient, unromantic lot. Their employees, the voyageurs, on the other hand, were French-Canadians from the Montreal and Trois-Rivières areas, and they were romantic, superstitious and easy-going. Moreover, they could sing; they could paddle great distances without tiring; they could carry heavy bundles or *pièces* over portages.

Wearing gay clothes — bright woollen cap with feather, deer skin leggings, blue capote, gaudy sash with pipe and beaded pouch attached — and guided by a devil-may-care philosophy, the voyageurs revelled in their service and made a legend of themselves.

Marie-Anne became a part of the legend.

Jean-Baptiste hired himself to the North West Company as a

voyageur. Because Marie-Anne was the first white woman to travel into *les pays d'en haut,* she received much attention, but there were no luxuries. A place was found for her among the bundles and there she sat motionless, for hours at a time, exposed to sun, rain and wind. She ate what the voyageurs ate – dried peas, salt pork and biscuits. At night, she slept in the open, folded in her blanket.

The excitement of the brigade of four canoes leaving Lachine was exhilarating; the short, husky crewmen, fourteen to a canoe, singing one of their favourite songs, and paddling as in a race, left no room for nostalgic memories of home. However, after the stop at Ste. Anne de Bellevue where the voyageurs prayed at the little church for a safe journey, a few tears may have been shed for family and friends left behind.

On the smooth ripple lifts the long canoe:
The hemlocks murmur sadly as the sun
Slants his dim arrows through.
Whither I go I know not, nor the way.[6]

At 2 A.M., Marie-Anne was roused each day by the call of *"Lève! Lève! Lève!"* the traditional early morning call of the voyageur. She would drag her aching bones from the hard bed, fold her blanket, and the canoes would be off within the hour. The canoemen paddled for some hours before breakfast, then stopped for a hearty meal. Except for a light meal at noon, there was no more food until supper, when camp was made for the night, at nine or ten o'clock.

The canoemen were given a break once an hour when they were allowed to smoke their pipes, but for the passenger there was no change of position unless they came to a portage, where goods and passengers were lifted from the canoes, and the canoes were carried or towed past the rapids. Although the voyageurs hated the portages because they had to carry the heavy ninety-pound *pièces* (two to a man), Marie-Anne came to long for these breaks which gave her an opportunity to stretch her weary limbs, and to escape the sun and wind for a time. At many of these portages, the water was too shallow for the canoes to touch the banks, and passengers as well as bundles were lifted out of the canoes by the voyageurs. Some women travelling in later days than Marie-Anne found this an embarrassment, but Marie-Anne did not mind, for she had Jean-Baptiste at her side. Indeed, she considered it an honour to be carried on the shoulders of a voyageur.

Express canoes could reach Sault Ste. Marie in two weeks, but Marie-Anne, travelling by freight canoe in brigade, took all of three weeks.

Sault Ste. Marie was a very old trading establishment. As early as 1777, the year that Molly Brant arrived at Fort Niagara, there was a picketed fort there, with as many as ten log houses. An Irishman, John Johnston, had settled at Sault Ste. Marie as a trader in 1794. He was married to the daughter of a Chippewa chief, and lived in a comfortable home with a good library and many of the comforts of civilization. As a day was always spent there by the canoe brigades, Marie-Anne may have had time to visit the Johnston menage, although a language barrier would have prevented any lively conversation.

The canoes were portaged there in order to enter Lake Superior, above the rapids. Proceeding westward with their cargoes, the brigades hugged the north shore for 420 miles. "The country along the shores of the Lake very barren and rugged, the fantastic shapes of the rocks, forming the chief variety."[7]

Heavy seas were as dangerous for the frail craft as were hidden rocks, and a forty-foot canoe, heavily laden, was in danger of having its back broken by big waves. During Marie-Anne's crossing of Lake Superior, the brigades encountered two furious tempests and some of the voyageurs were drowned. When Marie-Anne was ninety-five years old, the only vivid recollections she had of her whole journey from Montreal to the Red River were of these storms and drownings. In her extreme old age, she would look at the rosary which she had brought from Montreal, and remember how she had prayed to the Blessed Virgin for succour from the pounding waves.

On reaching Fort William, or any large post, it was customary for the crews, freshly shaven and "dressed in their gayest attire", to paddle briskly into port, singing one of their famous songs – perhaps *En Roulant Ma Boule* or *A la Claire Fontaine.* On Marie-Anne's voyage, however, the men were chastened by the loss of their companions, and the arrival at Fort William was sedate, even solemn.

The North West Company post at Fort William was newly built in the summer of 1806, the year that Marie-Anne passed through. It was not as splendid as it later became, but it was already an impressive post, set among the protective rugged mountains and islands of Thunder Bay — a company town in the interior. The sight of the fenced garden full of fresh vegetables, of the cultivated fields of Indian corn and potatoes, and of cattle, sheep and horses in the paddocks — first reminders of the parish of Maskinongé — must have made Marie-Anne at least a little homesick.

Marie-Anne had a few days' rest at Fort William. This is the one place where she could have changed her mind and returned to Maskinongé, if she had been faint-hearted, for this was the depot and the transhipment point where trade goods were exchanged for furs. From Fort William, the furs from the Northwest were taken in the big *canot de maître* to Montreal; at Fort William, the trade goods and supplies for the Northwest were transferred to a smaller canoe, called the "North canoe", designed for shallower waters.

. . .

If Marie-Anne had qualms about continuing her journey westward, she stifled them. Leaving Fort William, the brigade ascended the Kaministikwia to Dog Lake. A little beyond this lake is the height of land which divides waters flowing into the Arctic from those flowing to the south or east. The voyageurs always performed a ceremony at the crossing of the divide, a literal baptism for every newcomer to the north country. The newcomer was made to kneel and was liberally drenched with water showering from a cedar bough which had been dipped into a nearby stream.

No doubt, the voyageurs cut a lob stick for Marie-Anne, as they always did for special passengers. One of the men would climb a tall pine which stood out prominently, perhaps at a point in a lake or a curve of a river. The lower branches would

be cut off with an axe, leaving a tuft at the top, and the name
of the passenger cut into the trunk. As the crew paddled off,
the lob stick was saluted with three cheers and a discharge of
guns. The person so honoured was expected to acknowledge the
compliment by a treat at the first opportunity, and Jean-
Baptiste was not one to be indifferent to a compliment to his
wife.

Although Marie-Anne remembered little about the baptism
or the lob stick, she did not forget the hordes of insects, black
flies and mosquitoes, and the difficult, rocky country through
which they travelled before reaching Lake Winnipeg.

There were times when canoes were ripped by submerged
rocks or stumps, and even though lives were not endangered,
provisions were lost, and much time was spent repairing the
gashes. The route passed through a ghostly area of black
stumps, the remains of a large forest fire in the Rainy Lake
district.

There were many portages from Fort William to Lake of the
Woods, and some were completely fatiguing. Marie-Anne found
herself walking as much as seven miles in one day, under scorch-
ing sun and over log crossings which were so broken, uneven
and slippery that it was almost impossible to scramble past
them. How the voyageurs could manage to carry the canoes and
their *pièces* through this rough country is difficult to imagine.

The going was so bad along this route, by canoe and portage,
and the insects such a menace, that the voyageurs were paid a
bonus. The country, however, was magnificent — with its wild
falls, rugged hills, forests of spruce, pine and birch — and the
food was excellent. After leaving Fort William, the *hommes du
nord* no longer had to depend on pork; fish, Indian corn and
wild rice were the staples in the Lake of the Woods region; at
the Red River, there was pemmican, the dried buffalo meat.

When the Lagimodières arrived at Lake Winnipeg, they
paused at the North West Company post, Fort Alexander, at the
mouth of the Winnipeg River.[8] From this fort, the voyageurs
separated to travel to their lonely winter stations, and there was
always considerable celebrating before the men left for the
interior. At these Northwest parties, there were Indian girls to

dance with, and there was also a great deal of drinking. As the first white woman among these tough, untamed men, Marie-Anne, the girl from the quiet presbytère in Maskinongé, suddenly found herself in great demand as a partner. What she thought of the drinking we do not know, but she must have accepted it as a part of the way of the Northwest, for in her later years she never complained of the rowdyism which could not help but have distressed her.

At Fort Alexander, Jean-Baptiste and Marie-Anne left the voyageurs with whom they had travelled from Montreal, and headed south for Pembina, a Hudson's Bay Post on the Red River, just south of the forty-ninth parallel.

Moving easily up the Red River, enfolded by its rich timber stands, was a relief after the tortuous journey through the Lake of the Woods country:

> all was solitary and wild on the banks of the river, and in these immense solitudes, there was no cry but the sound of birds which flew up at the approach of the voyageurs.[9]

Gratefully, the party reached Pembina, the *Grand Camp,* in the last week of August, exactly two months after leaving Montreal. Jean-Baptiste pitched a tent for Marie-Anne near the Hudson's Bay post. Here, among the independents, hunters, traders and Métis, Jean-Baptiste prepared for the fall buffalo hunt while Marie-Anne Gaboury had her first lessons as a hunter's wife.

Marie-Anne immediately found herself in a difficult situation. Jean-Baptiste had previously left behind at Pembina an Indian woman who considered herself his wife. When he returned in 1806 with Marie-Anne, the Indian wife was understandably jealous, so jealous that she was determined to dispose of her rival. She prepared a potion that she believed would bring evil spirits around Marie-Anne and cause her harm. The Indian wife hid her jealousy and evil intentions and came to Marie-Anne apparently full of friendship, thus putting Marie-Anne off her guard.

Marie-Anne welcomed the woman, for during those first months the young French-Canadian bride was desperately lonely. Jean-Baptiste was off on the plains with the buffalo hunt. Although women were needed on the hunt to skin the buffalo and dry the meat, Marie-Anne, who knew nothing about the operation, would have been a burden rather than a help; and besides she was pregnant. So she stayed at Pembina, with nothing to do and with almost no companionship. Few of the Indian women could speak French, and Marie-Anne could not speak their language. She had plenty of time to weep for Maskinongé.

She might have been an easy prey for Jean-Baptiste's ex-wife, if the Indian woman had not unfolded her plan to the Indian wife of one of the Canadians. This woman was shocked. She warned Marie-Anne of the design to poison her, and advised her to move away from Pembina. On his return, Jean-Baptiste lost no time in moving his wife twenty-five miles up the Pembina River, where the Lagimodières stayed until the end of December.

It had been the custom for a quarter of a century, for white men in *les pays d'en haut* — there were 5,000 of them as early as 1777[10] to take Indian girls for wives. There were no clergy or *religious* in the country and so the marriages were informal, but usually lasting. A white man who married the daughter of a chieftain cemented a relationship which was of benefit to all. The girl found security; her people and the fur trader profited by good trading. Until Marie-Anne came in 1806, there had been nothing to jar or ruffle this comfortable pattern.

Twenty-four years later, another young bride, Frances Simpson, found herself in a dilemma similar to that of Marie-Anne Gaboury. When George Simpson, Governor of the Hudson's Bay Company, arrived at the Red River with his Scottish bride, he put aside his Métis wife, the daughter of one of the Hudson's Bay Company factors. Because so many had Indian or Métis wives, the Northwesters were openly indignant at the Governor's behaviour which seemed to discredit them all. The Simpson couple found themselves ostracised, and the atmosphere became so oppressive, socially, that they returned to Montreal after only three years on the Red River. Frances Simpson never returned to the Northwest.

.   .   .

In January, Jean-Baptiste arranged for temporary shelter in one of the Hudson's Bay Company houses at Pembina, and on January 6, a daughter was born to Marie-Anne Gaboury. She named the child Reine because she was born on the King's birthday.

For the first white child born and raised in *les pays d'en haut*[11] there was no church where her mother could take her for baptism; there were no ringing bells, no visits, nor congratulations from friends and family. Marie-Anne baptised the infant herself with Jean-Baptiste by her side, and dreamed of the day when the church would come to the Northwest. The birth of her daughter compensated Marie-Anne for the lonely, frightening, first days on the Red River.

Marie-Anne remained at the Pembina Post until spring. During this period, Jean-Baptiste spent much of his time hunting game which he sold to the trappers. It was a good year for game, and the trappers needed provisions.

In May, the Lagimodières left Pembina with three other Canadians; Chalifou, Bellegarde and Paquin, and their Indian wives and children. Their plan was to travel westward to Fort des Prairies, later called Fort Edmonton, and the journey by river was about 1,200 miles. Two canoes were bought, large enough to carry the women, children and provisions.

Did Marie-Anne wish she were safely back in Maskinongé? She must have had qualms at the thought of travelling so many more miles further from home, but she was not one to complain. She had chosen *les pays d'en haut* willingly, even stubbornly, and although Jean-Baptiste was something of a nomad, he was a good provider.

Marie-Anne's baggage was reduced to almost nothing. For the infant, she adopted the custom of the country and wrapped her in a moss bag. For herself, she continued to wear her Canadian style of clothing, and never once faltered in her determination to retain at least the appearance of civilization, no matter how nomadic her existence.

The party of two canoes travelled down the Red River to Lake Winnipeg, then north the full length of this large lake to the Saskatchewan River. Following the North Saskatchewan which cuts a giant trench across the Prairies, the four families travelled slowly, for there was nothing pressing them. Hunting was good along the course of the waterways, and they never wanted for food. There was an abundance of wild geese and ducks along the shores. This country was far north of the buffalo range, but they found deer, bear and beaver — gourmet dishes all; and few dishes could equal the sturgeon of the northern waters.

In the evening, after a spot was chosen for camp, the first task was to light a fire to dispel mosquitoes and discourage the wolves and bears. After the meal, the tents were set up.

Along the Saskatchewan at Fort Cumberland (a little south of today's Flin Flon), the natives had heard about the white woman and were both curious and frightened. They wondered if she were like Indian women, or whether she might have the evil eye.

The Canadian, Bellegarde, had gone ahead of his companions to the Fort, and when he heard all the talk about Marie-Anne, he told the Indians that the white woman was naturally *bonne,* but that she had very strong magic and that if anyone offended her she could make that person die simply by looking at him.

When Marie-Anne arrived at Fort Cumberland, she was met with great homage, presents and speeches, and the Indians cried to her, "Have pity on us. We only wish to look at you."

As we have said, Marie-Anne was a good-looking young woman with fair skin and regular features. To the Indians who had never seen beauty other than their own dark companions, Marie-Anne was a marvel, and they showed her great deference. Marie-Anne, for her part, enjoyed her role of white-goddess.

The beliefs of the Indians were not always so happily controlled and the Canadians were probably unwise in encouraging such beliefs. Not many years before, the factor of one of the neighbouring forts had given one of the young Indian boys a friendly pat on the head. Later, when the boy became ill and died, the tribe was convinced that the factor had put an evil spirit in him. The Indians surrounded the fort, and massacred all but one of the men.

The party was in constant danger from the wild animals in

the area. Shortly after leaving Fort Cumberland, one of the party was clawed by a bear. The man, Bouvier, who had joined the Lagimodières and their party en route, was dragged from his place beside the fire. Jean-Baptiste saved Bouvier's life by shooting the bear, but when Marie-Anne raised the injured man she found his face torn off, his nose and eyes gone. Marie-Anne nursed him until they reached Fort des Prairies. Everyone was subdued by the tragic mauling which could have happened to any of them.

Fort des Prairies was beautifully placed on the flats of the North Saskatchewan on a site sheltered by high, tree-covered banks. They had left the prairies behind them and trees were again a part of the landscape. Here the country was parkland, good for trapping. The Lagimodières reached the Fort at the end of August. The chief factor, or *bourgeois,* was Jim Bird whom Jean-Baptiste knew well. It was arranged that Marie-Anne and her child should spend the winter in the fort, while Jean-Baptiste hunted buffalo or busied himself with his traplines.

.   .   .

Fort life was secure, even agreeable. Although the men ran the business affairs, the women ran the fort; the Indian and Métis wives took pride in their position. They organized the fort efficiently, and they took good care of their children. Many of the men brought fiddles and there was dancing and singing, and usually plenty of food. Often the forts had small gardens; there was always plenty of fish — whitefish, trout, tollibees, sturgeon and pike — which was frozen for winter use; and there was pemmican.

It was no doubt because of his reputation as a good buffalo hunter that Jean-Baptiste, an independent, was able to establish his wife at the Hudson's Bay post of Fort des Prairies. Chief Factor Bird knew that the life of the Fort depended on a large supply of pemmican, and he knew that he could rely on Jean-Baptiste to supply him. It would be here that Marie-Anne learned how to cure the pemmican.

Christmas had little religious significance, but the people

devoted the holiday period to eating, drinking and dancing. Marie-Anne Gaboury was a religious woman but she was no spoil-sport. She certainly missed the traditional festivities and the solemn rituals of the nativity as celebrated in her native Canada, but she was adaptable. If this was the way that Christmas was celebrated in the new land, then she would not sit in a corner and mope. Marie-Anne said a prayer in her heart and joined the festivities.

New Year's Day was an even livelier occasion for the French and Scottish Northwesters. For this celebration, the Indians also came in large numbers to join their white brothers. New Year's Day gradually became the traditional open house for the whole Hudson's Bay Company organization.

In the spring of 1808, Marie-Anne left Fort des Prairies and went with Jean-Baptiste onto the plains for the buffalo-hunting season. Two hundred miles south of Edmonton, the country gives way to open rolling lands, bleak downs which are almost treeless and covered with stubby buffalo grass. Although the grass looks insignificant, it is nutritious, and here the male buffalo herds roamed. From an early period, white buffalo-hunters had penetrated this area, not for meat because there were no cows here, but for hides.

Bellegarde and his family accompanied the Lagimodières. Marie-Anne soon learned to ride all day long on horseback, carrying her child in a hide bag on one side of the saddle with a bag of provisions on the other.

These two families spent the summer roaming over the great, empty hills of the extreme southern part of what is now Alberta and Saskatchewan. By now, Marie-Anne was accustomed to the life of the nomad. Cooking stew in a pot over an open fire, setting up a tent, skinning a buffalo hide; all were part of a woman's life, and life was to be lived.

One day, while the two men were off hunting, a band of Indians came upon the tents and the two women. Bellegarde's Cree wife instantly caught up the Lagimodière child, ran to the nearby woods and hid, fearing that the Indians would run off with the pretty and unusual child. As for Marie-Anne, she thought her last moments had come; she kneeled in her tent and recited her rosary. When the Indian chief, who was Cree, opened the tent flap, he was astounded to see this lovely woman, and more astounded to see her posture. He was so amazed and touched that he stood at the tent-opening, staring but not entering.

Among the Indians was a Canadian named Letendre who had been adopted into the tribe. He had not seen a white woman for many years, and when he saw his countrywoman on her knees within the tent praying, he, too, was touched. He spoke to her in French, "I have been living among these savages a long time and I know them. I am sure that they will do you no harm. Don't be afraid."

Marie-Anne was reassured. However, she spent the day alone in the midst of these warriors, fearing for her life. In the evening, when Jean-Baptiste returned to see the warriors surrounding his tent, he feared that Marie-Anne was slain, and that he would suffer the same fate. From a distance he called out, "Marie-Anne, are you alive?"

"Yes," Marie-Anne answered, "but I am half-dead with fear."

Lagimodière knew the customs of the Crees, and spoke their language. He went up to them holding out his hand as a sign of friendship, and after smoking a pipe of peace, he begged them to camp at a distance because his wife was tired and ill.

The Indians assured him that they were friends, and moved their camp.

In August, the Lagimodière and Bellegarde families struck camp and began their return journey to Fort des Prairies. They were still travelling through buffalo country, and one day they came upon a sizeable herd. Horses used to the chase became excited in the presence of the buffalo, and sometimes took off in pursuit.

Marie-Anne was a good horsewoman but when her horse, a good hunter, started after the buffalo she lost control. Hampered by the child at her saddle, she could not rein in her horse and she was certain she would be thrown and trampled underfoot by the buffalo. All she could do was to hang on to the horse's mane and hope that her husband would come to her aid. Meanwhile, Jean-Baptiste was wasting no time. He forced his own mount through the stampeding buffalo, and with great skill, he cut Marie-Anne's horse from the herd and stopped the flight.

Marie-Anne was overcome by fear and fatigue, and so it was decided to set up camp. A few hours later, Marie-Anne gave birth to a son, her second child born in *les pays d'en haut.* Because the child was born on the prairie, she called him Laprairie. He was later baptised Jean-Baptiste.

Marie-Anne had a flair for the naming of her children, linking them to the events of her life. On this day, she had felt the vastness of the prairie, the great dome of the sky, the persistent push of the wind, the pitiless sun and the lack of shade. How insignificant the tiny new life was, before God and nature. She, Marie-Anne, was responsible. She had dared a great dare and she had won, so she called the child "Laprairie".

She was given a three-day rest and then, gathering the infant in her arms, she mounted her horse and the party proceeded to Fort des Prairies.

The winter passed without incident, but in the spring Marie-Anne almost lost her son — a pretty, fair, blue-eyed baby, much admired by the Indians. The Fort was built close to the river, but the banks were steep and the climb was not easy. Marie-Anne had to leave her two children in her house when she went to the river for water.

Some of the Blackfoot tribe were encamped near the fort, and Marie-Anne was accustomed to their wandering about. On this particular day she did not suspect anything unusual when she saw one of the Blackfoot women pass her, carrying a child under her hood.

When Marie-Anne returned to the fort after an absence of only ten minutes, she met the Chief Factor, James Bird, who asked her why she had dared to leave her children alone while the Blackfoot were camped in the vicinity.

"One of them has just run off with a child," he said, "I strongly suspect that it's yours. You had better hurry to make sure."

It only took Marie-Anne an instant to discover that her

infant son had disappeared in the cloak of the Indian woman. She did not stop to ask for help, but ran off in pursuit of the Blackfoot. The latter began to run, but Marie-Anne, with frantic energy, caught up with her and stopped her by grabbing her cloak.

"Give me my child," she demanded.

The squaw did not understand the words, but she did understand the gestures. At first, she tried to pretend astonishment, but when Marie-Anne opened the cloak, she found her child, smiling. The Blackfoot woman pretended that she had only wanted to play with the infant.

And so, Laprairie was rescued.

The following summer, Marie-Anne with her two children, again followed Jean-Baptiste to the prairies. She was, by now, thoroughly accustomed to the nomadic life, toughened to the hardships, and less frightened by its insecurity. Indeed, had she not enjoyed it she would have stayed in the fort.

In June, Lagimodière and his family were camped by a small lake where the game was abundant. One morning he found that his horses had been stolen during the night, and since horses were a prime necessity, he was very upset. He decided to go to an Indian encampment, some distance away. Marie-Anne was left alone, but she was probably more concerned, at this point, for Jean-Baptiste than for herself.

In the afternoon, a band of Sarcees, tattooed and armed with arrows and knives, obviously on the warpath, surrounded Marie-Anne and her children, alone in their tent. Marie-Anne did not know it, but these warriors were hunting their enemies, the Crees, and they had already wiped out the Cree families of Lagimodière's Canadian friends. The men who had been off hunting escaped to Fort des Prairies.

This time, Marie-Anne's white skin saved her, for the Sarcees saw at once that she was not Cree. However, the chief asked to see her husband, and when Marie-Anne told him that Jean-Baptiste would be back soon, he said, "We will wait for him."

Marie-Anne had learned much during her few years in *les pays d'en haut*. Instead of cowering before the Sarcees, she put on a bold face and treated them as friends. She knew that the greatest act of politeness to an Indian was an invitation to a feast. She had plenty of food stored away, and so she put out a spread of meat on the grass and gave them a little tobacco. The Sarcees marvelled at this reception, and as Marie-Anne had hoped, they were friendly.

Late in the afternoon, Jean-Baptiste arrived with his horses, and was amazed to see Marie-Anne's guests. However, he felt uncomfortable with them so near his camp, so he told them he was moving away from their camp so that his wife and children could sleep.

"Alright," said the chief, "but don't go far, for you are not going until five of our men being held at the fort are returned to us. If they come to harm, then you will pay for them with your head."

The Lagimodières went a few miles away and pretended to camp, but as soon as he felt certain that the Sarcees were asleep, Jean-Baptiste broke camp. He and Marie-Anne mounted their horses and fled for Fort des Prairies. They rode all night and part of the following day. They had not been inside the safety of the Fort long when the Sarcees, annoyed at being duped, arrived outside the palisade.

During the year 1809, Jean-Baptiste did not return to the prairie. Perhaps because of Indian tribal wars, the area was unsafe for hunter as well as family. In any case, he remained in the north in the park lands, trapping and hunting moose, elk and beaver. Marie-Anne spent the year in the fort.

The following summer, however, they were back on the prairie, the third summer for Marie-Anne. This year they travelled far to the southeast and were in the vicinity of the Cypress Hills, when Marie-Anne's third child was born. Again, Marie-Anne's sense of romance and drama aided her imagination, and she called the child "Cyprès". Later, the little girl was christened Marie-Josephte, but she was known all her life as Cyprès.

The little son, Laprairie, continued to be the object of admiration and envy among the Indians. One day a band of Assiniboine arrived on horseback before Marie-Anne's tent. The chief of the band, after looking at the little boy, approached the mother and offered her the best of his horses in exchange for her son. Marie-Anne refused his offer, of course, but the chief, thinking that his offer was not enough, said to her, "Take my two best horses and one of my children, in exchange."

Marie-Anne began to cry. "Please leave me," she said. "You can have my heart sooner than my child." The chief was touched by her tears and did not press her further.

This was Marie-Anne's last adventure on the prairies. The following summer, Jean-Baptiste took his family back to the Red River, for he had heard that a white colony was to be founded there.

Marie-Anne left Fort des Prairies without tears. Her great hope was to return to civilization, and if she could not persuade Jean-Baptiste to return to Canada, at least a settled colony on the Red River might have some of the advantages of Maskinongé. She would have a home of her own; there would be a church, and schools for her children; and other comforts would follow.

Nevertheless Marie-Anne had enjoyed her five years on the prairies and at Fort des Prairies. When she told her stories in later years to her children, and to l'abbé Dugas who wrote them down, she recaptured much of the drama and the romantic spirit of the Northwest. Her little tales are sprightly and exotic, unlike her later stories of the more mundane trials of colony building and settlement.

.   .   .

What did Marie-Anne find in the way of settlement at the Red River? Nothing. Nothing at all. When the Lagimodières reached their destination in the summer of 1811, they found no sign of a colony. Indeed, the enterprise had started off badly, with the advance party having been obliged to winter near York Factory on Hudson Bay. Marie-Anne's trials were a long way from being over.

There have been many books written about Selkirk's Colony on the Red River, and the story has so many sides that we

cannot begin to recount it here. Enough to say that the two
great fur companies, the Hudson's Bay Company which had its
terminus at York Factory on Hudson Bay, and the North West
Company with its terminus at Montreal, were deadly rivals.
When the Scottish nobleman, Selkirk, bought into the Hudson's
Bay Company enough shares to take control, he asked for and
received an immense grant of land which included the Red
River, the lower part of Lake Winnipeg, and the vast buffalo
hunting grounds. The grant had a threefold purpose; to give new
homes to the evicted Highland crofters; to provide a place of
retirement for the Company employees and their families; to
supplement the provisions of the various Hudson's Bay Company posts.

All the veteran fur traders, whether Hudson's Bay Company
men or Northwesters, were sharply opposed to the idea of Selkirk's colony encroaching on what they considered their pre-
serve; they believed that settlement and fur trading were
antipathetic. Besides, the Red River was so remote from world
markets that its economic future was doubtful, and it was
unbelievably difficult to supply. To the Northwesters, who
depended entirely on the pemmican from the buffalo hunting
grounds for food, this grant to Selkirk seemed to be a warning.
The planting across their trade routes of a colony belonging to a
rival company threatened not only their trade but human survival. In fact, no one was happy about the grant except Lord
Selkirk who, in the face of increasing difficulties, appears so
stubborn, as to be mad. It is difficult to believe that a man in
his right mind would cast hundreds of helpless people into such
remote lands, poorly organized and prepared, for supposedly
altruistic reasons. Most of the colonists suffered bitterly, many
died, but a small colony of Scottish, Canadian and Métis did
survive.

Marie-Anne, however, was not yet to become part of a
settlement.

Jean-Baptiste had planned to offer his services to the new
colonists as a buffalo hunter, but finding no one on the Red
River needing these services, he took his family upstream to the
fort at Pembina where they spent the winter. Here, during the

winter of 1811-12, Marie-Anne had a fourth child, a son, whom she called Benjamin, which means "son of good fortune". Perhaps she chose this name with the hope that her nomad's life was over and that she would soon have a home in the midst of a civilized community.

They passed the winter without incident, in the shelter of the fort. In the spring, Jean-Baptiste was hired by the Hudson's Bay Company to hunt for twelve months, for the sum of $30. He established his family on the Assiniboine River, nine miles west from its confluence with the Red. Here he built a small wooden cottage for Marie-Anne and the four children.

Their new home was close to the buffalo lands. The whole fur trade depended on pemmican, and the Assiniboine Indians, the Métis, and the freemen had made it their prime occupation to supply this need. The buffalo hunt was a highly organized operation with its "captains of tens". Jean-Baptiste had no alternative but to join the hunt, for this was his greatest skill. It meant, however, leaving Marie-Anne alone, for Jean-Baptiste was absent the greater part of the time. Used to fort life with its hustle, or the constant action and change of the prairies in the company of Jean-Baptiste, Marie-Anne found the isolation in her little cottage almost intolerable. For three years she was without neighbours, and without friends or relatives to visit her; she had only her children to keep her company.

In her loneliness, Marie-Anne was scarcely aware that some Métis families had settled only nine miles downstream at the fork of the Red and the Assiniboine Rivers, in anticipation of the Selkirk colony. So far, only a few Scottish families had arrived and preparations had been inadequate even for these. There were no plows to break the land, no blacksmiths, no houses, no land cleared, no livestock, and little food.

In January of 1814, when the food became scarce, Miles Macdonell, the governor of the new colony, issued a proclamation prohibiting the export of pemmican or other provisions from Assiniboia.

This seemed to be a direct challenge to the survival of the North West Company, and a threat to the Métis community, whose members lived off these buffalo lands. The survival of a large number of people was at stake. As the furor mounted to the level of warfare between the two great companies, with the Métis on the side of the North West Company, Jean-Baptiste continued to hunt buffalo for the Hudson's Bay Company.

How was it, then, that Jean-Baptiste, a freeman who also depended on the buffalo for his living, was not on the side of the Métis, and the North West Company?

Jean-Baptiste Lagimodière was an independent, and he considered himself aloof from the quarrel. If he chose to hunt buffalo for the Hudson's Bay Company because they paid him well, that was his business. He never considered himself an employee of the Hudson's Bay Company, though his preference lay with it. He had been well treated by the Bay Company factors at Pembina and at Fort des Prairies, and his family had been well looked after. If the Company needed his services, and paid him well, he was prepared to stand by them.

There are frequent references to "Lagimonière" in Miles Macdonell's journals.

> "(1812, Sat Dec 12) Send off Lagimonière my best hunter with his family three men and horses to the plains."
> "(1812, Sun Dec 20) Send a bag of oatmeal to the Forks for sheep. . . . and a man to Lagimonières for the horse bought from Belhumeur 32 dollars in goods."
> "(1812, Dec 31). Ishan sent near Lagimonière."

Buffalo hunters needed women to dress the slaughtered animals and to dry the meat. From the records that remain, it is impossible to discover whether or not Marie-Anne helped her husband with this formidable chore. With four infants to care for, she probably did so only in an emergency. Jean-Baptiste probably hired an Indian woman to handle this work.

In her isolation, Marie-Anne might have been unaware of the tense situation which had grown between the Hudson's Bay Company and the North West Company. Miles Macdonell's proclamation prohibiting the export of pemmican was taken by the Northwesters and the Métis as an act of war. By this time, there were some hundreds of Métis in the Red River area, many of them educated, and because of the buffalo-hunt, organized and well disciplined. They and the Northwesters persuaded thirteen families of the colonists to resettle in Upper Canada, and the others were terrorized into leaving their homes, which were then burned, and the crops trampled.

The Nor'westers had won the first round, but when Selkirk sent out a fresh group of settlers from Scotland in 1815, it became a war, not between the two companies, but between the men of *les pays d'en haut* and Lord Selkirk. The hapless colonists were to suffer most.

.   .   .

And now, Jean-Baptiste Lagimodière, the independent who had hoped to remain aloof, was caught in the web of the quarrel, and with him, Marie-Anne and the children.

In October 1815, Jean-Baptiste was approached by Colin Robertson, who had been sent by Selkirk to the Red River with a shock brigade. Robertson asked Jean-Baptiste if he would carry important letters to Lord Selkirk in Montreal, saying that the life of the colony was at stake. He promised Lagimodière a substantial reward if he succeeded and, so that he would not be anxious about his family, Robertson promised to provide for them in Fort Douglas, "the fort of the colony".

Lagimodière accepted the challenge and promised to reach Montreal if he were not killed or captured along the way. Marie-Anne left her isolated cabin on the Assiniboine and once more entered into the bustle of fort life. According to Robertson, Lagimodière arrived with his family at the fort on October 11.

One wonders why Lagimodière would toss away the security of his hunter's income, to accept such a dangerous challenge. Perhaps the reward was too substantial to turn down, or he may have been intrigued by the challenge. As for Marie-Anne, she probably considered any change from her isolated cabin to be for the better.

Although the Lagimodières were accustomed to a life of danger and excitement, this trip by foot to Montreal, during the winter months, was the most dangerous that Jean-Baptiste had undertaken. Not only was there the danger of travelling practically alone, in winter, through unknown country, but he must avoid the enemies of the Hudson's Bay Company who would be on the watch for all express messengers. Moreover, Jean-Baptiste would not be able to carry food, but must find it as he went. Great hunter though he was, travelling by winter meant the added dangers of starvation and exposure.

According to family legend, Lagimodière set out on October 17, 1815, by horse. He was accompanied by two others, an engagé named Benoni Marier, and an Indian guide. He carried with him letters for Selkirk and a letter of recommendation written by Robertson.

The recommendation said:

> Permit me to recommend Lagemoneer as a man worthy any trust you may repose in him, he is able to act as a Guide; the respect he is held in by his countrymen, is one of the principal [sic] motives I have for sending him with the Express, and also to discover the road to Montreal by way of Faun de Lac [Fond du Lac]. . . . He is a real honest man, but hard in his dealings and highly worthy of the confidence I have reposed in him.
>
> I have also promised that should any unforseen accident happen to this man while in Charge of this Express that the Earl of Selkirk and the Hudson's Bay Company allow his wife seven pounds pr annum for ten years. . . . I have also agreed to keep his wife and family at our establishment here until his arrival at Red River.

Sending Lagimodière by way of Fond du Lac (Duluth) was unusual, and was probably done to avoid the Northwesters. This provided Lagimodière with another problem; the route from Red River via Red Lake to Fond du Lac was unknown, and he would have to find it.

Colin Robertson reported later that Lagimodière and his companions left Red River from near Pembina, walked to Red Lake, embarked there in a small canoe, but was "taken by the ice in Lake Superior, from thence he walked to Montreal on foot where he arrived about the first of March". His route lay by way of the south shore of Lake Superior, then took him to Drummond Island, Georgian Bay and York. At York, he refused to walk any further – "he seemed not inclined to go on foot" – so the Company sent him the remainder of the way to Montreal by sleigh. No doubt, poor Jean-Baptiste was having trouble with sore feet at this stage of his journey.

He delivered his letters to Selkirk on March 10, 1816. Selkirk wrote in his diary,

> Lagimonière from Red River has recently come to Montreal – he brought with him a packet of letters. . . . Conditions at the Settlement are much worse than I expected. . . . I shall have to put my business in order and hasten forth.

Lagimodière remained in Montreal until spring break up, then started off for Red River with dispatches for Governor Semple. This time the Nor'westers were on the lookout for him, and at Fond du Lac he was stopped by some Indians and a negro named Bonga, beaten, and robbed of all he carried. Lagimodière and his companions were taken to Fort William and there released – without guns or clothing – and left to survive if they could.

Meanwhile, Selkirk had raised a small private army of disbanded Swiss mercenaries, the De Meurons, to whom he promised land in the new colony. With these he proceeded westward with the intention of following Jean-Baptiste's newly explored route by way of Fond du Lac and Red Lake. However, when Selkirk reached Sault Ste Marie, he learned of the capture of Fort Douglas, on June 19, and of the death of the governor and the soldiers, and the banishment for a second time of the unfortunate settlers. Selkirk revised his plan, moved on to Fort William, and in a bold manoeuvre on August 12, seized this important North West Company depot. He also captured some of the leading Nor'westers and the annual haul of furs. This was the death of the North West Company. With Selkirk astride its trunk line, the Company was literally strangled.[12]

Jean-Baptiste and Marie-Anne, caught up in Selkirk's great quarrel with the Nor'westers, managed to survive, barely. Jean-Baptiste and his companions were found on July 2, fifteen miles west of Fort Frances, by two Canadians. It was possibly from them that he first heard of the tragedy at Seven Oaks, and of the capture by the Métis of Fort Douglas where he had left his family. By the time the story had reached him, he was told that all the inmates of the Fort had been killed.

The family legend does not tell us how Jean-Baptiste mourned for his beautiful little family or his staunch Marie-Anne, but it is clear that he had little heart to return to the Red River. Instead, he went south from Fort Frances to Red Lake where he had left a horse the preceding year. He took his time, possibly finding solace in the wilderness, hunting and fishing, for he did not arrive back at the Red River until September.

There, wonder of wonders, he found Marie-Anne, with all her children, safely lodged in a small abandoned hut on the east side of the river. When Fort Douglas had been taken by the Nor'westers, she had fled with her children of whom the oldest, Reine, was nine years old. One of the Cree Chieftains[13] who knew Jean-Baptiste well, took Marie-Anne and her family into his tent and gave her food and shelter for the summer. When September came and there was no sign of her husband, she felt certain that he had died. Her future was bleak. The Hudson's Bay Company had promised her a pension in case of Lagimodière's death, but at that moment the Company was inoperative. Her children needed food then, not the following year.

How could they survive on their own in this hostile land?

The answer came in the flesh. Marie-Anne had scarcely completed her move from the crowded tent of the big-hearted, Indian chief to the little, abandoned house, when Jean-Baptiste returned to the Red River. There was a joyful reunion in the little hut beside the great river.

Fort Douglas was retaken by Hudson's Bay Company men late in 1816, and Selkirk himself arrived with his Swiss de Meurons in June, 1817. He spent a happy summer organizing his colony and making treaties with the Indians.

.   .   .

When he left, Selkirk took with him a petition, from the French Canadians of the Red River to the Archbishop of Quebec. The petition was a request for missionaries. Quebec church records tell the story that when Lagimodière had arrived in Montreal in

1816, to deliver the letters to Selkirk, he had been asked what kind of favour he wished in return, and Lagimodière said, "Priests: give us priests." In these words of Jean-Baptiste, we hear the plea of his wife, Marie-Anne.

When the colonists discovered that Lord Selkirk was responsive to the idea of Roman Catholic missionaries in his colony, it was Marie-Anne, the only white Catholic woman on the Red River who initiated the signing of the petition. At long last she could see her nomadic life ending. There would be a church and schools, not only for her own family, but for all the Scotch and French Métis families as well. And she was to have a home.

For his services to the Hudson's Bay Company, Lagimodière received a large tract of land on the east bank of the Red River opposite Point Douglas, bounded in the south by the River Seine. (It is a remarkable fact that the river front of the Lagimodière tract remains vacant land, although surrounded on all sides by Winnipeg and St. Boniface. There are plans to make it into a park in memory of the first settlers of St. Boniface.)

Jean-Baptiste began immediately to build a temporary log house in the fashion of the other colonists – a simple hut covered with thatch, with the crevices plastered with clay. Many of the trading posts were built in the same manner.

The following year, Jean-Baptiste built a larger, more comfortable house, the first real home for Marie-Anne. The Lagimodières worked the soil, and planted vegetables and a little wheat, and they had a cow, one of the few in the colony.

Two missionaries, Père Joseph Provencher and Père Severe Dumoulin, arrived in July, 1818, and were greeted by almost the whole colony. The priests were temporarily housed at Fort Douglas, and there they received the people, said mass, preached their sermons, performed marriages, taught catechism and baptised the small children. Marie-Anne was kept busy as god-mother, for she was the only baptised woman among the Roman Catholics. For a long time, all the children of Red River called Madame Lagimodière, *Ma Marraine.*

Shortly, the missionaries had their own building, and began a school for the children. In deep gratitude, Marie-Anne kept a sharp watch on the physical well-being of the priests, often sending them meat or milk. Indeed, Monsieur Provencher felt so sure of Marie-Anne's care and generosity that when he found himself with nothing to eat, he would say to Reine or one of the older children, "Listen, my child. Go and tell your mother that I have nothing to eat this evening." And Reine would hurry home to get *un petit sac de viande* for him.

There were some grim days ahead for the colonists as well as for the priests, for there were crop failures, year after year, sometimes from frost, sometimes from grasshoppers, sometimes from mice — and then from flood. Jean-Baptiste, the great hunter, not only provided for his family, but he provided for many of the colonists as well. If it had not been for Jean-Baptiste, and some others such as he, the colony could not have survived.

Selkirk did not come back, and when he died in 1820 the world shut its door on the Red River. A few French Canadian families came in 1818, and with the addition of the de Meurons, the colonizing period was over. Altogether, there were 419 people in the settlement in 1821, of whom 154 were female. The Scottish numbered 221, the de Meurons, sixty-two, the Canadians 133 (mostly white men with Indian wives), and in addition there were about 500 Métis at Pembina. There was little change in the settlement for the next fifty years, except for the addition of retired, well-to-do, company officials.

The community was very mixed, and the economy was casual and unplanned. The Hudson's Bay Company looked on with a fatherly eye, but did not interfere. After the great flood of 1826, some of the colonists, including almost all of the de Meurons, were discouraged and left for the United States. Among those who left was Reine, Marie-Anne's eldest daughter who had married a Canadian, named Lamère.

Marie-Anne was upset about the parting, and she tried to persuade her husband to move back to Canada, but Jean-Baptiste was resolved to remain in the Red River country, no matter what reverses of fortune were in store.

Ironically, the colony's misfortunes were his good fortune. His great skill was as a hunter, but his wife wanted a home for her children, six in all, and she wanted church and school and all the good things that come with a settled community. In the Red River, he could have it both ways. His wife could have her home, and he could hunt.

.   .   .

There is little to add to Marie-Anne's story. She lived to be ninety-five years old, and was almost never ill in her life. Her memory was good until the end. Her three sons became farmers, and her three daughters married. Although Reine moved away, the other two daughters remained.

Jean-Baptiste continued to act for the Hudson's Bay Company when a good man was needed, and the records show that, "Captain Franklin's express was sent off early this morning for Rainy Lake by Lagimonière and his son who was hired for the purpose." This was after Franklin's second expedition to the Arctic (1825-27). The old adventurer, Jean-Baptiste, must have found this errand a diverting one.

Community life droned on, prosperous after the 1826 flood but simple. The French-speaking and English-speaking people were on good terms. One of the St. Boniface women in her old age recalled the parties of her youth: "Many of the Kildonan [Scots][14] people and the other people across the river used to come to our parties, and we went to theirs. We knew them all."

Although the Canadians were mostly on the east side of the Red River, and the Scots on the west, there was one Scotch family, the Sutherlands, who lived on the St. Boniface side. Mrs. Sutherland, senior, had been one of the first women settlers. When ship fever struck the colonists, Kate McPherson's skill as nurse had saved many lives and she was held in great affection by the colony.

In 1920, Kate's granddaughter, Mrs. W. R. Black, recalling her childhood, remembered the Lagimodières well, and the story of Jean-Baptiste's great odyssey to Montreal with letters for Lord Selkirk, as well as his capture on the return journey.

"As a result of our being on the other side of the river [St. Boniface]," she said, "we were in closer contact with the French-speaking people, and my father and mother and our whole family came to speak French as well as English. . . . The French people used to come to the house constantly to consult my father about their affairs, and in that way he came to be a link between them and the Kildonan people."

In 1852 there was another great flood, and many houses were carried away; probably the Lagimodières lost theirs too, for their fields were low. It is a little uncertain when Jean-Baptiste died, but it was within a few years of this flood. He was nearing his eightieth year.

Marie-Anne outlived him by a score of years. In her last years she had one great joy and one sorrow. The sorrow was to see her grandson, Julie's son, Louis Riel, lead an unsurrection of Métis against the Government and the company. The joy was to have her daughter, Reine, return to St. Boniface after an absence of forty years. Marie-Anne died in December, 1875, but not before she saw the first influx of settlers from the east.

She died in peace and was buried at St. Boniface Cathedral. Among Marie-Anne's descendants, in addition to the history-making Louis Riel, are many substantial and noted Canadians, including William Lagimodière who was Secretary-Treasurer of Manitoba, and later MLA; the Honourable Roger J. Teillet, Minister of Veterans Affairs in the Pearson administration; and Canada's recent Ambassador to Denmark, Hector Allard.

Marie-Anne died content, for she helped to tame the wilderness. Without her and those hardy Scots' women, *les pays d'en haut* would have remained a nomads' land; the men would not have settled there. They would have continued to hunt there, and then retire in their old age in the east. Marie-Anne's gumption, determination and zest helped bridge the cultural gap between the two worlds, the European world and that of the Indian. How else could Amelia Connolly have become the First Lady of British Columbia?

Notes

1. Frances Simpson was the young wife of George Simpson, first "governor" of the Hudson's Bay Company after its merger with the North West Company, 1821. Frances travelled with her husband in 1830, by canoe, from Montreal to the Red River, and then to York Factory on Hudson's Bay. She kept a journal of her travels. See "Journey for Frances", *The Beaver* (Winnipeg: December, 1953), p. 50.

2. At first all fur traders were called *voyageurs*. In time, *voyageurs* came to mean the men who operated the canoes.

3. The name, Lagimodière, has had many variant spellings, but traces back to Lecomte Sieur de la Vimaudière, whose name crops up in French-Canadian records as early as 1755. The family today spell the name "Lagimodière".

4. La Salle set off from Lachine in 1669 on his explorations of the Ohio. The name, *La Chine,* is said to have been given to the spot by La Salle's men, in derision of his dream of a westward passage to China. A model of the *canot de maître* can be seen in the National Museum at Ottawa—full scale.

5. The depot was at Grand Portage until the border between Canada and the U.S. was fixed. The last meeting of the Nor'westers at Grand Portage was in 1802.

6. Marjorie Pickthall, "Père Lalement", *Drift of Pinions* (Montreal: 1913).

7. Frances Simpson's journal. *The Beaver* (Winnipeg: March, 1954), p. 13.

8. This post was named Fort Alexander by the Hudson's Bay Company. It had originally been a North West Company post, and was known as Bas de la Rivière.

9. L'abbé G. Dugas, *La Première Canadienne au Nord-Ouest* (Winnipeg: 1945), p. 14. All quotations are from Dugas except where indicated.

10. Grace Lee Nute, *The Voyageurs* (New York: 1931).

11. There was a white child born at Pembina a few months before Marie-Anne Lagimodière's arrival. An Orkney girl came out to Rupert's Land dressed as a boy. After several years her identity was discovered and she was sent as a cook to Pembina. After the birth of a child, mother and infant were shipped back to Orkney, and were gone before Marie-Anne arrived. See Hudson's Bay Company Archives, Winnipeg.

12. Lawsuits followed Selkirk's freebooting, and the North West Company won. However, Selkirk's capture of Fort William so upset the North West's economy that the company was in a poor position for bargaining at the time of the merger of the two companies. See M.W. Campbell, *McGillivray, Lord of the Northwest* (Toronto: 1962).

13. Or was it the famous Chief Peguis as some sources say?

14. Mrs. Henry Macdonald, *Women of the Red River,* edited by W.J. Healy (Winnipeg: 1923), p. 119. Most of the Selkirk Settlers were Highland Scotch from Kildonan, in south-eastern Sutherlandshire. They were Presbyterians and spoke Gaelic.

Bibliography

Bryce, Rev. George. "Selkirk, Simpson", *Makers of Canada.* Toronto: 1928.

Campbell, M.W. *McGillivray Lord of the North.* Toronto: 1962.

Dugas, L'abbé Georges. *La Première Canadienne au Nord-Ouest,* reedited. Winnipeg: 1945.

Gates, Charles M. *Five Fur Traders.* Toronto: 1933.

Glenbow Foundation, Calgary.

Healy, W.J. *Women of the Red River.* Winnipeg: 1923.

Hudson's Bay Company Archives, Winnipeg.

Mackay, Douglas. *The Honourable Company.* Toronto: 1949.

Manitoba Archives, Winnipeg.

Morse, Eric W. "Canoe Routes of the Voyageurs", *Minnesota Historical Society.* 1961. Also *Canadian Georgraphical Journal.* May, July, August, 1961.

Morton, A.S. *Sir George Simpson.* Toronto: 1944.

Morton, W.L. *Manitoba.* Toronto: 1957.

Nute, Grace Lee. "Journey for Frances", *The Beaver.* Winnipeg: December 1953, March 1954, Summer 1954.

Nute, Grace Lee. *The Voyageurs.* New York: 1931.

Nute, Grace Lee. *The Voyageurs' Highway* . St. Paul: 1941.

R.C.M.P. Archives, Regina.

Saint-Boniface Archives, Saint-Boniface.

Selkirk Papers, National Archives, Manitoba Archives.

6

Amelia Douglas

Our sons shall wed your daughters, and we shall be one people.
Champlain to Algonquins, 1603[1]

Amelia Connolly was born in one of the great furposts of the Northwest, the same year, 1812, that Marie-Anne Lagimodière returned from her years of wandering on the plains to settle at the Red River. Amelia was not a diplomat as Jeanne Mance and Molly Brant had been. She was a home builder, and her children possessed the land.

Like Marie-Anne, Amelia was born in British North America. Her father, William Connolly, an Irish-Canadian, had been born at Lachine and had entered the North West Company when very young. While he was at Rat River House, sited in the vicinity of today's Flin Flon, Connolly married Suzanne Pas-de-Nom, the daughter of a Cree chieftain. It was a happy marriage "according to the custom of the country", and there were five or six children who survived infancy.

William Connolly was an able fur trader. In the employ of the

Hudson's Bay Company, after its union with the North West
Company, he rose to the rank of chief factor, the senior position in the service. He served in one capacity or another in
many of the trading posts – York Factory, Cumberland House,
Norway House, Ile à La Crosse, Rainy Lake, and Fort St. James.
His family, of course, moved with him, criss-crossing the country by canoe or bateau, along the river routes.

Of all the homes of her childhood, the only one which
Amelia remembered with clarity was York Factory, the Company depot on Hudson Bay. As an old woman, she could still
recall a great mess room with a low ceiling, an enormous fireplace at one end; a mess table that ran the length of the room
with chairs ranged along the walls; French-Canadian chefs; and
food served from large, covered dishes of silver and pewter. This
great mess hall was the playroom of the Connolly children during the long winter days.

Perhaps her memories were linked with the tragic death of
her little sister. In winter, the children were dressed in heavy,
Hudson's Bay duffel. (When they went outside, they added fur
parkas and leggings as children do today.) The little girls hated
the duffels which were bulky and scratchy. One winter day, the
children begged to put on summer cotton frocks which had just
arrived from England. Their mother humoured them. The
smallest child flitted about the room before the firelight of the
great open hearth. As she whirled past the roaring fire, a lick of
flame caught the light dress and, a moment later, the child was
swept by flame. Although the Cree nursemaid snatched her up,
wrapped her in a rug, and carried her out to the snow, the little
girl died.

Grimly romantic Fort York! How could Amelia forget it?
Her youngest daughter, Martha, believed her mother was born
at Fort York,[2] but a death notice in *The Colonist,* 1890, says
that Amelia was born at Fort Assiniboia. Certainly the family
were at Cumberland House, one of the first of the interior
Hudson's Bay posts, in 1819, when Sir John Franklin was preparing for his first expedition to the Arctic. Franklin mentions
William Connolly many times. Amelia, who was then seven
years old, remembered the outfitting for the Arctic journey well

enough in later years to be able to describe something of it to her children. She remembered a young artist of the party, Lieutenant Back, even better, because he played with her and her sister, Julia. The children posed for a painting by him, and the painting is still believed to be in existence.

According to Hudson's Bay Company records, William Connolly was appointed to Lesser Slave Lake, north of Edmonton, after the merger of the two fur companies in 1821. Later, he was posted to York Factory. In the fall of 1824, Connolly was moved to Fort St. James in New Caledonia, deep in the mountains between the Coastal Range and the Rocky Mountain Range. In central British Columbia, it is today about as isolated a spot as can be found, but in fur trade days it was no more than four days from the Pacific and Fort Vancouver, via the Columbia. Four days, to a fur trader, was nothing.

William Connolly had been appointed Chief Factor at Fort St. James. With him, as clerk, was sent a young Scot named James Douglas, then about twenty-one. Douglas had already been about five years with the fur trade in Canada. He was determined, efficient, and ambitious. Once he set foot in *les pays d'en haut,* he never looked back.

During his first years at St. James, as clerk to Amelia's father, he was put in charge of the fishery. This was vitally important, for the only food that this isolated post had was fish — fresh white fish and dried salmon. Officers and clerks had a few delicacies such as tea, sugar, flour, rice or beans, and occasionally wine, but the men had fish and water. Sometimes the fish was scarce, but there was always water.

When Amelia came to Fort St. James, she was twelve, modest, very shy as most Métis and Indian women were, and already becoming beautiful. She was small with wonderfully fair skin, grey eyes and brown hair. She was called "Little Snowbird".

At Fort St. James there were all the ingredients for a first-class romance. The Fort was built at the southern tip of Stuart Lake and commanded a view of the surrounding country. Stuart

Lake is about fifty miles long, four miles wide and studded with beautiful islands. The western shore is low, irregular and wooded, but ridged by hills. The Rocky Mountains are visible from a high promontory on the east side of the lake. The top of the promontory was only a few minutes from the fort by horse-back.

To the beautiful scenery had been added two, handsome, young people—one a young Métis girl, and the other, a tall, good-looking, Scot. With the addition of danger and isolation, how could romance fail? Before Amelia was sixteen years old, the two were in love, and James had asked for Amelia's hand in marriage. The parents had no objection to Douglas as a husband, but they stipulated that the marriage should wait until Amelia was sixteen. Amelia Connolly and James Douglas were married April 27, 1828. It was a lifetime love affair; and though they were to live through many dangers and behold many dramatic events, their love for one another was always a sound anchor.

Amelia has usually been described as shy and reserved, but the fact of her Indian origin and her life-time spent in the Hudson's Bay posts is seldom taken into account. That she knew her mother's people, the natives of North America, better than she did her father's, should be self-evident. She did not see life outside the forts until she was past forty, and within the fort the only people she saw, besides the fur traders and clerks, were the wives, who, like herself, were either full-blooded Indians or Métis. To thrust Amelia into the outside world was almost like thrusting a middle-aged nun from a convent-run hospital into everyday life.

Amelia's life in the fur posts was a cloistered one – confined within walls, secluded, secure. The fur traders, those soldier-merchants, came and went. The nomadic Indians came and went. But the Indian and Métis wives of the white men remained securely in the forts. For a white man to drag his woman across the plains in nomad fashion, be she brown or white, was highly irregular, and it was only because Jean-Baptiste Lagimodière was a freeman that he had no secure base for his wife. Even he placed his family in one of the posts during the winter.

The Indian women who became wives of the white men did not object to fort life. They knew they would eat, be warm, and have enough clothes for themselves and children. There was gaiety in the fort, and an Indian woman married to a white man had great influence with her own people, as well as considerable influence among the white men.

The Hudson's Bay Company and the Northwest Company fostered peaceful relations between the whites and the Indians. This policy was in contrast to the vicious wars between whites and Indians recorded in United States history. The reason there were no wars in British North America is simple. The white men who traded with the Indians married their daughters.

The rank and file took Indian wives. The top brass did, too. Such men as Charles St. Etienne de La Tour of Acadia in the seventeenth century, Sir William Johnson in the eighteenth, and Sir George Simpson, Dr. John McLaughlin and Sir James Douglas in the nineteenth, had Indian consorts. Through these women, white men had influence among the native tribes and learned to understand them. In the United States, the Indians were vermin, to be exterminated. In Canada, the Indians were relatives, to be cultivated. Many prominent Canadians have Indian blood in their veins.

So with Amelia. From birth, life in the fur post was the only life she knew, but for her it was a good life. Her mother was the daughter of a Cree chieftain, her father a top-ranking officer of the Company. She was married to a hard-working, ambitious, young Scot of good family, who was devoted to her. Moreover, she was able to help him understand the ways of her mother's people and at one time, her quick action prevented a blood feud.

It was shortly after she was married. She was still very young. Her father was away from the Fort at St. James, and young James Douglas was left in charge.

On August 6, 1828, Douglas wrote cryptically in his diary: "Tumult with Indians."

Five years before, two Indians had murdered two Hudson's Bay Company men at Yale. One of the Indians had been captured and had paid for his crime. The other, who was still at large, turned up in the vicinity of Fort St. James in the summer of 1828, during Connolly's absence. Douglas went out to apprehend the man, and in the mêlée which followed, the culprit was killed, and so "wild justice" was served. However, the Indians who were related to the slain man wanted revenge. Some thirty or forty Indians rushed the fort, overpowered the Hudson's Bay men, and seized Douglas.

There are several versions of the story. However, there is no doubt that Amelia rushed from her own quarters to the defence of her husband. Her long hair was seized by one of the intruders, and a knife put to her throat. Her young brother, William, tripped up her assailant and she fled to the second floor of the fort. Quickly, with the help of the interpreter's wife, Amelia began throwing trade goods and tobacco out of the window. The Indians were placated by this gesture of compensation. Certainly, in this instance, Amelia saved the life of her husband, and perhaps of all those in the Fort, by her understanding of the Indian mind. Her quick action also avoided what almost certainly would have resulted in a vendetta between the Hudson's Bay Company men and the Stuart Lake Indians.

Douglas never again attempted to serve out "wild justice" to the Indians. He listened to his wife, and he came to learn that a council or parley held with the fiercest of Indians was more effective in dealing with them than reprisal. He found, too, that meeting unfriendly Indians in parley required far greater courage than did a sharp, armed sally. James Douglas had later to face the fierce Haidas in parley on several occasions, in tense situations, requiring from him every ounce of courage he possessed. From Amelia, he had learned his lesson well.

A few weeks after the incident in which Amelia saved the Fort by quick thought and action, the young Douglases acted as hosts for the fort, to George Simpson, Governor of the Company, who was on a grand tour of inspection. He arrived at St. James with his usual pomp in a party of about thirty mounted men with flags flying, bugles and bagpipes playing. Douglas, in Connolly's absence, did the honours of the Fort, and replied with cannon and musketry, all to the amazement of the Indians.

James and Amelia Douglas must have impressed George Simpson who had not, at this time, put aside his Métis wife. One can guess at his thinking: "Here is an ambitious, hardworking, courageous, young Scot. And that handsome, young woman, Amelia, has a sharp mind and a cool head. She will be a help to him and he will learn." So, when an opening came for a clerk at the great Company mart at Fort Vancouver, James Douglas got the promotion.

Fort Vancouver (near today's Portland, Oregon) on the Columbia River was the grand emporium, the rendezvous for the Hudson's Bay Company of all its Pacific interests. The first post had been at the mouth of the Columbia, but Dr. John McLoughlin, Chief Factor, had moved the post inland some ninety miles, in 1924, and there on fertile flats, had built a great medieval fortress. Here the Douglases spent the next sixteen years.

Amelia, about to have a child, was not able to travel with her husband when he left for his new post, early in 1830. The infant died, and later in the year, Amelia accompanied her father when he conducted the brigade carrying the winter's furs to Fort Vancouver.

The first four days were by canoe, down the Stuart River, and then the Fraser, to Fort Alexander. Here the goods were transferred to pack-horses for travel over mountain trails during the twenty-five day journey to Kamloops. There might have been as many as sixty-five horses in the train, carrying a possible eighty-five packs of furs from the various mountain posts.

Amelia was dressed as befitted the daughter of a Chief Factor. She wore a skirt of fine broadcloth with leggings and moccasins richly embroidered with beads. She rode a small horse whose trappings were equally gay with beads, quills, fringes and little bells. Her long hair was braided with ribbons.

Riding over mountain passes, through valleys, crossing fords, through some of the earth's most spectacular scenery, with cheerful company and good food, Amelia enjoyed the days of travel to the utmost, until the day the brigade reached the confluence of the Okanagan with the Columbia. The ford was shallow but the river swift. Her horse lost its footing, and the horse and girl were swept with the current towards the surging rapids below. A great rock in the river held them for a few moments, just long enough to be rescued by the horse-master. She threw him her bridle, and her horse was guided to the opposite shore. Once again on dry land, and safe in her father's arms, Amelia, the young woman with the cool head in moments of stress, fainted.

·   ·   ·

After a thousand miles of mountains and rivers, the brigade arrived at Fort Vancouver, and Amelia rejoined her husband. She must have been amazed to see the huge fort with its twenty-foot palisades, its bastions with cannon, the two inner courts with their forty wooden structures, the two-storey governor's house, the 3,000 acres of tilled land, the orchards, cattle and sheep. All these things must have seemed grand indeed to one who had lived most of her life in small fur posts. The cattle, sheep and the orchards would have been enough to make her wonder.

And what did Amelia remember of her arrival at Fort Vancouver? She remembered that James Douglas was disappointed because she was sunburned. He had been boasting about her white-skinned beauty, and she had arrived, after weeks of travel in sun and wind, as brown as a full-blooded Indian.

The other thing she remembered was that Mrs. McLoughlin was kind to her. Mrs. McLoughlin was Métis and the wife of the Chief Factor, "the Governor" of the great Fort. Amelia had said good-bye to her parents, and was putting her first step into a strange, new, cosmopolitan world. She was lonely and timid, and Mrs. McLoughlin was kind to her.

Fort Vancouver reached out to all the world. During the sixteen years that the Douglases were there, many interesting guests came to visit. There were sea captains from the Orient trading tales with *bourgeois* from the Mackenzie River; traders from India or England encountered traders from Montreal or York Factory. There was little boredom — that is for the men. They dined in style in the officer's mess, smoked and told stories in "Bachelor's Hall", rode horseback and hunted. The Fort was run like a military establishment; with the discipline went good comradeship.

For the women, all of them Métis or Indian, life was humdrum. "We never saw anybody," Eloise, one of Dr. McLoughlin's daughters later commented. The seclusion of the women may have been in part due to their shyness, but more than likely it was the result of the military bearing of the fort. Family life was not a recognized part of the Hudson's Bay establishment, but in the small posts it was an accepted fact. In Fort Vancouver, the Company pattern was blown up in scale. Women did not belong.

The first white women to visit were American missionaries' wives, Mrs. Spalding and Mrs. Whitman, who came in 1836 and stayed with the McLoughlin family. Women from another world must have been exciting fare for the Fort Vancouver wives. However, these women were only visitors and did not stay long. The same year, the Hudson's Bay Company official chaplain, the Reverend Herbert Beaver, and his wife, Jane, arrived. This woman felt herself too good to associate with the women of the Fort because their marriages had not been solemnized by the church. Her snobbish, unkind manners caused Amelia great pain.

Amelia's father, William Connolly, had retired from the fur trade the year after Amelia had left Fort St. James. Connolly took his family to his birthplace at Lachine, to settle there in retirement. He introduced his Cree wife, Suzanne, as his lawful wife to the principal people of the town, and she was known as Mrs. Connolly. Then, suddenly, Connolly married his cousin, Julia Woolrich of Montreal. He sent Suzanne to the Red River Settlement, and placed her in a convent there.

Not only was Amelia disturbed by her father's desertion of her mother, but she now had to consider herself as illigitimate. And what of her own children? Her marriage to James Douglas was the same kind of marriage as her parents' had been, "according to the custom of the country", which meant with the consent of the parents of the bride, and with some token of good faith by the groom in the form of a dowery paid to the parents. Might James Douglas someday renounce his wife, Amelia, to marry a white girl?

Mrs. Beaver's stupid snobbery on top of her father's re-marriage caused Amelia many anxious thoughts. However, James Douglas was not a William Connolly, and in February, 1837, the Reverend Mr. Beaver united James and Amelia in holy matrimony, according to the rites of the Church of England.

The senior officers of the Hudson's Bay Company objected strongly to any unfair treatment of Indian wives. Governor Simpson, who had a Métis wife, had set a bad example by marrying his cousin, Frances, and then bringing her out to the Northwest. William Connolly had lost no time in imitating his superior officer by marrying his cousin and discarding his faithful Suzanne. James Douglas was in agreement with the majority of the officers in considering his first marriage binding, even if it had been without benefit of clergy. When he later became Chief Factor, he was very firm in insisting that his subordinates honour their marital obligations, no matter how they had been contracted.

The sixteen years at Fort Vancouver passed, for Amelia, as if in a dream. The Beavers could not stick it, and after a year, returned to England. There were no other outside interruptions to disturb the domestic flow of family life in the fort. Although some of the older boys were sent away to school in the east or to Britain, the young children and the girls were educated in the Fort. In all, Amelia gave birth to thirteen babies, but only six survived childhood. Alec, her eldest, a bright little fellow, was killed in an unlucky accident. James Douglas had been away. When he returned, he grabbed up his little son and, in fun, threw him in the air. When the father caught the child again, the boy cried out in pain: "Oh Father, you've hurt me." He died soon after, probably from a broken neck. We are told that the parents were broken-hearted, but that the anguish felt by Amelia was bearable in comparison with the remorse her husband felt. Amelia had need of all her tact and understanding to help console him.

The women at Fort Vancouver became expert at tailoring European fashions. They had servants to do their cooking and cleaning, but the tailoring was to them a fine achievement requiring new skills which, blended with their native talent with a needle, brought much satisfaction. Nursing cares, including midwifery, also fell to their capable hands. During Amelia's early years at Fort Vancouver, there was a bad epidemic of typhus which carried off scores of whites and thousands of Indians. One of the Douglas babies contracted the disease, but survived. Amelia apparently did not suffer from typhus, but she had continual poor health while at Fort Vancouver, from fever and ague, especially in spring when the waters were high. Her illness was probably malarial, for when she moved to the pleasantly dry climate of Victoria, her health was restored.

Except when the fur brigades arrived each year, the Fort Vancouver community lived quietly under the capable command of Dr. McLoughlin, "The White Headed Eagle". Life went along so evenly, in fact, that Amelia and the other women were scarcely aware that revolutionary changes were taking place outside the community, almost within sight of the walls of the fort.

American missionaries were bringing in settlers to Oregon. Gradually a clamour mounted throughout the whole of the United States, demanding the entire Pacific Coast — "fifty-four/forty or fight." This included much of the area controlled by the Hudson's Bay Company. Even the president of the United States, James K. Polk, took up the cry, and said in his inaugural address, March 1845: "Our title to the country of the Oregon is clear and unquestionable, and already are our people preparing to perfect that title, by occupying it with their wives and children."

Again it was the old argument of colony versus fur trading. The Hudson's Bay Company men were too few in number to contend with the 3,000 American settlers who claimed the Oregon lands. The "wives and children" won. The boundary between British and American territory was set that year at the Forty-ninth Parallel. Oregon thus became a part of the United States, and the Hudson's Bay Company lost a great domain, including its base at Fort Vancouver. Dr. McLoughlin who disagreed with some of the policies of the Company resigned his position as Chief Factor and remained in Oregon. James

Douglas was promoted to his place.

Douglas had climbed the ladder by hard work and attention to duty. He had come to Fort Vancouver originally as a clerk-accountant. A few years later, he was promoted to Chief Trader and in 1840, he was made Junior Chief Factor. During these years, he made a number of long trips — an eight-month journey to York Factory; up the Pacific Coast to Alaska to arrange the take-over of the Russian fur posts; to California to confer with the Spanish Governor of Mexico; up the Pacific Coast again, this time with Governor Simpson; and to Vancouver Island to choose a site for the new Hudson's Bay Company headquarters.

When the final boundary line was drawn at the forty-ninth parallel, the Company was ready, for a new depot had been built and named "Victoria" for the new Queen of England. James Douglas was the Chief Agent for the Hudson's Bay Company in the Western Division — the new name for the old Columbia Division.

When the Douglases left Fort Vancouver, they went overland to Puget Sound, and there, according to the *Nisqually Journal,* Friday, June 1, 1849: "Mr. Douglas and family . . . embarked after an early dinner and the schooner dropped down with the tide in the afternoon."

.   .   .

In the beginning, life was not too different for Amelia at Fort Victoria from what it had been at Fort Vancouver, except that she was now the senior lady of the fort. Apart from sixteen acres of Company farmland, everything was within the Fort and its twenty-foot stockade. There was the large mess room, the open fireplace, the long table in the middle. Douglas maintained the traditions of Fort Vancouver, the refinements of civilization, good manners, good conversation. It was still a man's world, but the men ate from spotless linen, with "clean" knives and forks. There were decanters of wine, Windsor chairs to sit on — "everything from Europe." Douglas, now about forty-six, is described as "a handsome specimen of nature's nobleman, tall, stout, broadshouldered, muscular with a grave bronzed face yet kindly withal —"[3] The adjective "stout" apparently meant "sturdy".

The mess room served every purpose; church, councils, dances, entertainments, funerals, library and reading room. A large bell tolled for weddings, deaths, fires, and warnings, as well as for meals, when "it was assisted by a chorus of curs".

The Douglas family lived in one corner of the main building, off the mess room. The Songhees, a neighbourhood tribe of Indians, were uncertain in temper, and so the fort children were not allowed to roam. Life inside the fort was secure but horribly muddy. Amelia and the other mothers must have longed for days when they might roam the hills among the pines, smell the sea, and glimpse the white-capped mountains of the Olympic Range, across the Straits of Juan de Fuca. In the first days at Victoria there were probably quite a few tears shed for the memories which the mountains recalled.

During the first year, there were about 200 people in or near Fort Victoria; eight years later, the number had increased only to 800. The Hudson's Bay Company, fearing for its life and property, had asked for and received under its charter, sole possession of Vancouver Island, and the right to colonize. However, colonization and fur trading are not complementary, and the Company was not strenuous in its efforts to bring in settlers. It was the Red River Settlement all over again. The plan was to provide a place of retirement for Company officers and men, and their families. It is hard to guess what might have happened if the gold rush had not struck. Gold on the Fraser turned Victoria overnight into a metropolis. Land values soared from £1 an acre to £100. Miners poured in, followed by merchants. There were canoes, skiffs, carts, vans, and express wagons constantly loading and unloading freight, human and otherwise. All was excitement, and the Douglases were in the midst of it.

For Amelia, the excitement and clamour were bewildering. She had taken only a few, first, uncertain steps outside the fort, the only life she knew, when the onrush swamped her. Only a year or so before the gold rush began, James Douglas had moved his family into a house of their own, on property he had bought from the Company, south of James Bay. It was described as a "very grand affair the most up-to-date house in the colony". We are told that it was built of logs, and not of redwood lumber, as some of the later houses were, and that it was commodious, with wide verandahs, a charming informal garden and a stretch of greensward leading down to the pretty little Bay. The house burned long ago, but its site is beside the parking lot near the Provincial Legislative buildings.

We get a splendid glimpse at this period of Amelia's life, from Dr. John Helmcken who married Cecelia, the oldest Douglas child. Dr. Helmcken, who later became Speaker of the Legislature in the new colony, had come to Vancouver Island as surgeon for the Hudson's Bay Company. He immediately fell in love with Cecelia who was then about sixteen. In his own words:

> I had fallen in love with Cecelia . . . so I spent much of my courting there, particularly whilst the Douglas' remained in the fort. . . . Miss Cameron, Mr. Douglas' niece had arrived and was domiciled there and played propriety. The courtship was a very simple affair — generally in the evening when we had chocolate and singing and what not — early hours kept. Mrs. Douglas at this time was a very active woman, energetic and industrious but awfully jealous [of her daughters' beaux] She was very kind to outsiders and visited them when ill and in fact nursed them more or less. . . . The young Douglas' were very shy and very pretty . . . and were looked after by their Mother with sharpness. . . .

The end of Amelia's era of seclusion had come, and even her husband could no longer protect her from the snubs of people who felt superior. Helmcken wrote that Amelia ". . . and Mrs. Staines did not chum at all — there being too much uppishness about the latter, she being the great woman. . . ." In spite of her uppishness, Mrs. Staines, who was the Company Chaplain's wife, was considered a remarkably capable school teacher.

There were other slights. Perhaps the nastiest was by the famed journalist, Amor de Cosmos, who attacked Douglas through his wife: "Were a good Indian agent required it would not be too difficult to discover a suitable incumbent, qualified by long experience and intimate associations."[4] Society had begun to frown on white men who married Indian women.

In the early years there was little company to entertain, but the Douglas house was always open to all comers. Another young man who found himself at home in the Douglas living room, Arthur Bushby, wrote in January, 1859:

> They begged me to make myself quite at home which I did & before dinner set to and tuned the piano — dined quite en famille. Mrs. Douglas came to dinner. Seems a good old sole [sic] — Had music in the evening & a good deal of chaff with the girls. Had a polka with Agnes & she gave me a lot of toffey for my cold which unfortunately I left behind — the girls have promised to bind all my music with silk — & made me promise to go there on Saturday . . . the two girls are romping sort of things.

Bushby began to fall in love with Agnes, but when he asked for her hand, Douglas refused. According to the young man, the father objected because ". . . his daughter & I were both so young . . . & my income so small (why the d- does he not make it larger?)" Bushby, a young spark, was acting as private secretary for Judge Matthew Begbie on his first circuit in British Columbia. Decision about the marriage was deferred for a year. Although young Bushby had moments of indecision, Agnes, whom he described as "a stunning girl — black-eyed & hair & larky like the devil", finally won, and they were married the following year.

All the Douglas girls were handsome and spirited, and Amelia had good reason to be "jealous" of her daughters in a frontier world where there were far too many men and not enough girls. On weekends, riding parties were organized and James Douglas and his daughters, and other ladies of the community, would ride with husbands and admirers. Amelia evidently did not ride with the party, but as the roads improved, she enjoyed driving in her carriage, and did so until her old age. To the girl who had ridden 1,000 miles over the mountains on horseback, riding was no novelty, and perhaps, at middle-age, it seemed a little strenuous. Her last two children were born after she moved to Victoria. Martha, her thirteenth, was born in 1854. John

Helmcken seemed to think it odd that she never went riding, but surely he did not expect her to romp like her teenage daughters?

Besides the riding, there were card parties and balls or "dancing parties". With the naval base close by at Esquimalt providing a fluctuating supply of young men, parties were frequent. Sometimes the navy improvised and played host for a ball. The pursuit of pleasure was sometimes difficult, for it could not have been too jolly to escort a lady home ". . . through mud nearly up to the knees". Moreover, even in 1858, there were only about twenty unmarried women on the whole Island which made competition somewhat fierce. However, by this time, Amelia had the comfort of knowing that her two eldest girls were safely married, the third was spoken for, and Martha was still only a child.

In the early years at Victoria, Douglas assumed the two separate offices of Chief Factor for the Company, and Governor of the Crown Colony, representing Her Majesty; his duties involved him mainly with Company affairs, a small amount of land settlement, and disputes with the Indians. These disputes he handled with courage, firmness and sagacity. Amelia was pleased, and Cecelia's husband, Dr. Helmcken, wrote:

> Douglas was a cold brave man, he had entered an Indian's lodge to seize the murderer of Mr. Black. . . . There was something grand and majestic about Douglas — in the first place he was broad and powerful and had a wooden hard face when necessary, which said quite plainly, I am not afraid.

.   .   .

After the miners surged in, however, affairs became too complex to be handled by the Company's Chief Agent, and so Douglas resigned his position with the Hudson's Bay Company and, in 1858, he became Governor of the two Crown Colonies, Vancouver Island and the mainland "Gold Colony". His firm rule of the turbulent, mining country prevented anarchy and war between the whites and the Indians.

As Douglas grew with the job, so did Amelia with hers as first lady. The Douglases made themselves available to all who needed them. Amelia's years of community life at Fort Vancouver gave her an understanding of how necessary it was for people to cooperate. She realized, instinctively, that if the settlement were to prosper and endure, the women and children must make the land theirs. The Company had provided churches and schools, but the care of the sick and needy was left to chance. It was among these that Amelia made her real contribution to the new Colony.

Such service usually goes on quietly, unnoticed and unrecorded. However, we do get hints of her activities in old letters and memoirs — helping the Indians, remembering the poor, nursing the sick. There is also an unexplained letter from Amelia's sister who had become a Sister of Mercy. The letter was written in May, 1859, from Montreal, and talked of the anticipation that several sisters of the Order would be sent to Vancouver Island for missionary and hospital work. The germ of the idea must have originated with Amelia, who knew the need. However, the plan did not materialize. Teaching nuns of the Order of St. Ann were sent instead. Amelia carried on her work as best she could, by personal kindness and by example. In her obituary in the Colonist, 1890, was the phrase ". . . ministering to thousands". What greater contribution could a woman make?

She became Lady Amelia on the day James Douglas was given the rank of Knight Commander of the Bath when he retired as Governor in 1863. A grand banquet was held in the theatre by the people of Victoria with 200 men attending — the ladies looking on from the balcony. Later, at New Westminister, a lawn fête was held, followed by a banquet. Lady Douglas attended this banquet, and was presented with a medallion of her husband. This was the high, dramatic moment of Amelia's life. She, the little Métis who had been snubbed by the fine, white ladies, even by the wives of clergymen, was now Lady Amelia. Amelia was no snob, but she would not have been human if she had not felt a certain honest satisfaction in her role as the first lady of the Colony.

In his address at the banquet at New Westminister, Sir James said: "Envy and malevolence may be endured but your kindness overwhelms me." These words go far to explaining the kind of people James Douglas and Amelia were.

The Douglas family life was close-knit and affectionate. Many of the Douglas family letters have been preserved, but only one written by Amelia, and it was to thank someone for a gift. However, she is frequently mentioned in the letters of the others.

After Sir James retired, and after his grand tour of Europe (Amelia did not accompany him), he settled down happily at James Bay with his eight acres of garden. He kept himself busy with business affairs, overseeing his estate, reading. He was now probably the wealthiest man in the Colony. And he wrote letters. One daughter, Jane, was now living in England; son James was sent to England to school; and later, the youngest child, Martha, was sent abroad.

When Martha set out for England, Amelia was heart-broken. James wrote to his daughter:

> I hurried up from the garden gate where I bade you adieu, to comfort mamma, and found her in a burst of uncontrollable grief – I caught her in my arms, but her heart was full – she rushed wildly into your room and casting herself upon the bed, lay sobbing and calling upon her child. Mamma was at length exhausted and then I poured on words of consolation.

Martha was the youngest of Amelia's thirteen babies, and the last of her family to leave home. The house was empty. However, although all her daughters had left, there were grandchildren to console her. A few years before, when Agnes had given birth to her first born, Douglas wrote:

> I hurried to James Bay with the tidings. You may imagine better than I can describe Mamma's feelings, as she sat laughing & crying at one and the same time. She is now more composed & would like to pay you a visit . . . I suppose Arthur [Bushby] is three inches taller since the birth of his boy. I wonder if he has yet thought of getting him enrolled in the B.C. Volunteers for I fancy there is

about him, the making of a first rate trooper. Someday ere long, I must take a run up to see the little rogue. They all wish to know who he is like, to ladies in general a most interesting subject of enquiry.

Grandparents evidently do not change over the centuries.

And there were poor Cecelia's children. Cecelia and Amelia had attended some open air ceremony, and had both been chilled. Then according to Cecelia's husband, John Helmcken:

> Very little notice was taken of this, and my wife kept about as well as she was able, but soon pneumonia resulted and in a few days, the end unhappily came, after having given birth to a boy [the infant died]. . . . Mrs. Douglas and, I think Mrs. Irving, nursed her well, but I was but little home and probably underrated the extent of the disease.

.   .   .

Amelia herself became ill in the late '60's. ". . . Lady Douglas being now a great invalid." The family was baffled by her illness, for her husband wrote: "We might fancy her quite well if she would make an effort." The cause of her illness may have been emotional, for her brother, John Connolly, had brought suit against the heirs of William Connolly and Julia Woolrich. The action was instituted in Montreal in 1864, and judgement given in 1867. It was a famous test case and much talked of. The story was on every lip. The whole affair was incredibly distasteful and embarrassing for Amelia, and yet she was relieved and happy to see her mother vindicated. Sir James, writing to one of the lawyers, expressed his own feelings without mincing:

> I have to thank you for a copy of the Montreal Transcript, containing the judgement on the Connolly case — John is a noble fellow and has bravely won his rights, alone and unsupported by his family; but to me the most pleasing part is, that he has vindicated his mother's good name; and done justice to the high-minded old lady, now at rest in the peaceful grave, — and worthy of a kinder husband than poor Connolly.

The judgement in favour of the Connolly children set a precedent, for the Court found ". . . that there was a legal marriage existing between the late Mr. Connolly and the Indian woman" and also that ". . . a community of property existed between him and his Indian wife from 1803, the date of their marriage." In other words, the laws of Canada validate a marriage performed "according to the custom of the country" when, in the absence of any clergy, the vows were formally recognized by the bride's parents.

Shortly after the trial was over, Douglas wrote: "Mamma absent on a visit, her health improving," and at a card party, "Mamma in excellent spirits and enjoyed it immensely," and again, "Mamma is in excellent health though she will not think so. Up every morning at 6, she hustles about till breakfast time. The chickens now fill her mind with anxious care, and we look grave and appear to sympathize if mishaps occur. To laugh would be a serious offence."

Soon Amelia began stepping out again. "Mamma is in very good health and moved about with her normal activity, believing that nothing would go on prospering without her close attendance."

The Douglases held open house on New Year's Day and on one occasion, Sir James reported: "The calls on the first lasted from 10 o'clock till dewey eve. I was thoroughly tired out, and glad when the reception came to an end. Mamma was nicely got up, and won all hearts by her kindness and geniality."

A few years later, Sir James wrote of his wife: "Mamma wore her fawn silk, white and blue shawl and white bonnet — looked wonderfully young for a lady of 62." Although some of the young gallants, fresh from England, may have thought the ladies of Victoria none too fashionable, Sir James found no fault in Amelia.

Douglas lived to see the confederation of British Columbia with Canada. His opinions on this hot subject were unrecorded, but it was he, a decade earlier, who had planned a road over the mountains from New Westminster to the Red River. A railway from the east to the Pacific, he most certainly would have welcomed.

When Sir James Douglas died suddenly in August, 1877, from heart failure, Victoria turned out en masse for the funeral. After his death, Amelia retired from public and social affairs, but continued to live at James Bay, and certainly continued her undramatic, unrecorded "ministrations to thousands". Her youngest daughter Martha, who had married Dennis Harris, came to live with her, and the big house rang again with the voices of children.

Then, ten years after her husband's death, when Amelia was seventy-five years old, she gave a grand party. According to the *Daily Colonist* of January, 1887:

The Assembly Hall was comfortably filled with Lady Douglas' guests last evening, and to say the least, the affair was most enjoyable.

The hall was beautifully decorated with bunting, and evergreens and flags were festooned, forming several arches, and dividing the hall into two sections.

The scene was a brilliant one – a midsummer night's dream. Not until 4 o'clock in the morning did the last guests depart, and the one opinion voiced was that the ball was the social event of the season.

And one young lady[5] wrote in her diary: "Lady Douglas' ball – fine night – room very pretty and everything well done. Lots of funny people. My shoes went to pieces. We got home at 3.15 – felt very tired."

So, the curtain goes down on Amelia, the daughter of the "high-minded" Indian woman and the Hudson's Bay Company Chief Factor. Before the lights went out on Amelia's personal drama, she had shown that she could adopt the white man's customs, and carry them out well. She was a true blend of both cultures, and she was a colony builder.

Amelia died at Victoria in 1890. She was buried beside her husband in the Ross Bay cemetery overlooking the waters of Juan de Fuca and the white topped Mountains of the Olympic Range.

Of the six Douglas children, there is only one descendant left today bearing the name of Douglas, Miss Orsa Douglas[6] who, fittingly, is employed at the Legislative Buildings. There are many other descendants – McTavishes, Bullens, Harrises – but the proud name of this sept of the Douglas will survive only in the history books.

Within walking distance of the Legislative Buildings and the spot where the Douglases had their home, is Beacon Hill Park, which Sir James and Lady Amelia gave to the city of Victoria. Partly cultivated, partly wild, it extends to the Strait. From Beacon Hill mountain ranges can be seen at all points of the compass.

Emily Carr, the artist, whose family was among the first in the colony, grew up in the early Victoria. Her description of Beacon Hill Park as it was nearly a century ago, will easily describe the Park today.

> "The Hill itself was grassy, with here and there little thickets of oak scrub and clumps of broom. Beyond the Hill the land was heavily wooded. When you climbed to the top of Beacon Hill and looked around, you knew that the school geography was right after all and that the world really was round. Beacon Hill seemed to be the whole top of it and from all sides the land ran away from you and the edges were lost."[7]

The Park will forever remind the people of Victoria of the man and the woman who, more than any others, founded their city and the province. Amelia, in her quiet, unassuming way, probably did nearly as much as her famous husband to make the Colony triumph. This frontier community proved to be a strong base for women such as Selina Bompas and Martha Black, when they braved the Arctic.

Notes

1. Gustave Lanctot, *A History of Canada* (Toronto: 1963) p. 330.
2. Fort York (York Factory) is confused in the Douglas memoirs with Fort Churchill, but Connolly was never at Fort Churchill. Hudson's Bay Company Archives.
3. Author uncertain. For his description of Fort Victoria, see *Sir James Douglas* by Walter N. Sage (Toronto: 1930), p. 153.
4. As quoted by Marion B. Smith in "The Lady Nobody Knows", *British Columbia: a Centennial Anthology,* ed. by R.E. Watters (Vancouver, 1958), p. 478.
5. Miss Kathleen O'Reilly, niece of Sir Joseph Trutch, in her diary. British Columbia Archives.
6. There is one elderly surviving Douglas male in Britain — no heirs.
7. Emily Carr, *The Book of Small* (Toronto: 1942), p. 116.

Bibliography

Bushby, Arthur. "Journal", unpublished, B.C. Archives, Victoria.

Carr, Emily. *The Book of Small.* Toronto: 1942.

Coats and Gosnel. "Sir James Douglas", *Makers of Canada.* Toronto: 1928.

Douglas Letters. B.C. Archives, Victoria.

Helmken Letters. B.C. Archives, Victoria.

Letters and Clippings in B.C. Archives.

Lugrin and Hosie. "Lady Douglas", *The Pioneer Women of Vancouver Island.* Victoria: 1928.

Nesbitt, James K. *Daily Colonist,* p. 6, May 13, 1962.

Sage, Walter N. *Sir James Douglas.* Toronto: 1930.

Smith, Marion B. "The Lady Nobody Knows", *British Columbia, A Centennial Anthology.* Vancouver: 1958.

7

Charlotte Selina Bompas

Whether the wilderness is
real or not
depends on who lives there.

Margaret Atwood[1]

Although Charlotte Selina Bompas was tiny, she was durable. She had to be tough to travel into the Mackenzie River country, as she did in 1874. Hardy and enduring as the fur traders and explorers were, none was more invincible than Mrs. Bompas or her missionary husband, William.

On the heels of the fur traders, the first missionaries had penetrated the whole Mackenzie Valley by 1862, and had travelled as far as the Yukon River. Even a few white women, daughters of fur traders and married to fur traders, had come to the Mackenzie River posts by the time of the Bompases.

The education of their children, white and Métis, had always been a problem for fur traders in remote areas. The Hudson's Bay Company actively encouraged missionaries to go into the

northern posts for this purpose, and often engaged school-
teachers for the larger posts. It was a considered policy. If the
Company could promise some kind of education, academic and
religious, for the children of the Company's servants, then those
servants were more likely to be satisfied to stay put. A similar
situation exists today; the Canadian government tempts
teachers and government officials to the far north by providing
good housing and good schools.

William Carpenter Bompas, an Englishman, first came to Fort
Simpson on the Mackenzie River on Christmas Day, 1865, and
for the next eight years, he had a roving commission as missionary for the Anglican Church. He covered vast distances, from
the Peace and Athabaska Rivers to the mouth of the Mackenzie,
and over the Mackenzie Mountains into the Yukon River territory. He travelled in all kinds of weather, from the bitterest of
Arctic winters to the muggiest of Arctic summers, and moved
by dog team, canoe, snowshoe, and on foot. He ministered not
only to the isolated white people in the lonely fur trading posts,
but to the wandering tribes of Indians and Eskimos.

In 1873, he was recalled to England where he was conse-
crated Bishop of the Diocese of Athabaska, a territory which
took in the Athabaska and Mackenzie drainage systems, as well
as that of the upper Yukon – in other words, most of Alberta,
the Northwest Territories and the Yukon.

During this three months in England, he again met his cousin,
Charlotte Selina Cox, called "Nina" by her family and "Lena"
by the Bishop. Bompas was forty, and Lena a few years older.
In her youth, she had been a beauty, with dazzling white skin
and blue eyes that did not lose their sparkle even in old age. In
her forties, she was still good-looking and full of fun.

She had been educated in Italy. Her father, a London doctor
who suffered from asthma, had moved his family to the heights
above the Bay of Naples where he hoped to find relief for his
ailment. There, the three daughters and the son were given the
best educations that could be found in Italy. Besides music and
art and literature, there were also gay parties, picnics and
excursions. At Lena's coming-out ball, she had danced with the
King of Naples.

Lena was living with her sister, Emma, at Torquay, England, in 1874, when her cousin, William Bompas, asked her to marry him. He had asked her years before, but then she had put him off.

When young, she had had no interest in missions and said of herself:

> My brother, who was Vicar of Bishop's Tawton, Devon-shire, used to hold missionary meetings at the Vicarage, and I remember thinking them the dullest affairs, and the clergymen who addressed us . . . I looked upon as the most dismal old slow coaches it was anyone's unhappy fate to attend to.[2]

By the time she was forty, Charlotte Selina had changed her attitudes, and she now found herself fascinated by William and his missionary work.

"Are you going to the North alone, William?" She asked him.

"That depends on you, Lena?"

After she married William, her life was turned upside down. Instead of the polished, aesthetic milieu of the cultivated well-to-do, Lena found herself thrust into hardships of cold, hunger, fatigue, and loneliness; nevertheless, she stuck by William in his remote dioceses and became one of the most resolute of social workers in the mission field. Not only did she faithfully serve the Christian cause as teacher and nurse among the native Americans, but she was invaluable as a self-appointed promoter. Through her efforts, she was to raise thousands of dollars for the Northwest missions.

Moreover, she always had enough sense of humour to see herself as others might see her — as one of the "dismal old slow coaches".

Selina and her husband left England in May, 1874, three months after William Bompas had arrived. For William, the time had been a flurry of activity, conferences with the Church Missionary Society, consecration as Bishop, courtship, and marriage. Although Lena was self-willed and impulsive, she soon learned that her husband was self-willed and determined, and that he had one unshakeable purpose — to live out his life in his beloved north among the Indians and the fur traders.

To some, the far north is a cruel, fearsome enemy, but to a man like Bishop Bompas, it presents a challenge. Then, too, Bompas had a rapport with the Indians and Eskimos; not only did they love him, but he loved them.

This was the man that Selina married, and true frontierswoman that she was, she adopted the life of the north as her own. Until the Bishop died in 1907, she spent most of those thirty years on the Mackenzie or Yukon Rivers, often hungry, cold and lonely, but never complaining. Even at times of extreme famine, when her husband sent her "outside" to Winnipeg or to England, she returned as soon as she thought possible.

During the years from 1874 to 1906, she wrote sprightly, detailed letters to her sister, Emma, to her family and to her friends. The letters are full of anecdotes and household concerns, and as a picture of life in the north, they are a lucid treasure.

.   .   .

The journey from England to Winnipeg took two months; from New York, the Bompases travelled by train via Chicago to St. Paul, and then by flat-bottomed boat down the Red River. The remainder of the journey to Fort Simpson on the Mackenzie River, took two more months in open boats by the old Voyageur's Highway.

"I had come prepared for intense cold," wrote Selina Bompas;

> and we were destined to endure tropical heat. All up the Saskatchewan, Stanley and English Rivers the banks slope down like a funnel, and the July and August sun scorches with the vertical rays the heads of the travellers. We were seated in open boats, each with a crew of ten or twelve men, who spread our sails when the wind was fair, and took them in when the wind failed us. Eighty-six was on some of those days our average temperature, and I had come provided with the thickest of serge dresses, as none of my friends realized the possibility of anything but frost and cold in these northern regions.

The Bishop evidently did not think to warn his wife that the

Saskatchewan River runs through the same latitudes as England, but even if he had, he might not have been believed.

"Besides this," she continued,

> we had to encounter swarms of mosquitoes, crowding thick around us, penetrating our boots and stockings, and invading our robabou soup and pemmican. I remember the bliss it was in those days in camping time to escape from the rest of the party, and getting rid of boots and stockings, to sit with my feet and legs in the cool water to soothe the intolerable irritation of the mosquito bites.

The long journey by way of Lake Athabaska, Slave River, Great Slave Lake, and some hundreds of miles on the Mackenzie, was tedious and they were often short of provisions. Lena felt herself "on the point of knocking up" before they arrived at Fort Simpson, but here the welcome from the people at the Fort and the Mission was so genuine, and the beauty of the river so entrancing, that she quickly put the discomforts of the journey out of mind.

Fort Simpson had been a fur-trading post since 1804, and the Hudson's Bay Company had been established there since 1821. The site of the Fort on an island at the confluence of the Liard and the Mackenzie Rivers was a beautiful one. The great, solemn Mackenzie, here about a mile wide, flows on its way with mighty purpose for its last thousand miles to the northern sea.

The Hudson's Bay Fort was a large one for it served as depot for most of the Mackenzie area. The main building, built of huge squared logs, had twenty rooms, with the traditional great hall in the centre, off which were bedrooms, kitchen, and a room for visiting Indians. Outside the Fort were a few scattered huts, occupied by Métis and Indian servants, and two churches, Roman Catholic and Anglican, with their mission houses.

The Bompases arrived at Fort Simpson, September 21, and Mrs. Bompas writes:

> It was very exciting to catch sight of it at last – this great goal which we had so toiled after and suffered so much to attain! There it was! First, the Fort on a high embankment, some houses and tents clustering near, and

about a quarter of a mile distant, the cathedral! A pretty, really pretty, little church with spire all complete, of wood, of course, and native built.

As they drew near, they were spotted and immediately the red Hudson's Bay Company flag was hoisted. All the people of the Fort, the clerks, officers, wives, children, the carpenter, blacksmith and schoolmaster came down to the beach to greet them.

The greeting was so whole-hearted that it was some little time before Mrs. Bompas learned that the post was dangerously short of food, and that a few extra mouths to feed almost created a disaster. The men of the fort had to be sent away to provide for themselves, so that the few provisions left could be given to the women and children. One day came when there was no food left, but on that day, two Indians brought in fresh meat, and so the ever-optimistic Lena writes: "From that moment the supplies have never failed. As surely as they got low, so surely would sledges appear unexpectedly bringing fresh supplies." There were days to come, however, when the Mackenzie River inhabitants, white and Indian, literally ate their shoes.

For a year or more, the Bompases shared the mission house with the Reeves and their children. Reverend H. D. Reeve was in charge of the mission at Fort Simpson. The arrangement suited the Bompases well, otherwise Lena would have been left alone for months on end, while her husband moved about his enormous diocese.

Lena immediately set to work to organize her household. Because she had no cupboards, she had to arrange her provisions, her year's supplies, in the attic. She was not too well off for provisions, for during the journey from Winnipeg to Fort Simpson, the flour bag had to be opened when supplies became short, to feed the boatmen. The bag of rice had got wet and much of it had to be thrown away, and the remainder was unpleasant, indeed, according to Lena, "very nasty". Also, at Fort Simpson, the Bompases discovered that the main grocery box had been left behind, and they would not see it again until the following year. However, small presents of food turned up at the mission house – such as twelve pounds of good rice, a little coffee, some candles, a small keg of butter. They had their own tea and sugar. Lena found that by baking once a week, using five pounds of flour, she could make the bread last throughout the week with a little for all; the schoolteacher, catechist and servants included.

The Hudson's Bay Company provided them with meat and fish, for a price, and on condition that they did not trade with the Indians for fur. These provisions — mostly moosemeat which really became their staple diet — they ate as stew, for breakfast, dinner and supper. There were no vegetables. Lena soon observed, too, that her craving for fat had increased enormously. Only a few months earlier she had watched with disgust while Indians ate bread with a lump of moose fat, but now she felt that she could do the same with satisfaction.

With her household organized, she turned her attention to the little school class of Indian children who came each afternoon. She taught them singing and calisthenic exercises. One wonders at the amazement of these children of the wild, watching the tightly-corseted, over-dressed woman waving her arms in the air, bending and stooping with no obvious purpose. Before entering the schoolroom which was a part of the mission house, she made the children wash their faces and hands and comb their hair. Soon she was called affectionately by the title of "Yalti Betsani" which was Slavé for "Bishop's wife". She mentions no white pupils at this time, but only a few years later, some of the children of Chief Factor J. S. Camsell were sent to the Anglican mission school for the early grades. Charles Camsell who later became Deputy Minister of Mines for the Federal Government, and Commissioner of the Northwest Territories, remembered both the Bompases with respect and affection.

.   .   .

Bishop Bompas set out on a southern tour of his diocese on December 8, 1874, with the intention of being absent all winter. At Christmas, Lena wrote in her letter-journal that it seemed hard to believe that she was married at all. She kept busy, however, and began making Christmas preparations with gusto. Her grand effort was to decorate a Christmas tree for all the children of the colony, with a present for each one, white or Indian. Many of the gifts — little woolly lamb with black eyes, dolls painted and dressed, puppets, aprons and leggings — she made herself; and under her direction some of the men made dog whips, drums, balls and workcases. There were forty presents in all. Her greatest difficulty was to find candles, but this was solved when the chief officer at the Fort sent her six or eight pounds of grease, while the blacksmith made her some little tin moulds. With these, she made a number of candles large enough to burn for a half-hour. The children, white, Métis and Indian, were enraptured, but no more than the Indian mothers who squatted on the floor in a huddle, astonished and delighted. After all the presents were given, tea and biscuits were passed, and the schoolchildren sang some of the carols which Lena had taught them.

Her other big effort was a Christmas dinner for twelve old Indian wives, "dear old things", who came dressed in their best. Lena had laid out a table in the schoolroom with linen cloth, knives and forks, but the unaccustomed cutlery proved too much for the Indian women who soon resorted to fingers. The menu was simple, moosemeat and rabbit, but Lena surprised them all by producing a plum pudding. After tea was served, she indicated to them that they might light their pipes which to these natives was the *beau geste.* At the end of the meal, one old woman grasped Lena's hand and voiced the feelings of all by saying simply, "Merci! Merci!"

After the traditional gaiety of the New Year's festivities, when the Hudson's Bay Company posts held open house throughout the whole Northwest, the colony at Fort Simpson settled down to endure the long, dark, cold winter. Lena did not complain about the cold, or the food, or the absence of her husband, but she regretted the lack of household candles and the grease for making them.

She rose at six in the morning, spent a little "quiet time" before the fire in the adjoining room, and then dressed in total darkness. She worried over the Bishop from whom she had had no word, and even more she worried about her family in England from whom she had not heard since she had left home, eight months before. She allowed herself one small lament: "I feel so lonely and desolate at times. Still, I have a definite aim in life. . . ." and she busied herself learning the Slavé language. She was handicapped in this because the mission servants were Cree. She also had a household problem because the Indian male servants would not take orders from a woman, and this was disruptive to the whole mission.

So the dark winter passed. She took into her household, for a few weeks, the two small motherless children of the carpenter, Brown, while he was away.

Then, one Sunday morning during breakfast, the sound of sleigh bells was heard. Sleigh bells were certainly not unusual, but these were not the familiar sound of Indian sleigh bells.

"These dogs have such smart tapis, they must be strangers," said the schoolmaster.

A moment later, in walked Bishop Bompas, "looking quite handsome, with white, snowy beard fringed with icicles". He was two months earlier than had been expected, and, great joy, he had brought the English mail which he dropped into Lena's lap.

With the Bishop home again, life became tranquil. The household problems straightened out; there was plenty of moose and deer meat which meant more grease for candles and soap.

Sundays, of course, were the busiest days; there was Sunday school, and three church services, one English and two Indian, and Lena played the harmonium for all three services. As well as playing for the hymns, she had a small choir. In addition to her church work and the day school, Lena was also called upon to visit the sick, and as with Bishop Bompas, she found she must learn to diagnose and treat illnesses.

On March 19, 1875, there was headline news. A cow had calved and there would be a little milk for the colony. The sun on the snow was so bright that the blinds had to be drawn. In spite of the snow glare, it was pleasant to be out again, and Lena sometimes walked through the woods, visiting Indian camps.

The main events of the spring were the mail packet from Athabaska, the coming of the wild geese, and the hauling of the next year's wood. Wood-hauling occupied the whole colony, and made a pleasant counterpoint to the usual activities, with sleigh bells ringing all hours of the day and the great stacks of wood rising beside the buildings. By May, the sun was so high that the snow melted quickly, and wild flowers began poking up through the snow. The mornings were clear and bright, and daylight lasted until nine. It was a busy, active time, and everyone was cheerful.

In the journal, Lena tells many little anecdotes of her Indian neighbours, simple, colourful stories which show how personally involved the Bompases had become. One such story will illustrate. One bright little girl of about ten, Jeannie du Nord, who was motherless, ran away from her aunt and uncle who were perhaps none too kind to her. She headed for the bush where she knew her father had a camp, and she did not return. Although it was not winter, the weather was still cold. When Lena heard about the missing child, she told the Bishop, who immediately put on his duffle socks and snowshoes and, organizing a search party, set out to look for her. Jeannie was found twelve miles away, alone, in her father's camp. She had made herself a fire, but had had nothing to eat for two days.

The search, however, cost the Bishop much agony, for he had not dressed for such a long tramp, and he returned wet and cold, and wracked with pain.

Lena was much attracted to the little girl, and hoped that she could bring her into her household, but Jeannie's family needed her. A few years later, the girl died from overwork and exposure.

The months passed on into years. Although Lena was not able to take Jeannie du Nord into her household, she soon found another Indian girl, Julie, whom she trained as a servant, and at the same time taught her English and the catechism. Lena usually had two or three little girls living under the Bompas roof, and these she taught a little of everything; sewing, housework, English and singing. The children came and left again, as the parents wished, usually without warning.

The Bishop's wife also tried to substitute for her husband during his long absences. She tried not to worry about him, but sometimes his journeys were more than even his sturdy physique could bear. On one occasion, he was brought back by a faithful Indian companion in a state of collapse. The Bishop had gone off with some Indian hunters but, on becoming ill, he turned back alone. When he was missed, one Indian set out to look for him, and found the Bishop lying in the snow. If he had been left a few minutes longer, he would have frozen to death.

Lena felt that the hardships of mission life were light compared to the long separations from her husband, but these long absences she filled with the care of children. The Bompases adopted a delicate, orphaned baby whom they called Jeannie, and this, added to her other responsibilities, kept Lena too busy to reflect.

.   .   .

In 1876, the Bishop decided to move his headquarters from Fort Simpson to Athabaska, but as he first had to travel north to the Peel River and the Yukon, it fell to Lena to do the packing and moving of the mission. Although she trained a succession of girls to help in the mission, few could be depended upon, and most of the work she had to do herself. She often felt herself to be ". . . general servant to the mission".

The five-hundred-mile trip to Athabaska was begun at the end of June in a brigade of open York boats; included were some Hudson's Bay Company craft. Mrs. Bompas with the infant Jeannie, was seated in the stern-sheets of the mission boat. While travelling in the wilderness, the brigade got under way at four in the morning, to the old cry of "Lève! Lève! Lève!", and breakfasted at eight on salted deer's tongues and tea. The day's journey usually lasted about sixteen hours. Dinner, at night, was of pemmican which Lena described as "very good". When the brigades reached any of the forts, the party, which included the Chief Factor from Fort Simpson and his family, was given the full hospitable treatment of the Hudson's Bay Company. These were welcome interludes.

Although Lena described her tent as "pretty and comfortable", there were nights when the rain beat in, dampening her clothes, and what was worse, the dogs crept in, too, out of the storm. The rain and the cold, however, were almost better than the constant irritation of the mosquitoes which "maddened" the poor infant.

The Hudson's Bay post of Fort Chipewyan on Lake Athabaska stood prominently on a high rock, and was surrounded by a score of wooden dwellings which were occupied by the Company employees. The mission house, however, was not finished, and Lena found temporary shelter in a small, one-room hut with an attic reached by ladder.

"I did the best I could," she wrote, "to make it habitable, and placed the cooking stove in the yard enclosed in a skin tent or lodge. I find this a great comfort, and wonder why people at home in want of space do not make use of lodges."

What must her family at home have thought?

So, Charlotte Selina Bompas, ever adjustable, began making a new life for herself and household. She had with her as a servant, an Indian girl, Theresa, from Fort Simpson. Theresa had been one of the problem children at Simpson, but the Bishop said that it was among these that the effort of training was most needed. She was spiteful and jealous, and she hated the little Indian baby that the Bompases had adopted. Lena dared not leave the two alone.

The baby was sickly and required constant attention, and Lena seemed to cherish her more on this account. In addition to Jeannie, Lena also took into her house a little Métis boy whose father was away.

Food, which was scarce, consisted mainly of fish or berries which were obtained from the Indians in exchange for some tea or an item of clothing. Lena had the luck to be adopted by a Cree woman who kept her supplied with duck, beaver, and berries, for which the payment was sometimes a trifle, sometimes a petticoat, and once a treasured, red shawl.

The shawl was an old one, and well worn, but for Lena it had happy memories. When she learned that the Cree woman wanted it, Lena got it out, looked it over, and then folded it up and put it away again. How could she give away such an old friend? But her conscience bothered her, and so she took out the shawl again and presented it to the Cree woman. Although Lena was sorry to part with it, she never made a better deal. The Cree woman loved the shawl, and wore it until it was tattered, faded, washed, mended and tattered again. She wore it low on her shoulders, with a red and yellow, silk handkerchief on her head. She was a clever, pretty woman, and looked stunning in the shawl. Sometimes her eight-year-old daughter wore it in imitation of her mother. Later, it was used to wrap a newborn infant, and still later, as a baby's hammock tied to the boughs of a tree.

At Christmas, Lena became ill. Her Indian maid abandoned her in fear, and Lena was left alone in her house with the ailing infant. Madeline, the Cree woman who had been given the shawl, then came to help her. Not only did she care for Lena, but she nursed the infant.

The relief of no longer being alone was all that Lena needed to start her on the way to recovery, but little Jeannie had tuberculosis, and died before the end of January.

The Bishop returned after an absence of seven months, just in time to bury the child.

Lena's health had become seriously impaired, partly as a result of her illness, partly from the loss of the infant, but mostly from lack of proper food. During the Bishop's long absences, she was at times living literally from hand to mouth, not knowing where the next meal would come from. The Bishop seemed to live outside the sphere of physical hardships, and was scarcely aware of such comforts as a full stomach, a warm bed, to say nothing of the luxury of hot soap and water. While travelling, he carried an iron cup, plate and knife, one or two kettles. For sleeping, all he asked was a space, six feet by two ". . . a hole in the snow, a corner of a boat, wigwam, or log hut".[4]

Lena said of him that his diet was at all times abstemious. "He was a fairly good cook and breadmaker, and loved to produce a dish good and savoury for his friends, although eschewing all such dainties himself."

Unlike her husband, Lena did not live in a world of mind and spirit. She was unable to take the physical strain. When Bishop Bompas realized how poor her health was, he decided that she should be sent out of the country for a time, to recuperate.

"These extended travels prove inconsistent with domestic life," he wrote, "and Mrs. Bompas, being left alone in the rigorous climate, has lost her health from exposure to cold and insufficient food."

Famine was a serious problem in the north. Indians and whites were so near starvation that they survived only by stewing bear skins or moosehides. "Imagine an English lady taking her supper off her muff," the Bishop had written lightly to relatives at home.

Although he might treat the famine humourously in a letter, William Bompas was deeply concerned, and was particularly anxious about the well-being of his wife. So, when spring break-up came, Lena unwillingly found herself on the way to Winnipeg. En route, she travelled part of the way with His Excellency Lord Dufferin, Governor-General of Canada, and Lady Dufferin.[5]

·   ·   ·

The following spring, 1879, Charlotte Selina Bompas was on her way back to the north. The first part of the journey this time was by ox-cart, over incredibly rutted roads and through great swamps. The route was more direct than by river, but uncomfortable and bumpy. The nights were spent under tents, and the same pattern of travel was maintained as by boat, even to the familiar morning alarm of "Lève! Lève!" After six weeks by ox-cart, Lena and her companion, Miss Morris, continued their journey by boat, to Fort Simpson.

Miss Morris was sent out by the Church Missionary Society as school-teacher and assistant to the Bishop. Like the Bishop's wife, she was often stranded for months at a time during his absences, but Lena found in her a welcome companion, and tried to make her comfortable. After a year or two with the Bompases, however, Miss Morris fades from history, a vague character.

During the years 1881-2, Bishop Bompas went north to a remote part of his diocese, and Lena induced him to take her part way with him. She found herself, therefore, established for a time at Fort Norman, a mission and fur post on the Mackenzie River, several hundred miles north of Fort Simpson, and within view of the Mackenzie Mountains. She had adopted another Indian baby named "Owinda", and also had under her care two Indian girls and a boy.

With the Bishop away, she again found herself assuming responsibilities for which she did not feel adequate. The mission house was very small and poorly built, but she did her best to make it homelike, although she referred to it as "our little halting place". For the church she made an altar cloth. She also modelled a font from some white clay found in the district. An Indian convert, Allan Hardisty, was in charge of the local mission, and Lena assisted him with the school.

There was a continual shortage of food and, although Lena was learning to live with this worry, there were times when fear almost crushed her and then: "In my loneliness and isolation I talk a great deal to these grand old mountains, and they say much to me."

Bishop Bompas was late in returning, and when he did, he was almost dead from starvation. He had been caught by ice on the river. Too impatient to wait until freeze-up, he had continued his way on a small raft. Finally he was forced to leave the river and walk, but the Indians with whom he was travelling lost their way, and they went for days without food. When the Bishop came within a day's walk of Fort Norman, he could proceed no farther, but sent the Indians, themselves too exhausted to carry him, for help. The weather was thirty below zero. How he survived, Lena could only marvel.

The winter was a severe one, but with "dear William" home, Lena could always cope. The small house, roughly built and cold was "rather a cram for six", but the Bishop, fretting because he had brought these hardships upon his wife, kept busy by filling chinks and cracks with moss and paper, and hanging deer skins and old sail along the walls. Sometimes they had memorable meals, such as the dish of dumplings of flour with fish roe, but more often they were on short rations — thirty pounds dried meat for the whole household per week, and this without a single vegetable "to help out".

In the spring, Lena wrote of her hopes of a visit to England, in a year or two, when she thought she would be able to persuade the Bishop to go with her. She longed for England and yet she was determined not to go without William.

The following year Lena stayed at Fort Resolution on Great Slave Lake. There are no letters or journals that survive this period, but Bishop Bompas was away for nine months; hearing that she was ill, he returned to spend two weeks with her, and was then off again to the far North among the Loucheux on the Yukon, where he planned to spend a year. It was only then that Lena consented to return to England alone. She had been away for nine years.

Lena took with her the baby, Owinda, but the child became ill and died in England. (Later Lena installed a beautiful oak font in the church at Fort Simpson in memory of Owinda.) Heartbreak over the loss of the child ruined the pleasure of her visit in England, and Lena was back in Winnipeg again in 1885, and then on her way to the Mackenzie River.

The second Riel Rebellion, however, interrupted all travel across the prairies, including the movement of supplies for the northern posts. Supplies that had been stored in the Hudson's Bay posts were stolen.

> Think what the want of flour, tea, and sugar must be; of warm clothing; of fish-nets, and twine to make them; of soap and candles; of tobacco; and worst of all, of powder and shot without which it is impossible for the Indian hunters to bring us our supplies of moose, deer, or wild goat's meat.

Lena wrote this from "outside" at Winnipeg, fully understanding the desperate conditions of those in the northern posts. She, herself, with five others who were en route for the northern mission fields, impatiently sat out the year in Winnipeg while those in the north barely survived.

.   .   .

In the spring of 1886, the six who had been stranded in Winnipeg set out, this time on the new railway, for Calgary, and they were much impressed by the smooth journey, the view of the prairies, and the interesting small towns which had so recently sprung up along the way — Moosomin, Moose Jaw, Swift Current, Medicine Hat — where stop-overs were made for meals. After her many journeys across the prairies by boat or ox-cart, the change was exciting for Lena. To travel in fastidious comfort as a lady across those same plains where she had eaten by camp fire, slept under tent, and fought off mosquitoes, was something of a marvel, and she fully appreciated it as such.

From Calgary to Athabaska Landing, via Fort Edmonton, they were back to the old grind of cart by day, tent by night, through alternate periods of intense cold and suffocating heat.

The year of 1886-7 was again a year of famine, desperate famine, in the Mackenzie River system. During the previous year, there had been a shortage of supplies from the civilized world, supplies such as flour, tea, twine for nets, and ammunition, but this year there was a shortage of game and fish, and whole families of Indians starved to death. There were reports of cannibalism.

Lena wrote,

> We have been living for some days on flour and barley soup, and potatoes, twice a day. We are four in family, and William gives us all the giant's share and takes so little himself. One hears terrible accounts of the Indians all around, all starving, no rabbits or anything for them to fall back upon. Here many of them hunt for rotten potatoes thrown away last fall. Oh! it is heartrending!

In the spring, Bishop Bompas again sent his wife out of the country. "I tell the Indians and everyone else," he wrote her, "that I have sent you home against your will."

The Indians missed her and kept asking for her, but Lena did not return again to the Mackenzie River. She was absent from the North for five years, most of which time was apparently spent with her nieces at Montreal. There were probably several reasons for the long stay, although there are no letters available from these years, and we can only guess.

The Bishop would not allow her back until he had been able to make Fort Simpson, the base of the northern missions, independent in the matter of provisions. He had had some such project in mind for some years, but the disruption caused by the Riel rebellion and the following year of extreme famine made the matter urgent. Perhaps the fact that he had had to send his wife out of the country helped the idea to jell.

Bompas had spotted the Peace River district as good farm land and, encouraged by the success of a mission-farm at Fort Vermillion, he established two more in the Grand Prairie area of the Peace, one at Dunvegan and one at Smoky River. As these farms began to produce, he established a mission farm at Fort Simpson. In June, 1890, he wrote:

> I hope they will bring oxen with them and by this means might cultivate a large field in summer, haul firewood in winter, and by obtaining a boat load of fish in the fall from Great Slave Lake, and dry fish in the summer, the mission might be nearly independent.

The north was changing. Ox teams were supplanting dog teams, and steam boats were supplanting York boats. The Bishop felt that a small steamboat would simplify many of his problems, but before he did anything about it, the Hudson's Bay Company had built one. It was on the first trip of the *Wrigley* that Mrs. Bompas had left Simpson in 1887.

There was a further reason why Charlotte Selina Bompas delayed her return, for the Mackenzie diocese was to be split again. The missions were prospering, and there were far too many for Bishop Bompas to manage. His original diocese, Athabaska, had an extent equal to that from London to Constantinople. A large section had already been cut from the south, and now the Yukon River district was to be split from the Mackenzie River district, with the Mackenzie Mountains as the dividing line.

After this split had taken place, Bishop Bompas moved over the mountains to his new, smaller diocese, composed of what is now Alaska and the Yukon. Although Alaska was, by then, United States territory, there were no American Missions there, and the Anglican Missions from Canada, like soldiers in guard boxes, were strung out along the Yukon River and its tributaries.

Bishop Bompas established his base mission at Forty Mile on the Yukon River, just within Canada, near the Yukon-Alaska border. Here, while waiting for Lena to return to him, he continued his Indian translations of prayer book and Bible and, for entertainment, he poured over a Syriac Testament which Lena had sent him. As for the spectacles which she had sent ". . . I shall bless the day you were born."

.   .   .

So, Charlotte Selina found him at Forty Mile on the Yukon River, a thousand miles in from the sea, surrounded by mountains, serene among his Indians, and in surprisingly good health. The Bompases had been separated for five years, and the reunion was ". . . between crying and laughing".

Lena had reached Forty Mile by boat from Seattle, four weeks on the Pacific, and three weeks puffing up the Yukon River. The Bishop had come down river in a small boat to meet her, and so they travelled the last week up-river together during the beautiful Arctic summer, stopping at pleasant coves for wood, or at Indian villages for salmon, with the rugged mountains surrounding them and the blue sky overhead.

The Bompases had found their home. Their health improved. The food supply was better. They liked the climate, the mountain air, and the country. Their missionary work progressed. Until now, Lena's journals had had something of the tone of a good soldier with a stiff, upper lip. Now, there was a ring of joy to them. She was sixty-two with greying hair and in need of spectacles, but her inner self was still youthful.

There were some problems. Miners and prospectors had already penetrated the area in 1892, five years before the Klondike Gold Rush, and their influence tended to corrupt the Indians. Although the Bompases felt that their main work was among the Indians, they could not ignore the miners, far from home and church and the influence of their own families. Lena immediately set about organizing a club room for these men with magazines, books, and a little music. The miners appreciated this and were touched by her thoughtfulness. On Christmas Day a deputation came to her and presented her with a large gold nugget to honour her for being the first white woman who had wintered so far north.

The mission house was soon made moderately cosy by the lining of the walls with cotton drill, which was pasted on as if it were wall paper and then painted red, ". . . the red gets sobered down by degrees and looks warm and our pictures look well on it". Besides, Lena had her chairs and little tables, carpets, bookshelves and "all the dear home treasures of pictures and photographs". From the windows, she could see the mountains, range beyond range.

Forty Mile was a mining centre rather than a fur centre. There were two well-equipped stores, a good lending library, six saloons, several restaurants, a theatre, two doctors, two blacksmiths, a watchmaker, and one dressmaker. And there were, unfortunately, several distilleries where whisky was sold to the Indians.

The mission house was soon full of children. There were always four to six school children "boarding" with the Bompases. Lena paints a lively picture of the daily winter chores of bringing water and wood into the house. First the Bishop chopped a hole in the ice of the river. Then he filled a pail for each of the five or six older girls. They ran with the pails to the kitchen where the water was dumped into water-kegs, close to the stove. After this, the girls ran to the woodpile and filled a little sled which the Bishop had made for the purpose. This was hauled to the house, and then the wood was carried to the various woodboxes within. It was considered good fun by the young pupils.

Lena herself made all the bread for the household, and oversaw the cooking as she tried to teach her girls the art of good housekeeping. Besides, there were always the tasks of mending and altering clothes for the children. One winter, the temperature went to seventy-five degrees below zero, and she wrote: "Can you imagine the cold of the handle of a kettle on the fire being so intense that one cannot touch it, while the kettle itself is boiling."

She helped when needed in the schoolroom, and sometimes the pupils were adults, not only men, but women with babies. Lena did not mind helping in the schoolroom, but she felt that her main task lay in running the mission house, and she was relieved when an Irish girl, Susan Mellet, aged twenty-two, arrived as schoolmistress. A few years later, Susan married Reverend R. J. Bowen, and these two had the difficult task of building a church at Dawson City in the heyday of the Gold Rush. Nearly seventy years later, when an old lady living in London, Ontario, Mrs. Bowen's memory of Charlotte Selina Bompas was still vivid.

"She was a very spirited lady, very energetic and capable of many things," Mrs. Bowen said. "One wonders how such a frail, little lady kept up for so long." As Bishop's wife, Mrs. Bompas "had to be ready at all times to be all things to all".

Mrs. Bowen who spent two long periods with the Bompases, and knew them well, said that she did not believe that Mrs. Bompas had ever seen the inside of a kitchen before she went into the mission house at Fort Simpson. "She had an awful life; he was away so much."[3]

But Lena did not think she had an awful life. Many little things pleased her: her "quiet hour" early in the morning before the children were up: the strong flow of the Yukon: the first green grass in spring followed by the snow-birds, ducks, geese, snipe and "the dear swallows": the going-out of the ice and even the excitement when they were in danger of a flood: the piling of the winter's store of wood: the tender feel of a baby's face on her cheek — for Lena now had another Indian baby to love and care for.

Lena enjoyed having Susan Mellet at the mission for she was adaptable and a good sport, and the children were devoted to her. "One comfort," wrote Lena, "is that she has good health, and is not troubled with nerves."

Lena had reason to be wonderfully thankful of Susan because Susan saved the Bishop's life.

In 1896, Lena was called back to England because her sister, Emma, was dangerously ill. Emma recovered slowly, and Lena left England early in July, 1897, in order to catch the last boat from San Francisco for St. Michael. The boat, on which she had booked her passage months before, was the *Excelsior,* just returned from the Yukon River with the first news of the Klondike gold. Off the decks of this ship, the citizens of San Francisco had seen with their own eyes the Klondike miners lug suitcases, gunny sacks, blankets, so heavy with gold that they could scarcely be lifted. The *Excelsior* had docked on July 15, and Lena arrived in San Francisco on July 27. The excitement, which was to carry round and round the world during the next two years, and stir at least 100,000 people from their homes, had already become a kind of madness.

Lena found good accommodation in the Occidental Hotel, and she was lucky, for hotels and restaurants were taxed beyond their capacities; the streets were choked with people, and outfitters were opening up everywhere with hawkers advertising their goods.

Charlotte Selina Bompas, the missionary from the Yukon, was surrounded by the curious and by newspaper reporters. "The excitement about the Klondike gold mines has surpassed everything," Lena wrote. "I was interviewed at the hotel at San Francisco and perpetually questioned about Alaska and the Yukon.

"Alas! our tranquil North is invaded, no more peace there. The whole country is to be opened up."

All this within twelve days of the docking of the *Excelsior*!

The small steamboat that carried Lena up the Yukon River from St. Michael was uncomfortably overcrowded with ninety passengers aboard; it was built to accommodate forty. Unluckily, the river was extremely low, and the overcrowded boat was only able to get as far as Fort Yukon, several hundred miles short of Forty Mile where Bishop Bompas was waiting for her. Lena was forced to spend the next eight months at Fort Yukon at the mission house with the Reverend John Hawkesley. The Hawkesleys made her as comfortable as possible, but this family had four small boys in a small house, so Lena slept in a compartment curtained off the schoolroom though she ate her meals with the family. The schoolroom, she found, "very, very cold, and I feel lonesome at night, the northern winds whistling around me and dogs howling, with wolves prowling far too near to be agreeable".

Lena, as usual, hoisted her spirits by keeping busy, and she assisted Mr. Hawkesley with his school where they had fifty children. They were greatly handicapped by the lack of school material, for they had no slates and no copy-books. For writing material, they managed to scrounge brown paper from the Hudson's Bay Company stores. The desks were planks laid over empty packing cases, and the seats were blocks of wood.

While Lena was waiting out the winter at Fort Yukon, many in the upper reaches of the Yukon River were starving. The shallowness of the river in the autumn of 1897 made it impossible to deliver the winter supplies to Forty Mile or to the new community at Dawson City. There was plenty of gold but there was no food to buy. Many of the miners had left Dawson and were congregated around Fort Yukon.

The Bishop had written from Forty Mile that he had enough food for the winter. Lena did not worry about him, for Susan Mellet, the Irish girl, was with him. Later, Lena found that although he had plenty of food, it consisted mostly of dried beans. What little fresh food there was to be found, he must have given to the others at the mission, for in early spring he became dangerously ill from scurvy. He was so ill that he gave Susan his last messages, not expecting to live. At the time of flow and flood, Susan sent out some of the mission children to search for greens, and they came back with a half-cup of the spring's first growth. It was enough to save the Bishop's life, and very soon he was able to be about.

With the going-out of the ice, Lena was able to travel again, and she was soon home at Forty Mile. Her first task was to brew some spruce tea for the Bishop, to aid his recovery. Her gratitude to Susan was unbounded. She never left the country again without William beside her.

Charlotte Selina Bompas wrote in 1898: "The mining excitement does not affect us." Nevertheless, the Bishop was concerned about the impact of the white man upon the Indian. The Indians learned extravagant habits, become dependent on luxuries, and raised their prices for meat, fish and labour. Lena could no longer find Indian women to help her with housework.

Fearing for law and order in the mining towns, Bishop Bompas and William Ogilvie, Canadian Government surveyor, had each written to Ottawa at about the same time, asking for police help, and it was through their urging that the North West Mounted Police were sent to the Yukon. For the Bishop, however, law and order were not enough, and so he sent Reverend R. J. Bowen who had recently married Susan Mellet, to Dawson, to start a church there. Another church was started at Whitehorse. Always concerned for his Indians, Bompas himself started a mission at Moosehide near Dawson City. Travelling by dog-sleigh, Lena joined her husband at Moosehide in time to celebrate her seventieth birthday.

Lena had a severe bout of bronchitis that winter, and it told on her health and spirits. The Bishop wrote in March, 1900:

> I find Mrs. B. improving in bodily health but nervous and excitable and restless and fidgety and plainly not steady in the head which makes me anxious to give her rest. The boys [two young Indians in Mrs. Bompas' care] have been too much for her and she cannot now dismiss them from her constant care.

And again in June, Bompas wrote: "I think it best for her and me, for her to be separated if possible from these children as she fusses rather nervously over them."[6]

.   .   .

Although Lena may have begun to feel her years, she found that her restless husband still had his eyes on far horizons. The next move was to be to Caribou Crossing, renamed "Carcross" by the Bompases.

Charles Camsell, who had once been a pupil of the Bompases at Fort Simpson, saw the Bishop about this time: "One of my first encounters in Dawson, "Camsell wrote, "was with venerable old Bishop Bompas, whom I had last seen when I was a small boy at Fort Simpson. He was plowing through the slush of the city's streets holding in each hand a small Indian child. . . ."

The mission house and church which the Bompases established in the spring of 1901 at Carcross had one of the world's most beautiful settings, at the end of the blue-green Lake Bennett and enclosed by the white-clad peaks of the coast mountains. "On some evenings of summer," Lena said, "the reflections of the mountains on the water is so clear and vivid that one is tempted to doubt which is the reality and which is the shadow."

The mission, itself, was no shadow.

Although a railway had been put through from Skagway to Lake Bennett, the rush of the gold stampeders had passed on, and Carcross was relatively quiet. However, as soon as the Bompases set up their tent, Indians began arriving, and within days, the Bishop and Mrs. Bompas were busy cleaning out an old roadhouse for a temporary mission house and school. By 1908, the mission school at Carcross was described by one visitor as "so exquisitely neat and orderly, such method, quiet, and discipline in each department".

Although the Missionary Society soon provided two teachers for the school, Lena still found herself busy with extra cares, an orphaned baby and a deaf-and-dumb child, and there were always the sick. The Bishop and Mrs. Bompas could never agree on the treatment of the sick patients, and sometimes Lena wondered how these individuals recovered. "Of course," she adds dryly, "if he does, it is thanks to my remedies, and if he dies, vice versa!"

At Easter, 1904, Bishop Bompas and Mrs. Bompas left the north reluctantly to attend an Anglican conference at Winnipeg. Later, Lena went on to Montreal, and during the summer she addressed the Women's Auxiliaries at Montreal, Toronto, Ottawa and Quebec. She spoke of the mission work in the north, successfully repeating her British lecture tours. She was later presented with a gift of $800 towards the building of St. Savior's Church, Carcross, and other gifts followed. The little church was consecrated after her return to Carcross.

After the Bompases returned to Carcross, the Bishop's

strength began to fail and he asked to be relieved of his responsibility for the diocese. While waiting for his release, the Bompases were visited by Bishop William Ridley of Caledonia. He wrote:

> The Bishop's house [was] built of logs, on the sand. The flooring boards were half an inch apart, so shrunken were they that it would be easy to rip them up and lay them down close together. Then the roof; it was papered, with battens across the paper. I was anxious to see less of the light of heaven through the rents . . . Everything around is as simple as indifference to creature comforts can make it, excepting the books, which are numerous, up to date, and as choice as any two excellent scholars could wish.
>
> The question that has often sprung from my heart has been this: if this poor £30 affair is, by comparison, delightful, what of the contrivances that have sheltered them in the past forty years?
>
> Never in my life did I value hospitality so much, or feel so honoured . . . She, accomplished far beyond the standard one meets with in London drawing-rooms . . . he, a fine scholar, steeped in Hebrew and Syrian lore . . . live on, love on, labour on in this vast empire, little trodden but by the Indians for whom they live and will die.

The Reverend I. O. Stringer was appointed successor to Bishop Bompas; he had been at Carcross only a matter of days when Bishop Bompas suddenly collapsed and died of a heart attack.

"The blow has been very severe, coming as it did, so suddenly," wrote Lena. She was thankful to Bishop Stringer who helped her in many ways, not least by his sympathy and presence. He was able to ease the shock for her, perhaps in a way that her William could never have done. It had not been easy being married to an ascetic, but Lena had loved him devotedly, tenderly. For a time her life seemed empty, and without purpose.

.   .   .

There was no place left for her in the mission life of the Yukon. As the Bishop's wife, there was always a place and work to do, but for a seventy-six year old widow, there was not even a niche. Lena visited England with the Stringers for a short time, and then returned to Canada, where she settled near her two nieces, Beatrice and Lilian Bengough, in Westmount, Quebec.

Until her death, ten years later, she kept in constant touch with her friends in the Yukon, including many of her Indian girls, some of whom married white men. There was Ellen, for example. Ellen married a trader who, "gave me such a good account of his little wife".

To these girls she wrote and sent presents, and each year she made little gifts which she sent to decorate a Christmas tree for the mission school at Carcross. As long as she was able, she addressed meetings of the Women's Auxiliaries in Montreal and Ottawa.

In 1915, she fell and broke her hip. When the Archbishops and Bishops of Canada presented her with a wheel chair, she was deeply touched and she referred to it as "my chair, my beautiful chair".

She was back again on her feet within a year. "You see I am so hard to kill," she wrote to the Stringers. However, she had had several serious attacks of pleural pneumonia during her last years in the North, and in the end it was pneumonia which carried her off, in January, 1917.

According to her niece, she died in her sleep, ". . . her own loving and devoted spirit manifested itself almost to the last breath, for even when no longer fully conscious, she responded to any little service rendered her with gentle words of gratitude". She was buried at Milby, near Lennoxville, Quebec.

It is difficult, in this unsentimental age, to weigh the work of such people as Charlotte Selina Bompas. Their Victorian niceness and their sentimental phrases and jargon, such as *true soldiers of the cross,* alienate us, and we feel critical of their presumption in trying to Christianize the native peoples and encouraging them to adopt a European way of life.

There were other missionaries, both Anglican and Roman Catholic, as devoted as the Bompases. These teachers, and they were teachers in the most comprehensive meaning of the word, used the knowledge and means they had at their command.

Most of them had the highest ideals, and their purpose was not much different from that of the teachers of the 1970's; the missionaries, schoolteachers, Indian agents, police, nurses and doctors who work in the north to help native North Americans integrate with the white people who are pouring into the north, or to prepare them for job opportunities when and if the job opportunities come.

The emphasis is different, that is all. Charlotte Selina Bompas would have said that the aim was to save souls. Today we talk about integration. Certainly Charlotte Selina helped many Indian boys and girls to a better way of life, by teaching them simple hygiene and dietetics. Some of her girls married white men, and the children became integrated, continuing the pattern which was started by the Ursulines when they encouraged Frenchmen to marry the Indian girls from the Convent at Quebec.

If Charlotte Selina Bompas could, today, look at the federal schools at Fort Simpson, at Fort Norman, at Whitehorse, she would be thrilled to think that the little seed she had helped plant had grown to such a spectacular plant. She would be overjoyed to know that the Indian mothers are coming from the bush to the hospitals to have their babies, that infant mortality is decreasing, that more and more Indians are learning civilized skills and are less at the mercy of nature's uncertainties.

She would see drinking today as there was in 1900, and she would do something about it. At Forty Mile, she set up a Miner's Club with books, magazine and music for lonely men during their leisure. That is what she would do today. In the North there is almost no entertainment in the smaller communities, nothing for people to do between work and sleep. Lena would take one look, and she would have people organizing hockey teams, curling, libraries, movies, card parties, perhaps bingo — but she would do something!

Charlotte Selina made the land and the people hers by giving of herself to those around her. Her gentle influence made life more bearable for entrepreneurs like Martha Black.

Notes

1. M. Atwood, "Further Arrivals," *15 Canadian Poets* (Toronto: 1970), p. 174.

2. S.A. Archer, *Heroine of the North* (Toronto: 1929). All quotes are from this book or from H.A. Cody's *Apostle of the North* (Toronto: 1908) unless otherwise indicated.

3. Unpublished interview with Mrs. R.J. Bowen by W.E. Elliott, Goderich, Ontario.

4. Rev. W. Spendlove in *Apostle of the North* by H.A. Cody (Toronto: 1908).

5. Lord Dufferin was Governor-General of Canada, 1872-78. Lord and Lady Dufferin toured Canada from the Maritimes to the Pacific — by American railways when no Canadian transport was available. They were touring the Red River and Winnipeg area when Mrs. Bompas' party happened to fall in with them. Lady Dufferin, *My Canadian Journal* (London: 1891) Coles Reprint, 1971.

6. Unpublished letters (Whitehorse).

Bibliography

Archer, S.A. *Heroine of the North.* Toronto: 1929.

Berton, L.B. *I married the Klondike.* Toronto: 1954.

Berton, Pierre. *Klondike.* Toronto: 1954.

Black, Martha Louise. *My Seventy Years.* Toronto: 1938.

Camsell, C. *Son of the North.* Toronto: 1954.

Cody, H.A. *Apostle of the North.* Toronto: 1908.

Elliott, W.E. Unpublished interview with Mrs. R.J. Bowen.

Letters (unpublished), Fort Simpson and Whitehorse.

Stefansson, V. *The Friendly Arctic.* New York: 1925.

8

Martha Black

Mrs. Black retorted that she had crossed the Chilkoot in the company of several thousand men and hadn't the least objection to crossing the Atlantic with several thousand more.

Laura Berton[1]

Martha Black was the epitome of the women colonizers. Martha was like a diamond, hard, brilliant, and beautiful. She was both ornamental and useful. If the others seem less brilliant or substantial, it may be partly because their imprint has softened with time. Martha's trail is still sharp and clean. She belongs to this century. She lived to be ninety-one and died in Whitehorse, Yukon Territory, in 1957.

Martha Louise, the daughter of George Munger and Susan Owens, was born in Chicago in 1866 and was the ninth generation of American-born Mungers. The Mungers were enterprising and industrious at a period when the United States economy was shifting from agriculture to business and industry. Martha grew up in a rapidly changing society in which her family and friends were among the leaders. Her father ran a successful laundry business in Chicago, and the family was well-to-do. Her parents were firm but loving. There was only one other child besides Martha who survived infancy, a boy several years younger than she. It was a happy family and Martha had a happy childhood.

Her first vivid memory was of the Chicago fire of 1871, when she was about five. Her family were forced to flee with 100,000 others, and lost everything they possessed except for her grand-mother's silver spoons, some linen and a few jewels. When composing her memoirs, sixty-five years later, Martha could still recall the fear and confusion at the time of the fire — hysterical children, screaming horses, bellowing cattle, people pushing wheelbarrows or baby-carriages filled with possessions, people with black or blood-stained faces, the roar of the fire. Following the fire, the Munger family spent three days camping beside the lake, in the open. Later, the family lived in a tent until a new house was built. The whole adventure was fun to the five-year-old Martha who was, of course, too young to appreciate the tragedy.

George Munger raised some money and rebuilt his laundry business and prospered. Happy childhood days followed, some of them with the Munger grandparents. Martha Louise was fun-loving, ebullient but quick-tempered, and got into many scrapes. After a session in a "Select Seminary for Young Ladies" her father entered her at Saint Mary's at Notre Dame, Indiana, a Roman Catholic Convent school with a fine reputation. The Mungers were not Roman Catholic, but Martha's parents thought that the convent education and its disciplines were what their high-spirited daughter needed. Looking back in her old age, Martha Louise knew that her parents had been right. During her five years at the school, she loved it all, the physical beauty of the buildings and environment, the traditions, the mysteries of the religious life. It was during these years that she developed an interest in botany, an interest which was to stay with her all her life. By the time she graduated from Saint Mary's, she had become a decorous, young woman who could type, curtsy, play tennis and ride, but her marks for conduct were the lowest of her class.

After her debut and a gay winter, she became engaged to Will Purdy whose father was the President of the Chicago, Rock Island and Pacific Railway. After the marriage, Will's father gave him a job as assistant paymaster on the Rock Island Railway, and the young couple started out with a splash on a good salary ($1,000 per annum) in a house that was a gift from Martha's parents, completely furnished with wedding presents, and with a coloured maid. The next ten years went by in a social whirl. After Martha's two sons, Warren and Donald, had reached school age, she worked for various public causes. These activities were not enough to absorb the energies of Martha Louise however and she was soon bored.

.   .   .

Came the Klondike Gold Rush of 1897-98. Will Purdy was immediately infected by the gold fever, as were many of his friends, and indeed the whole world. Martha Louise caught the infection, too. What seems more remarkable, and a measure of the extent of the gold craze, was that Martha's parents approved whole-heartedly and offered to care for the two boys at Catalpa Knob, the Munger ranch in Kansas, while Martha went off prospecting. Martha's ostensible reason for going to the Klondike was to trace a million-dollar cache of gold dust which was allegedly being held in trust for a friend named Lambert. Papers were drawn up which provided that Martha or her children should receive fifty percent of the hoard.

Martha and Will Purdy were joined by four others, Mr. and Mrs. Eli Gage, Martha's brother George, and her cousin Harry Peachey. In Denver, they bought their clothes. Martha outfitted herself with Jaegar combinations, high Russian boots, a brown corduroy costume, which was five yards around the bottom and edged with brush braid and stiffened with buckram. Under the skirt she wore voluminous, brown, silk bloomers; the blouse had a high, stiff collar. The suit was topped by a straw sailor hat. The outfit was noticeably stylish, but utterly impractical for mountain climbing, as Martha soon learned. One wonders, today, how the woman could walk, let alone climb rugged mountain passes, loaded down with such clothes.

At Seattle, the party was augmented by three more, and then divided, for the Gages were to go by boat up the Yukon River to Dawson, while the others would go by Skagway over the Chilkoot Pass.

Then something happened that Martha Louise was unable to explain, even to herself. According to Yukon gossip, she was deserted by her husband. Martha's account in her memoirs says simply that Will was called to San Francisco on business. A little later, he wrote to say that he had changed his mind about going to the Klondike, and was instead going to try his fortune in the Sandwich Islands. He suggested that she had better go back to her people while he made up his mind.

Martha had already bought her ticket for the Klondike; moreover she was lured by that million dollars in gold dust. She was furious. She would not go to the Sandwich Islands. She would not go home. She was tired of the monotonous society life of Chicago. She felt that the North Star was truly her lodestar, her destiny.

Martha's brother, George, at first refused to take any responsibility for her going to the Klondike without her husband, and insisted that she go back home. Somehow, she persuaded him not only to allow her to continue with the party, now five men and one woman, but to keep her separation from her husband a secret from their father. She wrote to Will Purdy that she never wanted to see him again, and she never did.

Seattle, June of '98, at the height of the gold rush, was bedlam. "Over its wharves," Martha recalled forty years later,

> surged jostling eager crowds of miners, prospectors, traders, trappers, and adventurers, all dressed in the clothes of the trail — hideous red-and-yellow plaid mackinaws, overalls tucked into high boots and caps of all descriptions. Everywhere were piles of "outfits" — camp supplies, sleds, carts, harness, which together with dogs, horses, cattle, and oxen, were being loaded into the various boats, sailing almost every hour. These, too, were of all descriptions — steamers, sailing vessels, dories manned by stout hands — all to leave, some never to be seen of again others

to be dashed upon the rocks of bleak shores by the cruel waves of the "Inside Passage."[2]

.   .   .

The small coast steamer that Martha, her brother George, and the rest of the party booked passage on was unsightly, but was said to be seaworthy. For privacy, Martha booked a stateroom with three berths for $120, a moderate price indeed for that explosive period when people were known to pay $1,000 for a bunk. However Martha soon found that the extra money did not buy privacy, for the double lower was allotted to a gambler and his mistress, and the upper to a notorious character named "Birdie". When Martha protested, she was told to take it or leave it. The boat was dirty and crowded. Men slept anywhere they could find space. Gambling and drinking were continuous, and the captain was usually drunk.

Martha Louise showed up as the good trouper she was. Scenery and weather were splendid, the food was good, and she grew to like her cabin mates. The thousand miles of sea route by the inland passage to Skagway, snaking between myriads of islands, themselves tops of mountains, is today a favourite summer cruise. In 1898, it was a serious venture with scenery thrown in for good measure. Even so, the gold seekers seldom failed to be impressed by the rugged grandeur which became grander as they journeyed north through the narrow, twisting channels; the fjords were bound by lofty mountains often lost in mist at their peaks; now and then, there were glimpses of distant glaciers, and sometimes, a turquoise iceberg.

The party of six spent several weeks at Dyea, the jumping off place for the Pass – the men in tents, and Martha in a shanty, which a kind-hearted soul loaned to her. While arrangements were being made for the transport of their goods, they fished and mountain-climbed. Martha spent hours gathering wild flowers.

She was chief cook and soon learned that the dish-pan had to serve many purposes besides that of washing dishes, for it became bath, wash-tub and bread-mixer.

They had left Seattle June 23, and by July 12 were ready to leave Dyea to walk the forty-two mile trail over the Chilkoot Pass to Lake Bennett. Though many men carried their own packs of sixty to eighty pounds, the Munger party travelled light, but at great expense. Their goods weighed several tons, and were packed over the trail by carriers for $900. After Martha had herself traversed the 3,500 foot high trail, she felt that the $900 had been well spent. It took a man three months to carry a ton over the Pass by himself.

They started for the Trail as part of a procession of humans, horses, pack ponies, a few cows, and even an ox-cart — driven by a woman. The first few miles were along a good wagon road through shady woods, and then the trail became rockier as it pierced a valley of boulders where there was no vegetation. Martha began to feel the weight of her bulky clothes. In the afternoon, they stopped for refreshments at a cabin kept by a widow and son, and before the end of the day, they had struck the mountain trail which led to the foot of the Pass. Here, they began to see grim evidence of what the ordeal would be, of miners' caches and dead horses that had fallen down the mountain side.

They spent the night at Sheep Camp, and put up at the Grand Pacific Hotel which was little more than a woodshed. Martha was given the privacy of the only bunk which was partitioned from the main room, and she had a wonderful night's sleep on hay covered by grey army blankets.

After a hearty breakfast the following day, they started up the Trail, the first hour past a recent slide of snow, ice, rocks, where thirty people had been crushed a few weeks before. In the melting snow, Martha saw a bit of blue ribbon which she pulled out and found to be a baby's bootee. She knew there was tragedy in that small article, but she dared not stop, nor even to look around at the magnificent scenery, for the footing was every instant becoming more slippery with the melting snow. Sometimes they had to cross mountain streams on the thinnest of ice. The Trail grew steeper, the day hotter, the going more treacherous. Her stylish clothes became almost insupportable; the high collar, the tight corsets, the bulky bloomers, the heavy ankle-length skirt were no longer items of vanity, but burdens to curse.

"We clung to stunted pines," she recalled, "spruce roots, jutting rocks. In some places, the path was so narrow that, to move at all, we had to use our feet tandem fashion. Above, only the granite walls. Below, death leering at us."

Sometimes, she could go on no longer, and was forced to stop to rest, but never for long enough. "Then on with that cursing procession of men and dogs and horses, pulling sleds or toting packs. Mush on. . . . Mush on. . . . It beat into my brain. . . . Cracking of whips. . . . Wild screams of two heavily loaded pack horses which lost their footing and were dashed to the rocks below. . . ."

Near the summit, Martha slipped and toppled into a crevice in the rocks. Her boot was cut through and her foot injured. She wept.

Brother George was sympathetic at first, but soon became impatient and told her "to buck up and be a man!" This made Martha angry, so she pulled herself together and marched over the summit of the Pass. At the crest, she had an hour of rest, and George bought enough wood for a "five dollar fire", for here the glacial winds were chill, even in summer.

Then came the descent, with sheer precipices, sharp rocks to tear hands and boots to shreds, and spruce or pine roots to trip the weary. Even the stop at the half-way cabin for bean soup, ham and eggs, prunes, bread and butter, was little help to the weary woman. Her brother had to help her walk the last mile into Lake Lindeman. That night, she slept on a straw shake-down and felt like a queen. She had walked over the Chilkoot Pass. She vowed she would never do it again.

The Munger party spent two weeks at Lake Lindeman, two miles above Lake Bennett. From Bennett, the rest of the journey would be by water. While waiting for their baggage to catch up with them, and for their boat to be built, they hunted and fished.

Lake Bennett, its colour constantly shifting from glacial green to deep blue, enfolded by snowy peaks, has become famous as one of the world's beauty spots. It was at Carcross, on Lake Bennett, that the Bompases spent their last years together. And it was at Lake Bennett, that the Chicago socialite learned to make "sourdough" bread.[3] This method of making bread or pancakes by fermenting the dough to make its own yeast was so common during the early days of the gold rush, that the true pioneers of the Yukon, those who came in '98 or earlier, became known as "Sourdoughs".

After three weeks of enjoyable camping, the Munger party was ready to move on. Their boat, built of Alaska pine, was an oversized fisherman's dory, thirty-seven feet long. When loaded with all their luggage and the six people, the boat was barely above the water line. The first part of the voyage was relatively easy, for they sailed before a good wind, through a series of lakes which are the headwaters of the Yukon River. At Lake Taglish, they were searched and counted by the North West Mounted Police, and were checked through as the 14,405th boat since the previous May. Martha Louise was the 631st woman to pass.

The first real test of navigating skill came at Miles Canyon and the White Horse Rapids. There, the waters from the mountain lakes pour through canyons and rapids into a deep river channel. This is the start of the mighty Yukon River, nearly 2,000 miles long, and one of the world's greatest rivers.

The White Horse Rapids are the first of many hazards, for the river, flowing between rugged mountains with a deep and rapid current, has many dangerous narrows, sharp curves, and is full of murderous, floating debris. It was once said that no man who fell into the Yukon would ever come out, for if he escaped the violent current, he would perish in its cold. Nevertheless, the Yukon was the life-line of the north until the advent of the airplane.

The land of the upper Yukon River is a lonely land of rock, gravel, spruce, sky and silence. Even the mountains seem abandoned, for they are topless. Glacial action has rounded off the peaks, and the whole land has the appearance of a vast, wrinkled, heather blanket — a giant's counterpane.

Although many have written about the trials and dangers of river travel on the Yukon, Martha Louise had an uneventful,

even a pleasant trip, lasting twelve days from Bennett to
Dawson. She noted the wild flowers, the wild berries, the wild
animals, the Indians, and the varieties of boats, rafts, scows, and
canoes, travelling like herself, down river to Dawson. Of the
hazards, she reported nothing.

.   .   .

Dawson City, surrounded by the topless mountains and the
rugged hills, was built on alluvial flats at the confluence of the
Klondike and the Yukon. By the summer of '98, the population
had already grown to 20,000. Although the Mounted Police
kept law and order by the threat of the "blue ticket" to the
"outside", the city was nevertheless a frontier post without
conventional restraints, further seasoned by the contrasts of
hard living and sudden wealth. All kinds of people from all
around the world had been drawn to this Eldorado, and some
were the most unlikely candidates. Not only were there prostitutes, gamblers, dance-hall girls, prospectors, miners and
sharpsters, but there were philosophers, schoolteachers, doctors,
lawyers, English aristocrats; and there were people like Martha
Louise and her brother, ordinary people with a dream.

Even today, Dawson has a zany appearance. Although almost
a ghost town, it does not look decayed or sad. Rather, Dawson
City in the 1970's reminds one of a woman of spirit, a merry
woman who has had her day, and although now old, poor, and a
bit scrawny, can still put her hat on at a provocative tilt. The
anniversary of Discovery Day, August 17, 1896, is celebrated
each year with wild abandon by the inhabitants, although the
old-timers are now thinning out.

When Martha Louise arrived, she was far from being the first
of her sex. Charlotte Selina Bompas had been in the Yukon for
years. At least two other women were to write their
memoirs – Margaret Clark Shand who ran a hotel at Stewart
River, and Emily Craig Romig who came the almost impossible
route, by way of Edmonton, the Mackenzie River and the Rat
River Divide. There was the shrewd Irishwoman, Belinda
Mulroney. There was also Madame Emily Tremblay who had

been in the country mining with her husband before the gold rush, and stayed to run a dress shop. Many of the women who came were prostitutes and dance-hall girls, and many were quite ordinary women following their husbands. Some could not take it, and either left their husbands and went "outside" alone, or took their husbands with them. Rather than being unique, Martha Louise was typical of those who stayed; but more than any other woman, she adopted the land; the land and the people adopted her as well; and she called the Yukon home for her remaining sixty years.

The first thing to do after arriving in Dawson was to find a place to live. During the summer of '98, Dawson was a tent city. The main street was a bazaar, and it was lined with two-storey, log and frame buildings, which were mostly dance-halls, hotels, restaurants or saloons. Everywhere else, on the muddy flats, across the Klondike River on the hills, and even across on the west side of the Yukon, there was a profusion of tents, shacks, cooking utensils, people — soon 30,000 of them. Goods were no longer scarce, for stern-wheelers, literally by the dozens, came plying up the River from Vancouver and Seattle. Money was scarce and gold dust was the means of exchange; land and lumber prices had soared. The Munger party chose land on the south side of the Klondike, above the red-light district, and a mile and a half from Dawson; here the land was free; it was also hilly, a matter of vital importance, for in Dawson during the summer, many people died from typhoid, malaria and other illnesses related to fetid, swampy ground and poor sanitation.

The Munger cabin had built-in bunks for the men and a cubicle for Martha. After the men had pounded round, poplar blocks into the soil for a floor, the place was warmer and easier to clean. Furniture was made from whatever materials could be found, including packing cases, tree trunks. Martha had brought a bolt of cretonne, gay with red roses, which she made into curtains and cushions. She gathered wildflowers and put them in a bowl on the homemade table which had been covered with coloured oilcloth. As well as the cretonne, Martha had brought in over the trail two linen tablecloths, two dozen tablenapkins, and silverware. Finally the men built an arm chair for her from "willow withy branches", and she looked upon her home with satisfaction.

She was lonely for her sons, left behind in Kansas, but she had work to do, for she still had the task of tracing the million dollars of gold dust. Try as she might, however, she could not find the witnesses of the trust, the registration of the claims, to say nothing of the gold dust. Summer was slipping into the short Arctic autumn, and the time of the freeze-up was close, after which travel out by the River would be ended. Already the last down-river boat of the season had left for Seattle. Martha had spent money tipping government officials and others trying to locate the lost gold dust, and her funds were low. She knew it was time to leave the country with the last of the stragglers — but she could not. She was pregnant!

Martha does not make it plain in her memoirs by whom she became pregnant, but there is little doubt that it was her husband, Will Purdy, whom she had last seen in Seattle about three months before. The symptoms of pregnancy had shown earlier, but she had refused to recognize them. Now she had to face the fact that she would not be able to walk back over the Pass, the only way still open. She would have to spend the winter in Dawson. Her brother was shocked but there was nothing to be done but face the fact. And face it, Martha did. Her spirit soared in a kind of fervour as if to say, "Now is the time to prove yourself."

.   .   .

After the last boat had left Dawson for Whitehorse and the Pass, the people of Dawson prepared themselves for the long, dark winter. The winter of '98-'99 was not the starvation winter of the previous year when the city had been crowded with stampeders without the means of feeding themselves. Nevertheless, winter in the far north is an ordeal under the best of circumstances, and Dawson in '98 was only slightly better than Dawson in '97. During the summer of '98, no person had been allowed into the country without a year's supply of food but, needless to say, this was not fresh food.

With the coming of the steamboats during the previous summer. Dawson had gone on a building spree and, in a few months, it had changed from shanty town to a cosmopolitan city. Hotels had been built where impeccably dressed men and women could eat seven-course dinners at tables covered with fine linen, silverware and china, to the sound of fine orchestras. After the last tourists had left, the decorum was maintained, but as winter dragged on, the menus became scantier and scantier. Prices were staggering for everything except the "outfits" left behind by disillusioned stampeders who had returned to the "outside".

Martha's household now consisted of five, and they were soon reduced to rationing. They went without butter, sugar or milk. Flour was a dollar a pound, paid in gold dust, eggs three dollars a dozen, oranges, apples and onions a dollar and a half each – while they lasted. The price of fuel was exorbitant. Breakfast was cornmeal mush, prunes and tea (clear). The fine linen tablecloths that Martha had brought served another purpose, for she cut them up to use as baby clothes.

When it became known that a baby was on its way, Martha was showered with gifts, red flannel, white linen, homemade jam, and other delicacies. Martha never forgot these kindnesses, and if she had not already lost her heart to the people of the North, she did then.

When Martha inquired about the costs of hospital confinement at the Roman Catholic hospital, she learned that it would be $1,000. She did not have anything like that much money, and though the head of the mission would have trusted her until spring, she could not bring herself to go into debt. She decided "to get through alone", and quite literally she did. The baby, a boy, came ahead of schedule while she was alone in the cabin. The birth was easy, and it was all over quickly. When the men returned at night, they were amazed to find the little "Chechako" – Indian for tenderfoot – snug and cosy in his red flannel.

After the arrival of the baby, Martha was overwhelmed with attention and help, not only from her own household but from her neighbours. The men in the community brought in fresh

bread, fresh game, and gold nuggets, and stood in awe, sometimes even weeping, to see the infant. Uncouth miners crowded
the little cabin to watch the daily ritual of the bath, and the
infant, Lyman, grew to love them all. The baby brought so
many people to the cabin that it became a social centre, and
Martha and George soon brought out their guitars and mandolin
for jolly evenings of singing.

There were two principal annual dates in Dawson City – the
day the last boat left before winter freeze-up, and the day when
the ice began to move in the spring. Even today in Dawson, the
spring break-up is a matter of much excitement with everyone
in town betting on the exact minute that the ice will start to
move. However, the day the Yukon River moved in the spring
of 1899 brought Martha one of the most dramatic moments of
her entire life.[4]

She was sitting in front of her cabin, the baby asleep nearby,
both soaking up the spring sunshine. "Below, the Yukon was
heaving, crackling, and groaning, for the ice and snow were
melting fast. A warm, gentle breeze was scattering the yellow
pollen of the willow buds."

Martha heard a rustling above and saw movement in the
bushes. She thought it must be a bear and, quickly picking up
the baby, rushed into the cabin. After putting him on her bunk,
she gathered up all the firearms she could find, and with ammunition went out again, determined to shoot the bear. When she
looked again towards the hill,

> . . . to my horror I saw the whole hillside slowly moving
> towards the cabin, and gaining momentum. A landslide!
> The quick thaw had loosened the upper stratum of earth
> and made it into a river of mud that was carrying every-
> thing before it.

She rushed back to the cabin and grabbed the baby, then
stood, breathless, in one corner of the room. There was nothing
to do but to wait and pray.

A miracle happened, otherwise Martha Louise would not
have had a tale to tell. A clump of trees, well above the
cabin, caught some of the onrushing snow, rocks and small
trees. This clump formed enough obstruction to check the full

sweep of the avalanche long enough to divert it, half to one side of the cabin, half to the other. Two cabins lower down were carried with the slide, as well as all the outhouses and a large tree nearby. The hillside was wiped clean. Martha fainted.

Later, when she looked to the river, she saw ". . . a scene of magnificent beauty – enormous ice-blocks coursing down the river, swirling in swift-frothing eddies." Winter was over.

With the opening of the river, came fresh food; milk, salmon, eggs, oranges, lemons, and vegetables gradually began to appear in the food stores. And mail. Martha had letters from her family but none from her husband, so she decided that that chapter was closed. As summer came on, she spent long evenings on the hills gathering wild flowers and orchids while the men watched the baby. At the end of July, Martha's father arrived to take her home with him.

Martha went, but she had plans for returning. She had staked some placer claims. She promised her father that if these claims did not yield $10,000 she would forget about the Klondike.

But could Martha Louise forget the Klondike?

Leaving Dawson, Martha and her father went up-river by boat to Whitehorse,[5] and then transferred to a small steamer which carried them to the head of Lake Bennett. At Lake Bennett, they boarded a train to travel over the narrow-guage White Pass railway. This railway was newly built during the year that Martha had spent in the North. It was a most remarkable undertaking, paid for before it was finished, and still a paying railway through some extremely scenic country.

As Martha travelled by rail over the Pass, she caught glimpses of the old trail, and was deeply stirred. "I recalled vividly the agony of the year before. Once again in my memory I staggered up and up. Dead Horse Gulch brought back to me the screams of dying horses. . . ." The trip took only two hours over much of the same route which, the year before, had taken two days as well as much anguish for Martha, misery for thousands, and death for some.

.   .   .

Back at her father's ranch, "Catalpa Knob", Martha should have been happy, for she dearly loved her children and her parents, but she could not be satisfied. Love and security were not enough for this spirited woman. She needed a challenge and the Klondike called her. After a winter of drooping spirits, she received word from her brother George that her diggings had paid off. Almost immediately, she set off again for the North, this time with her eldest son, Warren. Her parents, with the two younger children, were to follow the next year. Martha was planning to set herself up with a saw mill and a quartz mill.

While she waited for her mill machinery to arrive, she entered into partnership with two men at a mining camp. Here, she worked as cook for the crew of sixteen men. When her father arrived in the summer of 1901, he set Martha up with the two planned mills on the left bank of the Klondike, about a mile from Dawson. When her parents left the following summer, they took Warren with them to be educated by his grandfather Purdy. Martha Louise was on her own, as manager of the mills.

The years passed quickly, and she prospered at the mill, but lost out in her mining claims. She had trouble only once with her mill hands because she was a "skirt", but in the usual non-chalant Martha Louise manner, she outmanoeuvred them. She lost all contact with her old Chicago friends and heard nothing more from her husband, from whom she eventually got a divorce. She had little to do with Dawson Society, and was totally absorbed with her work and her family. She made money from the sawmill, and furnished her home attractively from Simpson's and Eaton's catalogues. She dressed beautifully in Paris gowns brought in from France, or in clothes made-to-measure at White's, Woodstock, Ontario. She was not the only woman in Dawson to dress expensively by any means, but she was the smartest.

Laura Berton, who met Martha about this time, described her as a ". . . pretty, saucy-faced woman with steel-blue eyes and an expression of unqualified determination . . . a hard woman to cross."[6]

Mrs. Berton, who went to the Yukon to teach for a year, and stayed to marry, was slightly in awe of Martha, but always her admirer.

She was by all odds the smartest looking woman in Dawson. I never saw her disheveled. . . . On the hills out hunting with her husband, she was always dressed in the correct khaki outfit and she was never seen without a hat. She wore these hats at a rakish angle, pulled down low over one eye, her hair tightly close to her head.

Martha once said: "I love hats. I only wish I could wear a hat in my coffin".[7]

.   .   .

In 1904, Martha Louise married again. She first met George Black when she sought his legal advice over some mill matter. He was a young lawyer of United Empire Loyalist stock from New Brunswick who had caught the gold fever and come to the Yukon in 1897, along with a brother and an uncle, also lawyers. Martha Louise and George Black had much in common, not only their love for the rugged Yukon hills, for its people and its wild life, but each was also imbued with a strong streak of nonconformity. However Martha waited for two years after George first proposed before she finally agreed to marry him. In the fall of 1904 they moved into Dawson.

On the whole, it was a successful marriage, although Martha had a sharp bite to her tongue and George always had an eye for a pretty ankle. George was as fond of the boys as if they had been his own. Together the family went on many happy hunting excursions, and on these outings, George taught his stepsons all the arts of good sportsmanship. Lyman, the child born in Dawson city in 1898, later took the name of Black.

Besides being a lawyer, George Black was a politician, a member of the Conservative Party. It was for long years a common maxim in the Yukon to say that there were only two parties, the Liberals and the Blacks. Unfortunately, at this time, the Liberals were in the ascendancy, and the Blacks were out. As the heat went out of the gold rush, George Black found that he did not have enough law business to provide for his family, and so in 1909, the Blacks left for Vancouver, so that George could take the law examinations for British Columbia.

While in the Yukon, Martha had collected and mounted 464 varieties of Yukon wild flowers and plants. This collection came to the attention of officials of the Canadian Pacific Railway, and as a result, she was commissioned to collect floral exhibits for the Company hotels as a tourist attraction. With the boys safely stowed away on the farm of friends, Martha spent a glorious summer in the valleys and on the mountain slopes of British Columbia, doing nothing but gather flowers from remote places and mounting them. Her collections were later shown across Canada, at the Smithsonian Institute, and at Wembley, England. In 1917 she was made a Fellow of the Royal Geographic Society.

The following year, 1911, the Conservatives were swept into power across Canada, and George, good party worker, was given the position of Commissioner of the Yukon Territory. In March, 1912, the Blacks, including Donald and Lyman, returned in triumph to Dawson City to take up residence in Government House, a large, white-frame, colonial-style mansion, built on the bank of the Yukon, not far from the junction with the Klondike. The mansion stands idle now because it is too costly to heat (it cost the Blacks $2,200 a year, fifty years ago) but it still looks as if Martha Black had merely closed it up for a season.

Martha Louise enjoyed her years as chatelaine of Government House, and poured all her energy into the task. She planned all the redecorating, and did some of it herself. In one room, known as the Blue Room, she painted a border of blue birds.

When the house was ready, the Blacks gave a reception. In decorating for the affair, Martha made full use of white pillars against gold wallpaper and rich mahogony. Everywhere, she had placed bowls of scarlet poppies and hung streamers of scarlet and white.

The first reception given by the Blacks was no ordinary event. They had invited all the "right" people, of course, but they had also invited anyone who wanted to come. When Martha had ordered 1,000 sandwiches to be prepared, forty cakes, twenty gallons of salad and of sherbet, gallons and gallons of punch – the kitchen help had scoffed. However, 600 attended the reception, and there was no food left over. Many of the guests were miners, some dressed in evening dress, some in gum boots and overalls. According to Martha the reception began at 7.55; by midnight the rugs were taken up for dancing; the last guest left at 5 a.m.

During the years at government house, Martha became an enthusiastic gardener. She had the use of a greenhouse for starting seedlings, and the help of a gardener. Between them, they grew wonderfully large, sweet vegetables, the result of the long Arctic summer days. Martha even brought in mushroom spawn which was still producing twenty-five years later.

Besides growing vegetables, Martha and her gardener transplanted all the wild fruits they could find — currants, gooseberries, raspberries, cranberries — and all these flourished under cultivation. This was a great boon in the Yukon where fresh fruit was always scarce and expensive.

Most of all, Martha gloried in the growing of flowers, and from the beginning of the growing season to its end, the grounds were a mass of colour with almost every variety of flower belonging to the north temperate zone.

During George Black's tenure as Commissioner, the Blacks kept open house, and everyone was welcome. This deliberate disregard for established form frequently offended Dawson society, but the Blacks did not care at all. George was always loyal to his friends, poor or wealthy, and Martha thoroughly enjoyed shocking the snobs. George had no snobbery in him, and Martha was so much of a snob that she dared put herself above it. There are people today who remember her with pique. No doubt, over the years Martha lashed a few souls with her quick tongue, but most likely the pique resulted from her disregard of the accepted social code. Once she had the daughter of her washerwoman at one of her teas. On another occasion, Martha invited Diamond Tooth Gertie, one of the dance-hall girls who had married a lawyer friend of George, to an evening party at Government House. Dawson society was furious, but Martha enjoyed the sensation, especially as Gertie was a quiet, decent, young woman.

There is another story that Martha liked to tell of herself.

While Martha was organizing the first I.O.D.E. chapter in Dawson, one young woman asked her how long one had to be a Daughter of the American Revolution before becoming a Daughter of the Empire? To which Martha snapped back, "Only until one married George Black."

.   .   .

When the first World War struck, George grew restless, and sent in his resignation as Commissioner of the Yukon. He set about organizing a Yukon Infantry Company and was appointed captain, but it was not until the autumn of 1916 that the company left the Yukon. With him was Lyman, who was too young to enlist but somehow managed to be accepted. The two older Purdy boys had also joined the forces. Martha decided that there was nothing else for her to do but follow the Yukon infantry. This she did, all the way to England.

During the rest of the war years in England, she worked at various tasks for the Red Cross; gave 400 lectures on the Yukon; took care of the distribution of the Yukon Comfort Fund; and, probably most important, she acted as "Mother" to all the hundreds of lonely Yukoners, overseas. She took on this office with humility and delicacy which meant keeping her London apartment open to any boys on leave, writing countless letters, visiting the wounded in hospitals, and disposing of the Comfort Fund to the boys in the trenches. These years were certainly Martha's finest, which she herself appreciated as her finest, although in the pages of her stirring memoirs, they only amount to a few short chapters. Her heart was so filled during these years, that even when Lyman received the Military Cross and Martha was invited to the investiture at Buckingham Palace, the occasion was more interesting as an event than an emotion.

After the war the Blacks returned to Vancouver where George again took up his law profession. The position of Commissioner of the Yukon had been merged with that of Gold Commissioner, and the beautiful Government House closed.

When the federal election of 1921 was announced, George was offered the Conservative nomination for the Yukon, and he won the seat after a vigorous campaign. From then on, the Blacks lived for a large part of each year at Ottawa, and spent a great deal of their lives commuting back and forth between Dawson and Ottawa, which before the days of the airplane, took a lot of time.

They got along well in Ottawa. Martha Louise was a good hostess, and George was a charming fellow, and an interesting conversationalist. He rose through the ranks, until he was appointed Speaker of the House of Commons in 1930 — the "First Commoner". Martha delighted in this new role, for not only does the Speaker preside over the House, but he must act as official host for the House of Commons.

While preparing for his first session as Speaker, George became suddenly ill and was taken to hospital, leaving Martha Louise to make all the preparations for the big reception, alone. On March 5, 1931, she wrote in her diary ". . . called on Mrs. Adam Shortt after luncheon — broke down. I am so anxious about George." But Martha kept her chin up, and went that evening to see the O'Neill play, *Strange Interlude*. Before the opening of Parliament on March 12, George had recovered enough to be able to take his place, and of this occasion, Martha wrote in her diary:

> Opening of the House in the Senate by Senator Will-
> oughby — some very beautiful gowns — Miss Bennett most
> gorgeous in gold cloth — after speech from throne read by
> the Administration, Mr. Justice Duff went to our rooms
> where George and I held our first reception — nearly one
> thousand men and women shook hands with us. Lyman
> and Aimée [his wife] most ornamental — Lyman in full
> dress uniform, Aimée in white satin, scarlet gloves and
> slippers. Later George & I entertained at dinner — George
> stood the day very well — down to the House this morning
> about noon — many complimentary remarks about Aimée
> and her good French. She is sweet . . . Came home and
> rested before going out again. [8]

In step with her husband's success, Martha Louise became famous as an Ottawa hostess.

Back in Dawson City, the Blacks lived in a pleasant, cream, two-story building near the old Yukon Administration building which is now a Museum. The Blacks' old Dawson home has been unoccupied for years; in that splendid, dry Yukon climate, the house has not aged, but the flower garden which Martha planted has run wild.

Mrs. George Black had become a tourist attraction in her own right, and many summer visitors wanted to meet her. She liked nothing better than to be accosted on the street, especially if she were grubbing about in the town ditches hunting for her famous four-leaf clovers which she mounted on place cards for her dinner parties. After the visitors would ask where Mrs. Black could be found, and Martha had given careful directions, she would hurry home, put on a smart, new dress and leisurely greet her guests.

Martha had an everlasting sense of humour which she could turn on herself just as easily as on her friends. Although her sharp, quick mind and quick wit made her a little feared by many, she was also charming and kind.

According to her daughter-in-law Aimée, Martha was always feminine, and she was kind. She was a good manager but she was also extravagant.[9] She was a grand hostess and loved it. She was at home anywhere, and was just as happy to sit and eat a plate of beans with an old-timer as to be entertaining in Government House — just as at home and just as regal.

Her enthusiasms sometimes got her into trouble. Once, while chatelaine at Government House, Dawson, she played hostess to the Seattle Chamber of Commerce. The town was celebrating Dominion Day when the delegation arrived; flags of every nation were hanging before Government House, the Union Jack and Canadian Red Ensign having the prominent position. At the moment of the American delegation's arrival by river boat before the Government House, Martha Louise threw an enormous Stars and Stripes across the upper railing, outclassing all else. Needless to say, Martha had not meant her act to be disloyal; she had only wanted to appear hospitable. But the deed did not go down well among the townspeople.

Besides Martha's collection of Canadian wild flowers, for which she received the FRGS, Martha is still remembered by many people for her original place cards. These she made up by mounting dried wild flowers or four-leaf clovers which she was adept at finding. She had organized the first IODE chapter in the Yukon for matrons, and another for girls, and a third chapter was organized in her honour as the Martha Munger Black Chapter.

She wrote several charming little booklets which were for sale in Whitehorse, Dawson, and on the railway. One on *Yukon Flowers* was illustrated by photographs by George Black. A second, entitled *The Birth of Empire* was written by George and Martha. There were two others, *My First Christmas Memory During the Chicago Fire of 1871* and *Two Royal Elizabeths.* By this time, she had two honours, FRGS and OBE, both of which she used on the title pages.

While hostess for the Canadian Government, she entertained Prince and Princess Takamatsu of Japan, the British Ambassador to the United States, and Colonel and Mrs. Charles Lindbergh. She was entertained at No. 10 Downing Street, and she was received by the Duchess of York, now the Queen Mother. On this latter occasion, Martha recalled with some complacency the hours spent at St. Mary's College learning to curtsey.

.   .   .

In 1935 when Martha Louise was nearing seventy, her family affairs reached their lowest ebb, while her own individual efforts their highest. George had a serious mental breakdown and had to resign his seat. He slowly recovered but during this long illness the Yukon had no representation in Parliament. Martha was asked by the party to run in his place. She hurried back to the Yukon to campaign. There were 1,805 voters in an area of 200,000 square miles, and no radio stations. To reach the voters Martha had to travel by row-boat, motor-boat, steamer, horse, car, and on foot. In much of the Territory, she saw more caribou, game birds and bears, than she saw voters.

According to Martha herself, some of the younger women asked, "What can this damned old woman do for us at Ottawa?" and she replied, "You'll be lucky when you reach my age if you have my sturdy legs, my good stomach, my strong heart, and what I like to call my headpiece."

In the election the Conservative party was badly defeated nationally, but Martha retained the seat for the Conservatives and the Blacks, with a majority of 134. She was the second Canadian woman to enter the House of Commons at Ottawa.

A few weeks after she took her seat, her son, Lyman, who had stayed in the Services and was stationed at Brockville, was killed in an automobile accident. His wife, Aimée, was living with Martha and was also her secretary.

On that day, February 27, 1937, Martha wrote in her diary:

> We expected Lyman up for the week-end. He was motoring up with Bob Mimes. About three o'clock and a little later, Aimée commenced to be a little anxious as she felt Bob Mimes . . . was a very careless driver. About half past four, Mary Scott, wife of Col. Clyde Scott, military secretary to the Minister, called and meeting Aimée on the stairs, said, "Come with me. There has been an accident." – After a little conversation I took Mary Scott aside and said, "So Lyman's dead." She replied, "Yes, he was killed instantly just outside Brockville." We were stunned – beyond words – it was all *too* dreadful – Aimée's husband, my boy, the very light of our lives . . .

The following day, Martha wrote:

> Aimée slept with me – even tho we both took luminal we rested poorly – the poor child is so brave, beyond words, in her grief. She is *stunned* – the hard time for her will come later after the first shock is over. I have lost a dearly beloved son – but I am an old woman now with but comparatively few years left – while Aimée with her life before her will be lonely beyond words . . . my heart aches for her. She is brave. Another day gone – the world moves on no matter *what* happens.

George Black who was again practising law in Vancouver, flew east to Ottawa to attend the funeral. During the next days and weeks, Martha was deeply touched by the kindnesses of her friends and associates.

On March 12, she wrote in her diary:

> About 4 p.m. commenced a short talk on Yukon – spoke for twenty-five minutes and feel I did

fairly well tho not so well as I would like to do — was told
it was not necessary for me to speak but I felt that after all
it was what I was elected for. A splendid reception and
hearing in the Chamber — All members most considerate.

George, deeply crushed by Lyman's death, had already left
for Vancouver, and then Aimée left for Winnipeg with her
sister. "I did not go down," wrote Martha. "It would have been
too heart-breaking to say good-bye to Aimée in public. I love
her dearly — she is as a little daughter, has a difficult path ahead
of her — but is brave. I am *lonely*."

And the next day, "I am lonely. I feel bowed and broken for
the first time in my life. I can never forget the comfort Lyman
was to me two years ago when George was taken sick — he was
a tower of strength."

On the 15th, she wrote: "At the House — carried on as usual.
Somedays I feel fresh and able to go on — on others it is with
great difficulty that I can whip myself up to take any interest in
people or my work — but that will never do." Then, she adds,
"Thank God for my happy memories."

But the heartbreak could not be willed away. Days later, she
wrote: "I seem to have lost my grip. I am tired when I get up,
tired when I go to bed — tired in mind and body."

Martha Louise had scarcely recovered from Lyman's death
when she was stunned again by the death of her eldest son,
Warren, and the death of her brother, George, all three within
six months.

Even when she felt most heartbroken and lonely, however,
her thoughts were for others, for brave, little Aimée, for George
Black, who took the grief so "hopelessly", for Warren's little
children.

A strenuous election, to sit in the Commons for the first time
at the age of seventy, to face three tragedies all in a twelve-
month, would have fazed most mortals, but Martha's will and
determination carried her over her hardships and sorrows just as
triumphantly as when she was thirty, climbing the Chilcoot
Pass.

She served out her full term. At the end of the term, George
had completely recovered and was able to campaign for the

next election which he won. He returned to the House, and served until 1949.

.   .   .

When the capital of the Yukon was moved from Dawson City to Whitehorse in 1953, the Blacks moved with it. For some years after her death, Martha's hand could be seen in a neat one-storey house facing the river front, where the pleasant garden and green lawn made a small oasis in the dusty river valley of Whitehorse. The house was used for some years as living quarters for women working for the Yukon Administration but is now deserted. There are plans, however, for the Government House in Dawson to be restored.

Martha Louise spent her last seven years in a wheelchair, for she was crippled by arthritis. This handicap only slightly curtailed her activities. She continued to make her flower-mounted place cards and Christmas cards till she was past eighty-five. She continued to receive her guests, high and low, with a flair. Among the many visitors who came to see her in the little house at Whitehorse were Prince Philip and Governor-General Massey.

For one notable guest, Martha Louise stirred up another of her famous sensations. Lady Florence Eaton was visiting White-horse and was to be entertained by the Blacks at a large tea. Lady Eaton with her companion came a little early, so that she could chat with Martha Louise before the guests arrived.

Martha Louise had planned a tea party instead of a cocktail party because of the well-known Eaton taboo on drinking and smoking and so she explained to Lady Eaton that there would be no drinks. To this, Lady Eaton replied that she did not really mind a cocktail now and then.

At that moment, minutes before the guests were due to arrive, the tea party was converted into a cocktail party. George was sent out to buy liquor, fruit juices and cocktail foods. Because sandwiches had already been made and a tea table laid out, it was decided that tea and sandwiches would be served to those who did not drink, cocktails to those who preferred them.[10] Who but Martha Louise Black would have dared to make such a last minute switch?

When she was ninety, Martha brought her memoirs up to date, but did not live long enough to edit them. When she celebrated her ninety-first birthday, one Ottawa columnist wrote, "All Canada looked to the North with a bow."

She was still sparkling two weeks before she died, still able to complain with rich, lusty, swear words, when she did not like the treatment given her by the visiting nurse who came in to bathe her. Both Martha and George, like other old Yukoners, had always been hard drinkers, and liked their friends to drink with them. When Martha insisted that her nurse begin her duties by drinking a tall glass of hard liquor, straight, the poor woman found she had to dump it on the nearest plant, or she could not have carried on her day's work.

Martha died quite suddenly in the fall of 1957, and with her died an era.[11] She was the "Mother" of the Yukon, disliked by some, loved by many, admired by most. Perhaps she was admired because she would not become a martyr. If she wanted something, she went about the business of getting it, and she knew what she wanted.

Notes

1. Laura Berton, *I Married the Klondike,* pb. (Toronto: 1967) p.130.
2. Martha Black, *My Seventy Years* (Toronto: 1938). All quotes are from this book unless otherwise indicated.
3. "Sourdough" took the place of yeast in the early days of the north. The sourdough was made from a thin flour and water batter with a little rice water and a pinch of sugar added, then hung in a warm place for a few hours until the batter fermented.
4. Martha Black does not mention the great fire which razed the whole of Dawson in the winter of 1898-99, probably because she was not affected by it. The Munger cabin was on the other side of the Klondike River.
5. The stampede ended August 1899, when 8,000 went out in one week to a new rush at Nome. That same week some wild-eyed, starving stampeders arrived from Rat River. They had been two years en route from

Edmonton via the Mackenzie River. When they arrived at Dawson, the Klondike Gold Rush was over.

6. Laura Berton, *I married the Klondike* (Toronto: 1954), p. 41.

7. Laura Berton, *I married the Klondike* (Toronto: 1954), p. 136.

8. From Martha Black's Diary, Dawson Museum.

9. From interview with Mrs. Lyman Black, in Winnipeg, Sept. 1964.

10. From interview with Mrs. Martha Cameron, in Whitehorse, Aug. 1964.

11. George Black survived Martha by eight years. After Martha's death, he married Susan King and retired to Vancouver, where he died August 23, 1965, aged 92.

Bibliography

Alumnae News, Saint Mary's College, Notre Dame, Indiana. 1957.

Berton, Laura Beatrice. *I married the Klondike.* Toronto: 1954.

Berton, Pierre. *The Golden Trail.* Toronto: 1954.

Berton, Pierre. *Klondike.* Toronto: 1954.

Black, Martha. *My Seventy Years,* as told to Elizabeth Bailey Price. Toronto: 1938.

Black, Martha. *Dairy of Martha Black,* Dawson Museum.

Harris, A.C. *Klondike Gold Fields,* 1897. Coles Canadiana Reprint (paper).

9

The Quest Goes On

The map leaps up
from namelessness
to history
each place made ceremonial
when named and its name peopled!
events shouted!

Dorothy Livesay[1]

With Martha Black we come to the end of the trail which began with the dauntless, determined Gudrid. Among these echoes of Gudrid are the same qualities, the fearless resolution, the quest for the unknown, the contempt for failure. It almost seems that these women exulted in their hardships, in order to prove themselves, not martyrs, but fit to inhabit the land. None was content to merely endure, to live from day to day without improving conditions around them, as men living alone on the frontier would do. These women insisted on having schools, churches, hospitals, books, curtains on their cabin windows, silver and linen at the table.

Without these eight women, Canada would be a different

country today. Marguerite de Roberval proved that it was possible to live in a strange new land without help from Europe. Jeanne Mance kept a foothold in America for the French. Molly Brant built a solid base in Ontario, not only for her own people of the Six Nations, but for law-abiding British. Marie-Anne Lagimodière helped to establish church and school in the unsettled west. Amelia Douglas, who knew so little of European social customs, created stability in the rowdy Pacific Colonies by her personal example of good manners, kindness and hospitality. Selina Bompas helped to bridge the gap between the native peoples and the European, to prepare them for the later intrusions. Martha Black, with great vigour, did many things, but perhaps most significantly, she represented her beloved Yukon as a woman in Parliament.

When the quest began, not one of these women knew where she was going nor to what kind of life. The fears and hardships were accepted as the price of the journey. As each attained her goal, she took the land that she found, and made the improvements she felt were needed.

Other women took up the challenge, and the quest for newer frontiers went on.

Acknowledgements

I've had help from many people in many places. I am grateful to them all. Some people gave freely of their time; others offered me a single, crucial idea. Instead of lumping the names of those who assisted me together, I have divided the lists as they relate to the eight chapters in the book. I began collecting source material ten years ago, and some of the people who helped me during those years have since retired from their positions, or moved on to new ones.

First I am grateful to the Canada Council for the grant which made it possible for me to cross Canada from Atlantic to Pacific and from there north to the Yukon and the Mackenzie River area. As I travelled I visited the local archives of each area I was covering. My special thanks, therefore, go to those who sponsored my application to the Canada Council: Honorable Waldo Monteith, Dr. Northrop Frye, Wilfrid Gregory, QC, and the late Beth Hall Kaufman.

For general information I thank W. Kaye Lamb, Dominion Archivist, now retired, and Pierre Brunet, Assistant Deputy of Public Archives. Dr. Carl Klinck of the University of Western Ontario gave me the initial counsel and sponsored my guest application for use of University of Western Ontario Library, where I received much help, especially in the Regional History room. My thanks also go to the Reference Department of the Kitchener Public Library, Stratford Public Library, Toronto Reference Library and the University of Toronto Library. I would also like to thank Dr. Marcel Trudel, Associate Editor of the Dictionary of Canadian Biography; Martha Shepard and Ian C. Weese of the National Library; Christian Cauro, Attaché Culturel, Consulat Général de France, Toronto; and Professor G. Wilson Knight, Exeter, England.

For the chapter on Gudrid, I owe thanks to J.G. Channing, Deputy Minister of Provincial Affairs, Newfoundland; John V. Rabbits, office of the Archivist, Newfoundland Museum; Ian Whitaker, Professor of Anthropology, Memorial University, Newfoundland; Archie Munn, St. John's; Harold Horwood, Beachy Cove; Marjorie Mews, Chief Librarian, Newfoundland Tourist Division Office.

In the Maritimes, I received help from Dalhousie University, Halifax, and from Dr. George MacBeath at New Brunswick Archives, Saint John. In Quebec, my thanks go to Antoine Pelletier, Chief Librarian, Quebec Provincial Archives; Mère Marie Emmanuel, OSU, Monastère des Ursulines in Quebec City; Sister Allard, Le Centre Jeanne Mance in Montreal; and Madeleine Fohy St. Hilaire, Ottawa.

For the story of Molly Brant, I thank the many people connected with the Johnstown Historical Society, Johnstown, N.Y. and the Montgomery County Historical Society, Amsterdam, N.Y.; in particular, Mrs. Harvey Chalmers II, Col. Charles Briggs and Harold Catherwood. In Ontario, my thanks go to the Joseph Brant Museum, Burlington; Ontario Archives; Department of Indian Affairs; the Ontario Genealogical Society; Her Majesty's Chapel of the Mohawks in Brantford; and friends on the Grand River Reserve, particularly Marie Jamieson, Alma Green and Mrs. Joseph Logan. For genealogical data, I thank the Osborne-Kerr family and Walter Rutherford. Others who helped me significantly with the story of Molly are: Dr. William Fenton and Dr. Milton Hamilton, both of the New York State Educational Department; Dr. Isabel Kelsey, Glenn Mills, Pennsylvania; Dr. H.C. Burley of Bath, Ontario; Dr. H. Pearson Gundy, University Librarian, Queen's University; Marjorie Freeman Campbell, Hamilton; Dr. P.G. Cornell, University of Waterloo; Dr. Carl Klinck, University of Western Ontario; T.R. Millman, Archivist, General Synod of the Anglican Church of Canada; Verna M. Wilson, University Librarian, Queen's; R.A. O'Brien, Editor, Kingston Whig-Standard; Margaret Butterfield, University of Rochester; Henry B. Collins, Smithsonian Institution; Helen Rose Cline, Parish of Trinity Church in the City of New York, N.Y.; Reference Librarian Flora D. Colton, University of Pennsylvania; William G. Tyrrell, Historian, University of State of New York; Elizabeth Deily, Albany Institute of History and Art; New York State Archives, Albany; William G. Tyrrell, Historian, University of State of New York; R. Burnett, Superintendent, National Library of Scotland; R.J.F. Carnon, Sub-Librarian, Edinburgh University Library; Jane Gwyn, British Museum.

With Marie Anne Lagimodière, I received essential information from Irene Lane and Lionel Dorge of the Société Historique de Saint Boniface. I also thank Shirlee A. Smith and Alice M. Johnson of the Hudson's Bay Company Archives, and Malvina Bolus, former editor of the Beaver. Others who have helped me are Dr. Grace Lee Nute, Minnesota, authority on the fur trade; Hartwell Bowsfield, Provincial Archivist in Manitoba, and assistant archivist, Elizabeth Blight; K.L. Cosgrove, office of the Minister of Veteran Affairs; Hugh A. Dempsey, Glenbow Foundation; E.J. Holmgren, Alberta Provincial Librarian; C.W. Mudge, Superintendent Command Depot, RCMP, Regina; David J. Ross, Department of External Affairs; Mrs. Ross Haddon, Hawick, Scotland for permission to use parts of Lady Frances Simpson's Journal.

For Amelia Douglas, I thank Willard Ireland, Archivist, and the staff of the British Columbia Archives; and Hazel Mills, Washington State Library. I also wish to thank Miss Orsa Douglas, Victoria, B.C., who gave up some hours of her time to talk about the Douglas family.

For Selina Bompas, my thanks go to Reverend F.A. Peake, Director of Religious Education, Diocese of Huron; Reverend George Hamilton of Fort Simpson; and Reverend T.C.B. Boon, Winnipeg. A special thanks to Judy and Mary Ellen Whyard of Whitehorse for typing some Bompas letters for me, and to W.E. Elliott of Goderich for allowing me to use an unpublished interview he had had with Mrs. R.J. Bowen.

For Mrs. Black, I am grateful to Florence Whyard of Whitehorse for giving me many useful tips while I was in the Yukon; Martha Cameron and Ralph E. Hudson also of Whitehorse; Athol Retallack of Dawson City; the staff of the Dawson City Museum where I was able to read an old diary of Martha Black; Eva M. McBride of Vancouver; and J.E. Black of Montreal. My thanks also to Pierre Berton who gave me permission to quote from Laura Berton's *I married the Klondike*. I especially thank Mrs. Lyman Black for the interview in Winnipeg.

I owe particular gratitude to Louise McCaul for proofreading; to Madeleine Reeds and to Céline Johnston for translation of 16th century French; to my son, Dr. Hugh Johnston, and to my husband, Stafford Johnston, for their critical appraisal; and to my editor, Carol Martin, for her help.

Jean Johnston

General Bibliography

Adney & Chapell. *The Bark Canoes and Skin Boats of America.* Washington: 1964.

Brebner, J. Bartlett. *Canada.* Toronto: 1960.

Creighton, Donald. *Empire of the St. Lawrence.* Toronto: 1956.

Creighton, Donald. *Dominion of the North.* Boston: 1944.

Glazebrook, G.P. de T. *History of Transportation in Canada.* Toronto: 1938.

Kerr, D.G.G. *Historical Atlas of Canada.* Toronto: 1959.

Lanctot, Gustave. *Canada, From its Origins to 1663.* Toronto: 1963.

Lower, A.R.M. *Canadians in the Making.* Toronto: 1958.

MacLennan, Hugh. *Seven Rivers of Canada.* Toronto: 1961.

Olson, Sigurd F. *The Lonely Land.* Toronto: 1961.

Stefansson, Vilhjalmur. *Northwest to Fortune.* New York: 1958.

General References

Brown, George W. (ed.) *Dictionary of Canadian Biography.* Toronto: 1966.

Burpee, L.J. *Encyclopedia of Canadian History.* Toronto: 1926.

Storey, Norah. *Oxford Companion to Canadian History and Literature.* Toronto: 1967.

Wallace, W.S. (ed.) *Encyclopaedia of Canada.* Toronto: 1935-49.

Marie-Anne Lagimodière	— — — — — — — —
Amelia Douglas	— — — — — — —
Selina Bompas	- - - - - - - - - - - - -
Martha Black	— - — - — - — - — - — -

Labels on map: Yukon R., Forty Mile, Dawson, Fort Norman, Great Bear L., Mackenzie R., Liard R., Fort Simpson, Great Slave L., Fort Resolution, Fort Chipewyan, L. Athabasca, Peace R., Fort St. James, Athabasca R., Fraser R., Flin Flon, Saskatchewan R., PACIFIC OCEAN, Victoria, L. Winnipeg, Winnipeg R., Assiniboine R., Fort Vancouver, Columbia R., Fort Douglas, Red R.

D. McELROY